Intelligent Computing Everywhere

T0134488

Alfons J. Schuster

Editor

Intelligent Computing Everywhere

 Springer

Dr Alfons J. Schuster
School of Computing and Mathematics
University of Ulster at Jordanstown
Northern Ireland, UK

British Library Cataloguing in Publication Data
A catalogue record for this book is available from the British Library

ISBN: 978-1-84996-682-5   e-ISBN: 978-1-84628-943-9

Printed on acid-free paper

9 8 7 6 5 4 3 2 1

Springer Science+Business Media
springer.com

Preface

Morpheus: "The Matrix is everywhere. It is all around us. Even now, in this very room. You can see it when you look out your window or when you turn on your television. You can feel it when you go to work ... when you go to church ... when you pay your taxes. It is the world that has been pulled over your eyes to blind you from the truth."

(THE MATRIX, 1999)

The sequence from the cult science fiction film "The Matrix" reminds us that the creation of artificial entities and artificial environments exhibiting human intelligence or other forms of intelligence has been entertaining the human mind for quite some time.

In a modern science context, artificial intelligence (AI) is a discipline that deals with many of the issues involved in creating such intelligent entities and environments. At the moment, AI is enjoying a kind of renaissance actually. One of the reasons for this is the sometimes revolutionary progress in technology, a progress that seems to stand synonymously for our age. Unquestionably, information technology, which itself is intrinsically related to computing and AI of course, is part of this revolutionary progress.

This edited book focuses on this relationship more deeply and studies, in a timely investigation, the connection between AI and what we consider to be modern strands of computing. The field of modern computing is incredibly rich, and although several other strands of modern computing may have deserved to be included in this book, the strands considered include ambient intelligence, artificial intelligence in space, cognitive neuroscience, brain-computer interfaces, bioinformatics, DNA computing, and quantum computing, for example. Quite naturally, then, this book is not bound to technical details and applications only but also explores novel computing models and philosophical dimensions associated with computing and AI.

It goes without saying that a book like this cannot come into existence without the help and contributions of others. I therefore want to use this opportunity to express my sincerest gratitude to the various authors who have contributed to the book. I am also thankful to Beverley Ford, Helen Desmond, and Frank Ganz at Springer, and Springer itself, for their guidance and kind support throughout this project. Finally, it is a pleasure to thank the following individuals for their assistance in the review process of this edited book: Juan Carlos Augusto, Daniel Berrar, David Bustard, David Glass, Kieran Greer, Gaye Lightbody, Edward Keedwell, Mark McCartney, Sally McClean, Paul McCullagh, David Patterson, Mary Shapcott, and Klaus-Peter Zauner.

Belfast, June 2007   *Alfons Schuster*

Contents

List of Contributors

Juan Carlos Augusto
University of Ulster at Jordanstown
School of Computing & Mathematics
Co. Antrim, Northern Ireland
jc.augusto@ulster.ac.uk

Niels Birbaumer
Eberhard Karls University
of Tübingen
Institute of Medical Psychology
and Behavioral Neurobiology
Tübingen, Germany
niels.birbaumer@uni-tuebingen.de

Gustavo Deco
Universitat Pompeu Fabra
Department of Technology
Barcelona, Spain
gustavo.deco@upf.edu

Mathäus Dejori
Siemens Corporate Technology
Information & Communications
Munich, Germany
mathaeus.dejori@siemens.com

Zoheir Ezziane
University of Dubai
College of Information Technology
Dubai, United Arab Emirates
zezziane@ud.ac.ae

Daniela Girimonte
European Space Agency
Advanced Concepts Team
Noordwijk, The Netherlands
daniela.girimonte@esa.int

David H. Glass
University of Ulster at Jordanstown
School of Computing & Mathematics
Co. Antrim, Northern Ireland
dh.glass@ulster.ac.uk

Klaus Haagen
University of Trento
Department of Economy
Trento, Italy
khaagen@economia.unitn.it

Dario Izzo
European Space Agency
Advanced Concepts Team
Noordwijk, The Netherlands
dario.izzo@esa.in

Colin G. Johnson
University of Kent
Computing Laboratory
Canterbury, Kent, England
c.g.johnson@kent.ac.uk

Subhash Kak
Louisiana State University
Department of Electrical &
Computer Engineering
Baton Rouge, LA, USA
kak@ee.lsu.edu

Mark McCartney
University of Ulster at Jordanstown
School of Computing & Mathematics
Co. Antrim, Northern Ireland
m.mccartney@ulster.ac.uk

Andreas Nägele
Siemens Corporate Technology
Information & Communications
Munich, Germany
andreas.naegele.ext@siemens.com

Edmund T. Rolls
University of Oxford

Department of Experimental
Psychology, Oxford, England
edmund.rolls@psy.ox.ac.uk

Alfons Schuster
University of Ulster at Jordanstown
School of Computing & Mathematics
Co. Antrim, Northern Ireland
a.schuster@ulster.ac.uk

Eric Steinhart
William Paterson University
Department of Philosophy
Wayne NJ, USA
steinharte@wpunj.edu

Martin Stetter
Siemens Corporate Technology
Information & Communications
Munich, Germany
stetter@siemens.com

Part I

Introduction, Philosophical Issues, and Novel Computing Models

1

Intelligent Computing Everywhere

Alfons Schuster

School of Computing and Mathematics, Faculty of Engineering, University of
Ulster, Shore Road, Newtownabbey, Co. Antrim BT37 0QB, Northern Ireland,
a.schuster@ulster.ac.uk

Summary. This chapter introduces this edited book. It aims to set the context in
which we discuss the relevance of AI (artificial intelligence) to what we consider to be
modern strands of computing, including, amongst other areas, pervasive or ubiquitous computing, autonomic computing, bioinformatics, DNA computing, neuroinformatics, brain-computer interfaces, quantum computing, and quantum cryptography.

1.1 Introduction

> *Man is the measure of all things, of those that are that*
> *they are, and of those that are not that they are not.*
> (PROTAGORAS, AROUND 480–410 BC)

A few years ago, an imaginary Greek sophist may have witnessed the burst
of the e-commerce bubble and the decline of the telecommunications industry
happening roughly at the same time and still happily maintained that working
in IT can be one of the most exciting and challenging working experiences
in which to be involved. Why is that so? To answer this question requires
consideration of another term inseparable from IT, namely the notion of
"computing". Computing is the basis for IT, and the steady, sometimes
revolutionary progress in computing is the basis on which our claim rests.
It is of course easy to associate IT and the telecommunications industry
with computing and hence the classical or traditional theory of computing.
However, the view maintained here reaches beyond this simple association. It
recognizes that modern computing is touching, and influencing many areas of
everyday human life and human endeavor on increasingly more sophisticated
and challenging levels. One of the reasons for this phenomenon lies in the
fact that progress in various engineering fields has resulted in increasingly
cheaper and increasingly more powerful hardware for IT and computing
equipment. For example, at the time of writing, IBM's BlueGene/L, a machine
incorporating an astonishing assembly of 32,768 processors and a sustained
performance of 70.72 teraflops, tops a site listing the top 500 supercomputers.

Quite naturally, the availability of such powerful hardware led the development of applications into hugely complex and extremely powerful dimensions. According to IBM, potential applications of BlueGene/L include projects in fields as diverse as hydrodynamics, quantum chemistry, molecular dynamics, climate modeling, and financial modeling, for example. The BlueGene/L example not only represents the hardware and software evolution evolving over the last couple of decades but also illustrates that modern computing is no longer a task undertaken in small projects by a small number of people—modern computing includes large-scale projects and is inherently interdisciplinary, collaborative, and global. Another observation central to our investigation is the involvement of AI on the modern computing stage. It enters this stage in different appearances. For example, a project may be set up as a project in AI in the first place; alternatively, a non-AI project may raise issues and questions or produce problems that the AI community has been aware of for some time. For instance, huge amounts of data present the bioinformatics community with enormous challenges in terms of data storage, data management, data maintenance, and performance. In order to deal with these problems, bioinformatics research considers Grid computing technology [TCH+05] and the data warehouse approach [SHX+05] as viable options. Besides these challenges, data warehousing is also committed to supporting high-level decision-making and data mining, which are both typical AI areas. Investigations in forthcoming sections are going to show that similar arguments, challenges, and relationships apply to several other modern strands of computing, too. Section 1.2 provides a first taste of the many challenges involved in studying these relationships by looking at the seemingly harmless question of what computing is in the first place.

1.2 What Is Computing?

> ... *"Forty-two!" yelled Loonquawl. "Is that all you've got to show for seven and a half million years' work?" "I checked it very thoroughly," said the computer, "and that quite definitely is the answer. I think the problem, to be quite honest with you, is that you've never actually known what the question is."*
> (DOUGLAS ADAMS, THE HITCHHIKER'S GUIDE TO THE GALAXY, 1978)

We encounter a dilemma when we try to find an answer to the question of what computing is because there simply is no unified, generally accepted definition of what computing is. The dilemma should not be too disturbing, though, because it is the type of dilemma we humans face every day and actually cope with quite well. For example, many organisms are alive at this very moment, but the very basic concept of life itself still is an enigma in many respects. The dilemma actually holds for several other concepts cognate to computing; information, meaning, knowledge, complexity, or intelligence, to name a few, all share the same fate [Flo04]. Although some dilemmas are not too disturbing, there is no reason to neglect them entirely. After all, the quest for knowledge is a defining human quality. It is possible to approach the dilemma in two ways. One way is to look at existing definitions for computing, and the other way is to have a look at what people working in computing actually do. Both attempts, the first intentional and the second extensional, should provide us with a set of boundaries within which computing should fall. There are various routes to obtain this information. One possibility is to use the vast literature chronicling the evolution of computing and computing machines, as well as the main concepts and the key people involved [Gre01]. Another possibility is to run a quick search on the Web. Such a search may return the following:

Computer science: "the branch of engineering science that studies (with the aid of computers) computable processes and structures."

Computer: "a machine that can be programmed to manipulate symbols. Computers can perform complex and repetitive procedures quickly, precisely and reliably, and can quickly store and retrieve large amounts of data."

Although there are other possible query outcomes, most searches probably reveal the connection between computing, computers, and computer science. Unfortunately, for the new terms, computer science and computers, the dilemma immediately strikes again because these terms also lack generally acknowledged definitions. It is possible, however, to link the three terms by saying that one of the aims of computer science, amongst other aims, is to investigate the processing (or computing) possibilities and limits of what computers can perform. Theoretical computer science usually undertakes such an investigation in a rigorous, abstract, mathematical way, with the help of virtual entities called machines or automata. Interestingly, many of these theoretical investigations were carried out even before the first computers had been developed. Nevertheless, some of the insights gained from these investigations led to profound and intriguing consequences. For example, the Halting Problem, which is a decision problem, investigates the following problem: "Given a program and an input to the program, determine if the program will eventually stop when it is given that input." As it turns out, the Halting Problem belongs to a category of problems that are unsolvable or undecidable. The great Alan Turing, the man often praised as the father of modern computer science, made this discovery. Turing was also instrumental to AI by devising the "Turing Test" [Tur50]. Essentially, the Turing Test examines a machine for its capability to perform human-like conversation. Although some criticize the test, many still regard it as a useful procedure for testing machine intelligence. The well-known Loebner Prize, for instance, offers prize money of $100,000 for the first computer to succeed in the test.

Of course, theoretical investigations are essential for the establishment of a thorough understanding of a subject. If promising enough, they may inspire attempts at putting theory into praxis. Currently, the huge efforts undertaken in the fields of quantum computing, quantum encryption, and DNA computing are good examples of this. Grover's database search algorithm [Gro96] and Shor's algorithm for factoring large numbers on a quantum computer [Sho97] drew great attention to the fields of quantum computing and quantum encryption. In DNA computing, Adleman's contribution to the "Hamiltonian Path Problem" [Adl94], and Lipton's proposal to the "Satisfiability Problem for Propositional Formulas" [Lip95] are equally important. Another high-level view thinks of computing simply as a three-step "input-processing-output" process. On this basis, any entity or system demonstrating this three-step process is a computer. Consequently, not only is an ordinary desktop PC a computer but also any living organism, for example. Not surprisingly, one of the contributions to the "Grand Challenges for Computing Research" initiative investigates nonclassical computing paradigms, including research on how nature computes [SBC+06]. In this nonclassical (natural) computing view, centrifuges, for example, exploit differences in density to separate mixtures of substances in a kind of gravitational sorting, and industrial magnets perform a sorting task by separating ferromagnetic objects from other junk. With some imagination, even our universe represents a computer shuffling information in a cosmic program whose output is time, space, particles, and us—humans. Black holes appear naturally in this universal computer as subroutines in the program, sucking in matter and information, hiding it from the rest of the universe, but eventually evaporating their output [LJ04]. In an AI context, the input-processing-output process is related to the "Information Processing Metaphor". This metaphor takes the input-processing-output process from the perspective of the brain, where it is assumed to equate to a corresponding three-step "sense-think-act" process [PS00]. Another well-known AI metaphor, the "Computer Metaphor", considers the relationship between brain and mind and between computer hardware and software. There are many more facets to computing, but we have mentioned AI several times now and so it may be appropriate to look at this subject in a bit more detail.

1.3 Artificial Intelligence

... A strange multiplicity of sensations seized me, and I saw, felt, heard, and smelt, at the same time; and it was, indeed, a long time before I learned to distinguish between the operations of my various senses.
(MARY SHELLEY, FRANKENSTEIN, 1818)

Artificial intelligence as we conceive it today does not date back as far as the creation of Mary Shelley's legendary monster. Actually, its defining moment is often associated with a conference held at Dartmouth College in New Hampshire in 1956, where key figures of the field, including Marvin Minsky, Herbert Simon, John McCarthy, Claude Shannon, and Alan Newell, for example, met, and the term "artificial intelligence" was coined. Since then, AI has progressed continuously and along its way stimulated fruitful discussions and activities in many fields. Understandably, it is not possible here to provide a complete account of AI and its numerous subdisciplines or to discuss the many exciting and sometimes controversial contributions AI has made to a diverse range of fields. Instead, this section focuses on a few selected topics only, including the relatively young field of "new AI", which is closely related to "embodied artificial intelligence" and "robotics" [PI04]. We may see new AI as a natural progression of traditional AI, but it should be clear that it is not possible to discuss the two totally separate from each other. A crude distinction between the two could be that traditional AI investigates intelligence and cognition from an algorithmic, computational point of view, whereas new AI investigates intelligence from the viewpoint of a creative interplay between one or more entities, so-called agents, and a complex, real-world environment. For example, chess and checkers are typical classical AI domains, but a so-called humanoid robot roaming around as a waiter at a dinner party may stand for a project in new AI. It also may be possible to say that new AI is a more modern incarnation of "weak AI", which itself is a less ambitious form of "strong AI". Strong AI has the extreme goal of building machines capable of human thought, consciousness, and emotions, a view degrading humans to no more than sophisticated machines. Weak AI is a bit more moderate. Its approach contains a strong element of engineering. Theories of intelligence are first developed and then tested on real working models and artifacts. New AI, in a sense, pushes weak AI to the limit. It exploits and profits from cheap and powerful high-tech hardware and software and quite consciously strives for the actual creation of real working systems that are "clever" or "smart". The "DARPA (Defense Advanced Research Projects Agency) Grand Challenges", mentioned later in this chapter, are good examples of this.

New AI is a stimulating field in many ways. Some of its appeal may stem from the excitement and accessibility provided by robotics, which historically has been a popular test field for AI. Robotics research is highly accessible due to the availability of cheap and relatively powerful hardware and software. Already on a smaller scale we find professional low-cost, low-spec commercial platforms such as the "Lego Mindstorms Robotics Invention System", for example. Large-scale robotics research, ideally with some industrial backup, is a different thing, however. Humanoid robots such as P3, Asimo, QRIO, or AIBO, created by Honda and Sony, demonstrate this difference quite well. These robots have the concrete aim of functioning in the immediate, natural environment of human beings, where they can even provide company and be a partner for people. Another reason behind the popularity of robotics might be the evolutionary "build-test-immediate feedback-improve" development approach typical of many robotics projects. This approach provides quick feedback and quality assessment, and in some cases the possibility for on-the-fly modifications to an application. The well-liked RoboCup competition, where robots are tested for their ability to play soccer, is a good example of this. Today, the competition features innovative humanoid robots engaged in sophisticated tasks such as a penalty shootout against a human goalkeeper, for example. Unsurprisingly, the great ambition of RoboCup protagonists is

to create a team of fully autonomous humanoid robots that can win against
the human world soccer champion team by the year 2050. Other examples
demonstrating (successful) cutting-edge robotics research are the DARPA
challenges mentioned earlier. The early 2004 and 2005 DARPA challenges
offered a substantial amount of money to the team that builds an autonomous
ground vehicle that can run from Barstow, California, to Primm, Nevada,
across the Mojave Desert. On this journey, vehicles had to navigate through
130- to 150-mile routes in an intelligent manner, avoiding or accommodating
obstacles, including nearby vehicles and other impediments, without human
intervention. Although in 2004 all participants failed to complete the task,
2005 witnessed a very different outcome. From 23 finalists 5 vehicles completed
the course, 4 within a 10 hour time limit and 1 outside the limit. Without any
doubt, this is a great result for robotics and AI. It may be similar in magnitude
to the successes of IBM's "Deep Blue" supercomputer and the "Deep Fritz"
chess engine. The former is the machine that recorded the first win in a game of
chess against a reigning World Chess Federation Champion (Garry Kasparov
in 1996), and the latter is the commercial chess engine that triumphed 4-2 in
December 2006 against the then-reigning champion, Vladimir Kramnik, in a
six-game match. However, like many other fields, AI is a continuously evolving
and progressing field. This is why the current DARPA challenge has raised
the bar considerably by taking the challenge from an off-road environment
with only limited interaction with other vehicles to an urban environment
with moving traffic. Essentially, the "Urban Challenge" asks teams to build
autonomous vehicles able to complete a 60-mile urban course safely in less than
6 hours. In the current discussion, it is worth mentioning that the large-scale
dimension in which AI operates today is not bound to Earth alone. NASA and
ESA, for example, already pursue large research programs in space in which
AI plays a significant role, be it in the design of life-support systems, satellite
path planning, or the development of an integrated system for coordinating
multi-rover groups with the overall aim of collecting planetary surface data,
for example [RJS+07, IPG07].

However, from a higher perspective, our examples demonstrate an important trend in AI research. It is no longer sufficient to simulate or demonstrate
intelligence on a PC sitting on a desk in some office or lab. Modern robotics
and AI research envisages systems that demonstrate intelligence but also
engage, interact, roam about, explore, and reason in a complex environment
in which they have to function. The main new AI concepts of scalability,
robustness, real-time processing, embodiment, and situatedness connect directly to this challenge. Scalability assumes that many AI applications work well
in small so-called microworlds but may fail to generalize in more complex
and elaborate situations and environments. The Mojave Desert mentioned
before surely scales up beyond common lab confinements. The DARPA
challenges also explain the importance of real-time processing. In a complex
environment, the sense-think-act metaphor mentioned earlier can require
considerable resources in terms of information processing; for example, for

tasks such as obstacle recognition and avoidance, planning, and learning. This is why AI exploits parallel computing architectures and systems. It also explains why quantum computing and DNA computing are interesting for AI. Embodiment and situatedness work on the assumption that traditional AI neglected the importance of a container or body for intelligence. This body is not a PC running idly in some lab or abstracted microworld. Rather, it is a dynamic body engaging and adapting in various interactive modes with a complex macroenvironment using a range of devices (sensors, motors, and actuators) where the design of a device influences the experiences a body can have. Finally, robustness is a feature of paramount importance [Sch07]. AI systems are software systems, and so we are inclined to think about robust software. This is fine, but we need to be aware that robustness is a problem in almost all large-scale software development projects and that the majority of these projects do not contain any AI at all. AI is an additional layer of complexity on top of this. Consequently, and we are going to see this several times shortly, making AI systems fault tolerant or robust increases the challenge significantly.

1.4 Pervasive Computing and Autonomic Computing

> Dave: "Hal, switch to manual hibernation control."
> Hal: "I can tell from your voice, Dave, that you're badly
> upset. Why don't you take a stress pill and get some rest?"
> (ARTHUR C. CLARKE, 2001: A SPACE ODYSSEY, 1969)

It may not be the most comfortable argument around for pervasive computing, but Arthur C. Clarke's Hal epitomizes the idea behind it quite well. Pervasive computing, also sometimes called ubiquitous computing, is the brainchild of the late Mark Weiser, who expressed his view on the topic by rationalizing that computer technology devices are going to weave themselves into the fabric of everyday life until they are indistinguishable from it [Wei91]. Weiser's perspective separates pervasive computing from traditional computing in several ways. For example, traditional computing often perceives a computer as a machine that runs programs in a virtual environment in order to achieve a task. Whenever the computer has fulfilled this task, it stops. By contrast, pervasive computing regards a device as a potential portal into an application-data space and not only as a repository of custom software that a user must manage. It also considers an application as a means by which a user performs a task and not simply as software written to exploit the capabilities of a device. Pervasive computing therefore regards a computing environment as an information-enhanced physical space where communications, computing, and rich media converge, and not only as a virtual environment that exists to store and run software [HMNS03]. In this information-enhanced physical world, interfacing between applications and users is often regarded as the single most important challenge today, not only of pervasive/ubiquitous computing but in computer science as a whole [SM03]. There is a great dynamism and optimism in the field of pervasive computing. A good indicator for the general belief in the potential of the field are several projects involving major businesses and universities such as IBM, Microsoft, Hewlett-Packard, Siemens, AT&T, or MIT. Under closer inspection, these projects show that advances in distributed computing and mobile computing, the development of powerful middleware, and a growing number of devices featuring electronics have been responsible for the creation of a rich environment in which pervasive computing was able to take root. Four players have major roles in this environment: complex networks, intelligent sensors, actuators and devices, and, last but not least, human users. The Internet is the prime example of this. It involves a multiplicity of users webbed together through numerous applications. Communication between these applications is happening through a variety of modes, including keyboard, speech, and vision. From a user's perspective, these modes of interaction are getting more and more demanding, often requiring more sophisticated and perhaps intelligent solutions. AI is involved in this challenge in several ways and plays a relatively large role where networks interface with human users via intelligent sensors and devices. So-called ambient, intelligent, or smart "homes" summarize this effort quite well [AN06]. Intelligent homes are equipped with a large number of so-called smart sensors, microelectronic devices, wireless gadgets, and computers [CM04]. Typically, these devices communicate via RFID (radio frequency identification) technology [Wan04]. In such a home, computing could be blended invisibly into everyday tasks. For example, homeowners may use intelligent bags to alarm users in case they are about to forget a wallet or car keys. Other systems may adjust or prepare a home for particular events such as a garden party or a relaxed evening, for example. Intelligent homes also bear great potential for health care. Twenty-four hour noninvasive tracking of the well-being of people in their own homes may revolutionize the practice of medicine, and a health-related infrastructure in the home may allow effective preventative medicine, helping doctors to monitor health, exercise, and nutrition and to identify problems before they become critical. The University of Nottingham (UK) actually has conducted a Big Brother style study with a family of four living in a hi-tech future house. The study monitored the family closely for a period of six months in a house equipped with some of the technologies just mentioned. Today, the future home market has attracted interest beyond the university landscape. IT businesses such as Microsoft, Siemens, and Philips, for example, are all heavily involved and generally consider the area a very lucrative market.

1.4.1 Autonomic Computing

Not too long ago, autonomic computing emerged as a reaction by the IT industry to tackle the increasingly challenging software complexity crisis. IBM, regarded as the parent of autonomic computing, realized that "This increasing complexity with a shortage of skilled IT professionals points towards an inevitable need to automate many of the functions associated with computing today". IBM and the IT industry as a whole concluded that managing today's software systems goes beyond the mere administration of small software environments [Mur04]. Instead, the IT industry has to deal with extremely large and complex systems, where secure management increasingly approaches a level beyond human ability. For instance, it is impossible for administrators to have a clear idea of what is happening on the Internet at any particular point in time. Neither is it possible for such a person to have a clear picture of its large-scale topological organization [Sto01]. It is reasonable therefore to research solutions where managing such systems may no longer be undertaken by human administrators alone. Autonomic computing aims to tackle the problem via a new type of networked communication system that can manage itself to various degrees given high-level objectives from administrators [KC03]. These systems are autonomously controlled, self-organized, radically distributed, technology-independent, and scale-free. Autonomic computing, like pervasive computing, seeks inspiration from systems as they appear in the natural world. The autonomic nervous system is a key analogy, and self-configuration, self-healing, self-optimization, and self-protection are some of the key concepts autonomic computing exploits in this analogy. Autonomic computing, with its ambition of creating distributed networks that are largely self-managing, self-diagnostic, transparent to users, and able to adapt to new situations when new resources become available, involves many challenges that the AI community has been dealing with for many years. Soft computing and evolutionary computing-based techniques, for example, correspond to autonomic computing quite well. Interestingly, the autonomic computing community has a relatively positive view of AI. The community understands the motivation and achievements of AI, as well as its problems, quite well, and there seems to be a realization that AI is too useful to ignore.

1.5 Bioinformatics and Artificial Synthetic Life

> ... "If you weren't an android," Rick interrupted, "if I could legally marry you, I would."
>
> (PHILIP K. DICK, DO ANDROIDS DREAM OF ELECTRIC SHEEP?, 1968)

Although legal and ethical issues play a role in bioinformatics, initially we may describe the field loosely as "any use of computers to handle biological information". When it comes to practice, people are sometimes more specific and use the term synonymously with "computational molecular biology"—the use of computers to characterize the molecular components of living things [Les05]. The latter term indicates that bioinformatics combines two fields, molecular biology and computer science. Understanding this combination requires looking at the spectacular history of genomics, which involves Darwin's findings on the origin of species, Mendel's discoveries of the laws of inheritance, the study of chromosomes, and the revelation of the double-helix structure of DNA by Watson and Crick, for example. The genomics endeavor achieved its main goal on June 26, 2000, with the publication of a first draft of the human genome by the Human Genome Project team [HGM01] and a team spearheaded by Craig Venter [Ven01].

In simple terms, the human genome consists of DNA. DNA itself is assembled from basic nucleotides called adenine (A), guanine (G), cytosine (C), and thymine (T), which combine or bond to form DNA sequences. Other important terms include the terms gene and genome. Genes are particular DNA sequences and play a fundamental role in the evolution and production of organisms; for example, the development of a human being. DNA is a code and, like any code, contains instructions and information; for example, for the building of complex, three-dimensional proteins. The genome contains the full set of instructions. Understanding the code and related information is a major goal in bioinformatics. Naturally, computer science, with its long tradition of studying codes and information, is heavily involved in achieving this goal. Unfortunately, the task is not easy. The human genome contains an estimated 3 billion bases and about 32,000 genes. It also contains a substantial amount of redundant DNA or DNA whose purpose is still unclear. Even the role of the code is a mystery in itself. For example, for some time researchers saw the genetic code as maximizing efficiency and information density, but nowadays the code is examined from the point of view of providing maximum fault-tolerance or robustness, protecting life from catastrophic errors [Hay04]. It is also not wise to confine the bioinformatics challenge to the analysis of biological data alone. The Human Genome Project is a global project where materials and methods are available to the whole world and where everybody is encouraged to join in. Bioinformatics therefore includes the development and maintenance of computational resources to facilitate worldwide communication and collaboration between people of all educational and professional levels to support research, development, and education in the field. Facilitating this requires standards, definitions, and conventions. For example, the community at large needs to communicate in a coherent language, data have to be structured coherently, standardized databases are important, and tools, algorithms, and applications need standards, too, to allow cross-utilization. Hardware and software also need to be built that can cope with the huge volumes of data produced in biological research. This entails a powerful Web-based infrastructure to allow database queries, data transfer, and data visualization to happen in an economical way.

Although data analysis techniques from traditional mathematics, statistics, and computing permeated bioinformatics right from the beginning, over time it also transformed into a rich application area for AI [KN05]. Bioinformatics uses AI for prediction, classification, visualization, and several other tasks. Application areas include the analysis of genetic regulatory pathways, which is crucial for a thorough understanding of biological processes such as gene regulation and cancer development; for microarray gene expression analysis, which is important for drug development and medical treatment; for gene sequencing, which has similar goals; or protein folding, the transition from genes to complex three-dimensional structures. In terms of applications, bioinformatics seems to have no limits for AI.

1.5.1 Artificial Synthetic Life and Synthetic Biology

So far, we have seen AI as a means for problem solving in molecular biology. In return, we may ask "What can AI learn from computational molecular biology?" The relatively young fields of artificial synthetic life and synthetic biology may provide some feedback [Hol05]. Briefly, these fields aim for the creation of new life forms from nonliving chemicals in the lab. Long-range goals include the design and fabrication of biological components, systems, and artificial cells that do not already exist in the natural world from nonliving, raw material and programming them with the desired chemical functionality. The field also envisages the redesign and fabrication of existing biological systems [RCD+04]. Artificial synthetic life and synthetic biology are taken quite seriously, and there are strong beliefs by many practitioners that artificial cells will eventually be created. For example, Craig Venter, who was instrumental in sequencing the human genome, is involved in the field. Another fundamental research aim of artificial synthetic life is the discovery of the "minimal genome", the smallest set of genes needed to support a simple living cell [Ain03]. From an AI perspective, these ambitions are all extremely interesting. For example, the production of a minimal cell may involve some intelligent processing. This processing may involve some form of artificial intelligence, as well as modern strands of computing (e.g., DNA computing-based optimization techniques). Questions may arise such as "How much artificial intelligence or computing is needed for the construction or support of an artificial cell?", and concepts such as "minimal cell intelligence", "minimum cell computation", and "minimum cell information" may also emerge. Overall, artificial synthetic life and synthetic biology address several fundamental AI challenges. We should not be too surprised therefore to see AI researchers increasingly involved in the field in the foreseeable future.

1.6 DNA Computing

A sonorous voice said, "Welcome to Jurassic Park. You are now entering the lost world of the prehistoric past, a world of mighty creatures long gone from the face of the earth, which you are privileged to see for the first time."
(MICHAEL CRICHTON, JURASSIC PARK, 1991)

Although the input-processing-output metaphor mentioned earlier implies that DNA computing was secretly around when dinosaurs walked the Earth, in a modern sense, DNA computing is a relatively new computing paradigm. The basic idea in DNA computing is to use the information-processing capabilities of organic molecules in computers to replace digital switching primitives [PRS98]. Section 1.2 already mentioned the powerful demonstrations of DNA computing on the Hamiltonian Path Problem and the Satisfiability Problem for Propositional Formulas by Adleman [Adl94] and Lipton [Lip95]. Both studies were instrumental in showing the potential of DNA computing, which essentially relies on parallel-processing capabilities, for computationally expensive problems. For instance, when the time required to perform a task involves expressions such as 2^n, 3^n, n^n, or $n!$, then a solution will be impractical for datasets containing even a small number of data items. Since these early demonstrations, DNA computing-based solutions have been proposed for various other tasks, including relational database modeling [Sch05] or the creation of a programmable three-symbol, three-state, finite automaton [SYK+05]. DNA computing is a relatively complex domain, as it draws from computing, chemistry, and biology. This section tries to explain some of the major principles of the field, including, how programs are coded for a DNA computer, what the basis is for the strength of a DNA computer, what engineering is involved in building a DNA computer, and also what the main differences are between a DNA computer and a standard PC.

In simple terms, DNA computing uses the properties of DNA (deoxyribonucleic acid) to perform computational tasks. Execution of these tasks benefits from two major advantages nature provides for free: parallelism and Watson-Crick complementarity [WC53]. Although DNA computing and classical computer science share many similarities in conducting theoretical research, when it comes down to physical realizations of DNA computers, things could not be more different. The basis for a standard PC is silicon technology, whereas a DNA computer is more akin to a biochemistry laboratory. This difference is sometimes expressed by saying that for a standard PC computing is "computing with bits", whereas for a DNA computer it is common to say that computing is "computing with molecules". The biochemistry environment in which DNA computing happens relies on solid engineering foundations and revolves around the design, manipulation, and processing of molecules called nucleotides. Essentially, nucleotides are chemical compounds including a sugar, a phosphate group, and a chemical base. The four main nucleotides employed in DNA computing are adenine (A), guanine (G), cytosine (C), and thymine (T). These nucleotides can combine or bond as single-stranded DNA or double-stranded DNA. Single-stranded DNA forms through the subsequent bonding of any of the four types of nucleotides. A string of letters (e.g., AGCCAAGTT) typically represents single-stranded DNA. Double-stranded DNA forms from single-stranded DNA and their complementary strands. This type of bonding follows Watson-Crick complementarity, which says that base A only bonds with base T, base G only with base C, and vice versa. For example, TCGGTTCAA is the complementary strand for the strand AGCCAAGTT mentioned before. Often, the resulting double-stranded DNA appears in one picture as two parallel strands, for example as $\frac{AGCCAAGTT}{TCGGTTCAA}$, with the fraction line symbolizing bonding. In order to build a DNA computer, DNA computing uses the four nucleotides to form an alphabet Σ; for example, $\Sigma = \{$A, G, C, T$\}$. This alphabet can be used for the production of a language L. If a set of instructions and operations is available for this language, then it is possible to specify algorithms and to execute programs. In practice, in a DNA computer, these programs compose, design, and manipulate DNA strands in a series of carefully orchestrated biochemical events. These events are usually mediated by molecular entities called enzymes, and include processes such as lengthening, shortening, cutting, linking, or multiplying DNA [PRS98]. It is possible therefore to view a DNA computer as a biochemical machine or pool where hardware, software, input, and output coexist together. Soreni's work on a biomolecular, programmable three-symbol, three-state, finite automaton, can be used as a pointer for current achievements in the field [SYK⁺05]. Soreni's work not only indicates the potential of DNA computing for powerful applications, such as the theoretical execution of 137,781 syntactically distinct programs on the automaton mentioned before, but also provides a taste for the many engineering challenges associated with DNA computing, such as time performance, for example. An extension of this view into the AI landscape may see the integration of DNA computing-based AI algorithms in biomechanical devices (e.g., sensors and actuators), which brings us back to pervasive and ambient computing, for example [Hag00]. There are several other relationships between DNA computing and AI. For example, the "input-processing-output" paradigm mentioned in Section 1.2 applies to DNA computers, too. This means, theoretically, that practical algorithmic AI research on DNA computers can be a reality. The formulation of DNA-based algorithms for rough set analysis, which is a machine-learning technique, points in this direction [Sch03]. In addition, historically, nature has always been a great source of inspiration for AI. The fundamental fact that DNA is part of the human genome intrinsically relates DNA computing to investigations on how nature works. Current research relates the genome itself to the human mind. DNA computing research therefore may increase our understanding of the human mind and provide further insights on how nature computes. Certainly, AI can only benefit from such contributions.

1.7 Neuroinformatics

> *By exact count, there are exactly 75234 operations necessary for the construction of a single positronic brain, each separate operation depending for successful completion upon any number of factors, from five to hundred and five. If any of them goes seriously wrong, the "brain" is ruined.*
> (ISAAC ASIMOV, I ROBOT, 1967)

In many ways, neuroinformatics is analogous to bioinformatics. Section 1.5 mentioned that bioinformatics combines the fields of molecular biology and informatics. Similarly, neuroinformatics combines the fields of neuroscience and informatics. Neuroinformatics also logically complements bioinformatics. Bioinformatics includes data and tools from different biological levels of organization. In an upward fashion, these levels may be molecules, genes, more complex cell formations, organs, and, on the highest level, complex higher organisms, including human beings. Neuroinformatics complements this chain in a natural way by investigating the cognitive functions inherent in such organisms. The phrase "from molecules to cognition" therefore is sometimes used to summarize the field. Neuroinformatics is not easy to define. Most definitions, however, involve the terms informatics, neuroscience, and computational neuroscience. Neuroscience is concerned with the study of the fundamental principles that explain how biological nervous systems, most notably the human brain, work. The field also aims to acquire an understanding of behavioral constructs such as attention, learning, memory, emotion, or cognition. Computational neuroscience supports neuroscientists by providing computational techniques, resources, and metaphors for the modeling, simulation, experimentation, and investigation of neural structures, their functioning, and neural relationships. Neuroinformatics, like bioinformatics, has to deal with many data-related issues. Arbib reflects on this issue by defining neuroinformatics as a discipline integrating data-related issues and computational neuroscience, with the former including data storage, data structuring, data visualization, and data analysis tasks [Arb01].

Historically, the discipline of neuroinformatics stemmed from the Human Brain Project. Launched in 1993, this project aims to create a complete understanding of the human brain via the exploitation of a promising supplement—informatics [HK97]. The incentive came during the 1980s and 1990s when neuroscientists realized the need for enormous computational resources in order to come to grips with the rapidly growing volumes of data and information produced in their field. Requirements for more and more sophisticated models simulating different aspects of the brain and its functions also seemed to escalate. In order to overcome these problems, researchers realized that success in neuroscience corresponds directly to the exploitation and further development of computing resources. Thus, neuroinformatics and bioinformatics have similar origins—information overload and complexity. On a practical level, neuroscientists and computer scientists work on projects all over the world. The Blue Brain Project, for example, which is a collaboration between IBM and EPFL (Ecole Polytechnique Fédérale de Lausanne) has the vision that "The Blue Brain Project marks the beginning of a long journey to study how the brain works by building very large scale computer models". The ultimate goal of the project is to build a single model for the simulation of the entire electrical circuitry in the human brain. This involves the modeling of functions such as memory, vision, hearing, or speech and explains the involvement of IBM's Blue Gene supercomputer, mentioned earlier in this chapter, in this quest. Many neuroscience researchers believe that having such a tool at hand may help them attain a better understanding of the brain. They also believe that society as a whole may benefit from findings in neuroinformatics, as it may lead to a better understanding of and the possible discovery of treatments against diseases such as depression, Alzheimer's disease, or addiction.

Of course, there are many other fascinating projects. The important thing here is that AI relates directly to many challenges in these projects. For example, the view of the brain as a computing device is at the heart of AI. Pioneers such as McCulloch and Pitts, for instance, considered individual neurons as computing devices as early as 1943. Subsequent research has gone far beyond single-neuron networks, of course. General-purpose brain-computer interfaces, for example, already allow humans to control devices and to produce actions such as moving computer cursors or reading email via their minds [SMH+04]. If this is possible, then doing the reverse, creating artificial thought in a person's mind, might be possible, too. The increasing quality of current computer games may be an indicator of this. The level of sophistication some (often virtual reality) games have reached has left philosophers and AI practitioners working in virtual reality and related fields arguing that the wall between the real and virtual worlds is already crumbling. The link between AI and the brain also raises ethical issues. Strong AI, for example, has the clear goal of building machines capable of human thought (a goal that some say degrades humans to sophisticated machines). This view, combined with the steady progress made in various other fields in computing, lets some people contemplate the separation of body and mind plus the possibility of storing the mental life of a human being on disk [Mar03]. Ultimately, the debate may contemplate immortality or transhumanism and involve questions about when human life begins [Gaz05]. For example, some see the moment of conception as the beginning of life and others the moment when the brain starts functioning. Sometimes the duration of 14 days is important in the latter context, which is about the time when the fertilized egg begins to generate a nervous system. Along parallel lines, AI is familiar with similar questions. It is common to ask "At which stage does an intelligent machine come to life?" or "In case there ever is an intelligent machine, should it be granted human rights?". Although conclusive answers to these sorts of questions are notoriously difficult to find, efforts in neuroinformatics and AI should enrich the debate with their findings.

1.8 Quantum Computing and Quantum Cryptography

It was at ten oclock today that the first of all Time Machines began its career. I gave it a last tap, tried all the screws again, put one more drop of oil on the quartz rod, and sat myself in the saddle.
(H.G. WELLS, THE TIME MACHINE, 1895)

In case H.G. Wells's time traveller ever arrives in our time, researchers in the field may explain to him that a quantum computer is a physical device that demonstrates results derived from computer science, information theory, and quantum physics, and that the theory behind it is called quantum computing or quantum information theory [BEZ01]. If the time traveller wishes to learn more about the field, however, he could find that it may take some time to get his head around these subjects. For example, information theory and quantum mechanics, the theory describing the elusive world of the quantum, have a reputation for being notoriously difficult to understand, technically as well as conceptually [Ald07]. Although there are well-established conceptual and mathematical frameworks describing both theories, many of the very basic concepts of the theories still lack a total understanding. Information theory, for example, is discussed in exotic areas such as holographic universes [Bec05], and the interest in quantum mechanics rests, at least to some degree, on conundrums such as the well-known double-slit experiment or EPR (Einstein-Podolsky-Rosen) paradox, to name just a few. Nevertheless, despite these challenges, the importance of both theories is widely acknowledged today. Some of the important concepts necessary for an understanding of quantum computing include qubits, entanglement, teleportation, measurement, and quantum algorithms [SR00]. A quantum bit, or qubit, is the quantum analogue to a classical bit. A classical bit can be in one of two states, it is either on $= 1$, or off $= 0$. A register consisting of n classical bits can be in 2^n distinctive states. At any particular point in time, the register can be in one and only one of these 2^n states. Qubits are fundamentally different in this regard. A feature called quantum superposition allows a single qubit to be in both states (on and off) simultaneously. A register consisting of n qubits therefore can be in 2^n states at the same time. A quantum computer exploits this feature by operating on all superpositioned states at the same time. This so-called quantum parallelism can lead to significant performance increases. There is, however, a catch. The so-called measurement problem in quantum physics imposes the rule that whenever a measurement on a quantum system is made, only one state of the many superpositioned states can be measured. The crux behind any quantum algorithm therefore is relatively simple. Manipulate the superpositioned states in such a way that, when a measurement occurs, states providing a solution to a particular problem have a higher likelihood or probability of being measured than those states not contributing toward a solution to the problem [RP00]. The operations and manipulations on a quantum system usually have a particular goal in mind. The two best-known problem solutions for a quantum computer are Grover's database search algorithm [Gro96] and Shor's algorithm for factoring large numbers [Sho97]. Today, many consider quantum computing as the next big revolution in computing. If this revolution happens, it will also have an impact on AI. Computational AI involves algorithms. The power of quantum computers lies in its exploitation of parallelism. This power allows it to execute computationally complex algorithms efficiently. Typical candidates for AI therefore are algorithms or areas where a solution to a problem involves a high degree of parallel computing. It is no surprise then that there are already quantum-inspired algorithms for artificial neural networks [BNS⁺00] and genetic algorithms [HK00], as well as investigations into quantum game theory [DJL05], for example. Then again, neural networks connect quantum computing and neuroinformatics. Just take the case of the long-existing conjecture whether it is necessary for the brain to perform operations based on principles of quantum mechanics [Teg00]. Surely, this debate is highly relevant to AI. Another area that potentially could bring AI and quantum computing together is the area of quantum cryptography.

1.8.1 Quantum Cryptography

Cryptography is one technique, amongst several other techniques, that aims to bring security into networked environments. In a cryptographic system, an encryption algorithm uses an encryption key to transform the original data (plain text) into cipher text. A decryption algorithm then uses a decryption key to transform the cipher text back into plain text. A cryptographic system must address several needs, including confidentiality, privacy, authentication, integrity, and key distribution, for example. These features are important because, amongst other things, there has to be user assurance that data really come from the correct source, that the information is inaccessible to anyone but the sender and receiver, or that the data have not been tampered with in transit. Key distribution has to be secure, too, because knowledge about the key is usually the privilege of special system users. Quantum cryptography is the most current, most sophisticated, and arguably most heavily researched approach to providing network security [Sti05]. A future with powerful quantum computers having enormous capabilities for breaking current codes is one incentive for this effort. Ultimately, quantum cryptography is a child of quantum mechanics. In principle, the technique enables the generation and distribution of unbreakable cryptographic keys. It allows users to establish and communicate keys on public communication channels that provide means to guard and detect attempts by eavesdroppers trying to spy on a data stream traveling through a channel. Today, quantum cryptography has matured from theoretical research, through to experimental research, toward commercial products already on the market. Its technical use grew from point-to-point networks that were 30 centimeters apart, to the first money transaction over a network spanning 600 meters [UJA⁺04], to a network covering a distance of several kilometers through air [PYB⁺05], a distance that could make satellite-based quantum communication feasible. Quantum cryptography is not without challenges, however, as research on the idea of a quantum Internet and how hackers might attack such a network already indicates [And04].

It is not straightforward to link quantum cryptography and AI. There are efforts under way researching AI and computer security in traditional non-quantum environments. One area is evolutionary computing techniques applied to the detection of network attack patterns [IH04]. Biometrics, which applies neural networks for user identification tasks, is another area where AI and traditional security overlap. The previous section mentioned that quantum computing-based solutions for some of these techniques already exist in theory. It is possible therefore to look forward to a future where the elusive worlds of quantum cryptography, quantum computing, and AI finally converge.

1.9 Summary

> *All human beings are pregnant in body and in mind, and when we*
> *reach a degree of adulthood we naturally desire to give birth.*
> (PLATO, THE SYMPOSIUM, AROUND 360 BC)

The aim of this chapter has been to introduce this edited book. In order to do so, the chapter initially investigated the notion of computing itself and then moved on to the subject of AI, reflecting on its motivation, achievements, and many challenges. Subsequent sections reported on the many relationships AI holds with various strands of modern computing. We understand the possibility, and perhaps the need, to say much more about each of these subjects, and that several other subjects may have deserved mention here. Our apologies therefore to those readers whose favorite topics are not included here. On the other hand, this gives us a reason to look forward to the forthcoming contributions in this edited book. Overall, we hope that this short introduction has produced some appetite in the reader to further explore our claim that intelligent computing is (almost) everywhere.

References

[Adl94]   L.M. Adleman. Molecular computation of solutions to combinatorial problems. *Science*, 266:1021–1024, November 1994.

[Ain03]   C. Ainsworth. The facts of life. *New Scientist*, 178:28–31, May 2003.

[Ald07]   M. Alder. Help wanted: philosophers required to sort out reality. *Philosophy Now*, 59:12–15, January/February 2007.

[AN06]   J.C. Augusto and C.D. Nugent, editors. *Designing Smart Homes—The Role of Artificial Intelligence*, volume 4008 of *Lecture Notes in Artificial Intelligence*. Springer-Verlag, Berlin, 2006.

[And04]   M.K. Anderson. The secret is out. *New Scientist*, 180:24–27, November 2004.

[Arb01]   M.A. Arbib. Neuroinformatics: the issue. In M.A. Arbibaa and J.S. Grethe, editors, *Computing the Brain: A Guide to Neuroinformatics*, pages 3–28. Academic Press, San Diego and London, 2001.

[Bec05]   J.D. Beckstein. Information in the holographic universe. *Scientific American*, 15(3):74–81, 2005.

[BEZ01]   D. Bouwmeester, A. Ekert, and A. Zeilinger, editors. *The Physics of Quantum Information: Quantum Cryptography, Quantum Teleportation, Quantum Computation*. Springer-Verlag, Berlin and London, 2001.

[BNS+00] E.C. Behrman, L.R. Nash, J.E. Steck, V.G. Chandrashekar, and S.R. Skinner. Simulations of quantum neural networks. *Information Sciences*, 128(3–4):257–269, 2000.

[CM04] D.E. Culler and H. Mulder. Smart sensors to network the world. *Scientific American*, 290:53–59, June 2004.

[DJL05] J.F. Du, C.Y. Ju, and H. Li. Quantum entanglement helps in improving economic efficiency. *Journal of Physics A: Mathematical and General*, 38:1559–1565, 2005.

[Flo04] L. Floridi, editor. *The Blackwell Guide to the Philosophy of Computing and Information*. Blackwell Publishing, Malden, MA, Oxford, Carlton, 2004.

[Gaz05] M.S. Gazzaniga. What's on your mind? *New Scientist*, 186:48–50, June 2005.

[Gre01] M.W. Greenia. *History of Computing: An Encyclopedia of the People and Machines that Made Computing*. Lexikon Services Publishing, Antelope CA, 2001.

[Gro96] L.K. Grover. A fast quantum mechanical algorithm for database search. In *Proceedings of the 28th Annual ACM Symposium on the Theory of Computing (STOC)*, pages 212–219, New York, NY, USA, 1996. ACM Press.

[Hag00] M. Hagiya. Theory and construction of molecular computers. In J. Van Leeuwen, O. Watanabe, M. Hagiya, P.D. Mosses, and T. Ito, editors, *Proceedings of the International Conference IFIP on Theoretical Computer Science, Exploring New Frontiers of Theoretical Informatics*, volume 1872 of *Lecture Notes in Computer Science*, pages 23–24. Springer-Verlag, Berlin, 2000.

[Hay04] B. Hayes. Ode to the code. *American Scientist*, 92(6):494–498, November–December 2004.

[HGM01] The international human genome mapping consortium. A physical map of the human genome. *Nature*, 409:934–941, February 2001.

[HK97] M.F. Huerta and S.H. Koslow. The Human Brain Project: past, present, and promise. In S.H. Koslow and M.F. Huerta, editors, *An Overview of the Human Brain Project*. Erlbaum Associates, Mahwah, New Jersey, 1997.

[HK00] K.H. Han and J.H. Kim. Genetic quantum algorithm and its application to combinatorial optimization problem. In *Proceedings of the 2000 Congress on Evolutionary Computation CEC 2000, San Diego, CA*, pages 1354–1360, Piscataway, NJ, 2000. IEEE Service Center.

[HMNS03] U. Hansmann, L. Merk, M.S. Nicklous, and T. Stober. *Pervasive Computing*. Springer-Verlag, Berlin, 2003.

[Hol05] B. Holmes. Alive. *New Scientist*, 185:29–33, February 2005.

[IH04] P. Isasi and J.C. Hernandez. Introduction to the applications of evolutionary computation in computer security and cryptography. *Computational Intelligence*, 20(3):445, August 2004.

[IPG07] D. Izzo, L. Pettazzi, and D. Girimonte. A path planning technique applied to satellite swarm. In D. Girimonte, D. Izzo, T. Vinko, S. Chien, and V. Kreinovich, editors, *Workshop on Artificial Intelligence for Space Applications at IJCAI'07*, pages 29–30, Hyderabad, India, January 2007. IJCAI.

[KC03]   J.O. Kephart and D.M. Chess. The vision of autonomic computing. *IEEE Computer*, 36(1):41–50, January 2003.

[KN05]   E. Keedwell and A. Narayanan. *Intelligent Bioinformatics: The Application of Artificial Intelligence Techniques to Bioinformatics Problems*. John Wiley & Sons, New York, 2005.

[Les05]   A. Lesk. *An Introduction to Bioinformatics*. Oxford University Press, Oxford, 2005.

[Lip95]   J.L. Lipton. DNA solution to hard computational problems. *Science*, 268:542–545, April 1995.

[LJ04]   S. Lloyd and Y. Jack. Black hole computers. *Scientific American*, 291:30–39, November 2004.

[Mar03]   P. Marks. The story of your life ... on a laptop. *New Scientist*, 180(28):32, October 2003.

[Mur04]   R. Murch. *Autonomic Computing*. IBM Press, Yorktown Heights, NY, 2004.

[PI04]   R. Pfeifer and F. Iida. Embodied artificial intelligence: trends and challenges. In F. Iida, R. Pfeifer, L. Steels, and Y. Kuniyoshi, editors, *Embodied Artificial Intelligence*, volume 3139 of *Lecture Notes in Artificial Intelligence*, pages 1–26. Springer-Verlag, Berlin, 2004.

[PRS98]   G. Paun, G. Rozenberg, and A. Salomaa. *DNA Computing: New Computing Paradigms*. Springer-Verlag, Berlin, 1998.

[PS00]   R. Pfeifer and C. Scheier. *Understanding Intelligence*. The MIT Press, Cambridge, and London, 2000.

[PYB+05] C.Z. Peng, T. Yang, X.H. Bao, J. Zhang, X.M. Jin, F.Y. Feng, B. Yang, J. Yang, J. Yin, Q. Zhang, N. Li, B.L. Tian, and J.W. Pan. Experimental free-space distribution of entangled photon pairs over 13 km: Towards satellite-based global quantum communication. *Physical Review Letters*, 94:15051, 2005.

[RCD+04] S. Rasmussen, L. Chen, D. Deamer, D.C. Krakauer, N.H. Packard, P.F. Stadler, and M.A. Bedau. Transitions from nonliving to living matter. *Science*, 303:963–965, February 2004.

[RJS+07] L.F. Rodriguez, H. Jiang, K. Stark, S. Bell, and D. Kortenkamp. Validation of heuristic techniques for design of life support systems. In D. Girimonte, D. Izzo, T. Vinko, S. Chien, and V. Kreinovich, editors, *Workshop on Artificial Intelligence for Space Applications at IJCAI'07*, pages 5–6, Hyderabad, India, January 2007. IJCAI.

[RP00]   E. Rieffel and W. Polak. An introduction to quantum computing for non-physicists. *ACM Computing Surveys*, 32(3):300–335, 2000.

[SBC+06] S. Stepney, S.L. Braunstein, J.A. Clark, A. Tyrrell, A. Adamatzky, R.E. Smith, T. Addis, C. Johnson, J. Timmis, P. Welch, R. Milner, and D. Partridge. Journeys in non-classical computation ii: initial journeys and waypoints. *International Journal of Parallel, Emergent and Distributed Systems*, 21(2):97–125, April 2006.

[Sch03]   A. Schuster. DNA algorithms for rough set analysis. In J. Liu, Cheung, Y.M, and H. Yin, editors, *Intelligent Data Engineering and Automated Learning*, volume 2690 of *Lecture Notes in Computer Science*, pages 498–513. Springer-Verlag, Berlin, 2003.

[Sch05]   A. Schuster. DNA databases. *BioSystems*, 81(3):234–246, 2005.

[Sch07]   A. Schuster. Robust artificial intelligence. In D. Girimonte, D. Izzo, T. Vinko, S. Chien, and V. Kreinovich, editors, *Workshop on Artificial Intelligence for Space Applications at IJCAI'07*, pages 29–30, Hyderabad, India, January 2007. IJCAI.

[Sho97]   P.W. Shor. Polynomial-time algorithms for prime factorization and discrete logarithms on a quantum computer. *SIAM Journal on Computing*, 26(5):1484–1509, October 1997.

[SHX$^+$05]   S.P. Shah, Y. Huang, T. Xu, M.MS. Yuen, J. Ling, and BF.F. Ouellette. Atlas: a data warehouse for integrative bioinformatics. *BMC Bioinformatics*, 6(34), 2005. Available at http://www.biomedcentral.com.

[SM03]   D. Saha and A. Mukherjee. Pervasive computing: a paradigm for the 21st century. *IEEE Computer*, 36(3):25–31, March 2003.

[SMH$^+$04]   G. Schalk, D.J. McFarland, T. Hinterberger, N. Birbaumer, and J.R. Wolpaw. Bci2000: A general-purpose brain-computer interface (bci) system. *IEEE Transactions on Biomedical Engineering*, 51(6):1034–1043, June 2004.

[SR00]   A.M. Steane and E.G. Rieffel. Beyond bits: the future of quantum information processing. *IEEE Computer*, 33(1):38–45, 2000.

[Sti05]   G. Stix. Best-kept secrets. *Scientific American*, 292:65–69, January 2005.

[Sto01]   S.H. Stogatz. Exploring complex networks. *Nature*, 410:268–276, March 2001.

[SYK$^+$05]   M. Soreni, S. Yogev, E. Kossoy, Y. Shoham, and E. Keinan. Parallel biomolecular computation on surfaces with advanced finite automata. *Journal of the American Chemical Society*, 127(11):3935–3943, 2005.

[TCH$^+$05]   F. Tang, C.L. Chua, L.Y. Ho, Y.P. Lim, P. Issac, and A. Krishnan. Wildfire: distributed, grid-enabled workflow construction and execution. *BMC Bioinformatics*, 6(69), 2005. Available at http://www.biomedcentral.com.

[Teg00]   M. Tegmark. Why the brain is probably not a quantum computer. *Information Sciences*, 128(3–4):155–179, 2000.

[Tur50]   A.M. Turing. Computing machinery and intelligence. *Mind*, 59:433–460, 1950.

[UJA$^+$04]   R. Ursin, T. Jennewein, M. Aspelmeyer, R. Kaltenbaek, M. Lindenthal, P. Walther, and A. Zeilinger. Quantum teleportation across the Danube. *Nature*, 430:849, August 2004.

[Ven01]   J.C. Venter et al. The sequence of the human genome. *Science*, 291: 1304–1351, February 2001.

[Wan04]   R. Want. RFID—a key to automating everything. *Scientific American*, 290:46–55, 2004.

[WC53]   J.D. Watson and F.H.C. Crick. Molecular structure of nucleic acids. *Nature*, 171:734–737, April 1953.

[Wei91]   M. Weiser. The computer of the 21st century. *Scientific American*, 265:66–75, September 1991.

2

Infinitely Complex Machines

Eric Steinhart

Department of Philosophy, William Paterson University, Wayne, NJ 07470,
steinharte@wpunj.edu

Summary. Infinite machines (IMs) can do supertasks. A supertask is an infinite series of operations done in some finite time. Whether or not our universe contains any IMs, they are worthy of study as upper bounds on finite machines. We introduce IMs and describe some of their physical and psychological aspects. An accelerating Turing machine (an ATM) is a Turing machine that performs every next operation twice as fast. It can carry out infinitely many operations in finite time. Many ATMs can be connected together to form networks of infinitely powerful agents. A network of ATMs can also be thought of as the control system for an infinitely complex robot. We describe a robot with a dense network of ATMs for its retinas, its brain, and its motor controllers. Such a robot can perform psychological supertasks—it can perceive infinitely detailed objects in all their detail; and it can formulate infinite plans; it can make infinitely precise movements. An endless hierarchy of IMs might realize a deep notion of intelligent computing everywhere.

2.1 Introduction

We discuss a variety of infinitely powerful machines and their infinitely complex operations. We won't argue for the existence of such machines.[1] Our only purpose here is to start to map out the logical space of all possible machines and minds (see [Doy91]). If we have a map of that logical space, we can locate ourselves there. We can then ask questions about our cognitive powers. For instance, if our brains are only finitely powerful machines, we can ask whether that finiteness is necessary or merely contingent (e.g., on the fact that our brains are made of certain stuff). And if we have a map of that logical

---

[1] It has long been traditional in Western thought to argue that the theistic God is an infinite mind. Hence the old arguments for the existence of God would be arguments for the existence of an infinite mind. For good introductions to divine infinity, see Leblanc [Leb93] and Achtner [Ach05]. However, their discussions are primarily historical. We do not appeal to the old arguments for the existence of God, and we do not see any easy way to link the modern Cantorian theory of the infinite with traditional theism.

space, we can study the upper bounds on the powers of our artifacts. Perhaps we can make artificial intellects far more powerful than our brains. They could use entirely different physics (e.g., quantum mechanical computers). If these artifacts are only finitely powerful, we can wonder why. If they are infinitely powerful, then having a map of the logical space of all possible intellects helps us understand what they can and cannot do. So a map of the logical space of possible intellects is useful in several ways.

2.2 Infinite Progressions

2.2.1 The Progression of Ordinals

We all know that the series of whole numbers (natural numbers) is endless. We can write 0, 1, 2, 3, and so on. We all know that for any natural number n, there exists a next natural number $n+1$. Natural numbers are more precisely known as *ordinals*, so we'll talk about ordinals rather than natural numbers. Although it's well-known that the series of finite ordinals is endless, it's less well-known that the endless finite series is bounded above by the first *limit ordinal*. The first limit ordinal is the first transfinite number. The ordinal number line thus extends beyond the finite into the transfinite. A useful description of the ordinal number line is given by Cantor's three number-generating rules. For a more complete description, you'll need to look at the full development of the ordinals in set theory (see [Dra74] or [Ham82]). The rules look like this:

1. Initial Rule. The initial ordinal is 0. The initial ordinal 0 is the set of all ordinals less than 0. There are no whole numbers less than 0. So 0 is the empty set {}.
2. Successor Rule. For every ordinal n, there exists an ordinal $n + 1$ that is greater than n. The ordinal $n + 1$ is the successor of n. It is a successor ordinal. Each ordinal $n + 1$ is the set of all ordinals less than itself. It is the set $\{0, \ldots n\}$. For instance, $1 = \{0\}$, $2 = \{0, 1\}$, $3 = \{0, 1, 2\}$, and so it goes.
3. Limit Rule. For any endlessly increasing series of ordinals, there exists a limit ordinal greater than every ordinal in the series. Since the series of finite ordinals 0, 1, 2, 3, ... is endlessly increasing, there exists a limit ordinal ω greater than every finite ordinal. The ordinal ω is the set of all ordinals less than itself. It is the set of all finite ordinals. It is $\{0, 1, 2, \ldots\}$. Since ω is an ordinal, it has a successor $\omega + 1$. And so it goes.

2.2.2 The Progression of Zeno Points

We'll say that a *progression* is a series of objects defined by three rules. An *initial rule* that associates the initial ordinal 0 with some object. A *successor rule* that associates each successor ordinal $n + 1$ with some object. And a *limit rule* that associates the limit ordinal ω with some object. For example, consider the following progression of fractions:

1. Initial Rule. The progression starts with the initial object 0. $Z_0 = 0$.
2. Successor Rule. For every object Z_n in the progression, there is a successor object Z_{n+1} in the progression. $Z_{n+1} = Z_n + \frac{1}{2^{n+1}}$. Hence we get the series $Z_1 = \frac{1}{2}$, $Z_2 = \frac{3}{4}$, $Z_3 = \frac{7}{8}$, $Z_4 = \frac{15}{16}$, and so on.
3. Limit Rule. The progression ends with a limit object Z_ω. The limit object is the limit of the Z_n as n goes to ω. So $Z_\omega = 1$.

The progression Z_0, Z_1, ..., Z_n, Z_{n+1}, ..., Z_ω is the *Zeno progression*. If we think of the fractions in the Zeno progression as points on a spatial line, they are *Zeno points*. If we think of them as fractions of a time interval, then they are *Zeno moments*.

Zeno progressions are useful for defining supertasks. A *supertask* is an infinite series of operations done in some finite region of space-time. Although some supertasks are ill-defined (and thus seem to be paradoxical), many supertasks have consistent recursive definitions and converge to well-defined objects at transfinite limits [EN93, KA97]. We can think of a supertask done in the temporal interval $[0, 1]$ as a progression of finitely complex (*finitary*) tasks done at Zeno moments during that interval. The first task is done by time $\frac{1}{2}$, the second by time $\frac{3}{4}$, and so on. At time 1, as many tasks have been done as there are natural numbers.

2.3 Some Supertasks

2.3.1 Drawing the Royce Map

A system or agent that performs a supertask is said to *accelerate* (see [Wey63, p. 42], [Gru69], [BJ89, pp. 14–16]). We'll follow convention and say that *Zeus* is an agent able to perform supertasks. We'll informally describe some supertasks for Zeus. Our first supertask is drawing the *Royce Map*. Royce describes a perfectly accurate map of England drawn on the surface of England, see [Roy99, pp. 506–507]. Since the map has to exactly describe the part of England on which it is drawn, it contains an exact copy of itself (which contains an exact copy of itself ...). The Royce Map contains an endlessly nested series of exact copies of itself. It is endlessly recursive.

For simplicity, say England is just a square crossed by a north-south road and an east-west road. Zeus is going to draw the perfect map of England. He writes with a special pencil that can always write twice as thin and that never runs out of graphite. He can always write twice as fast and twice as precisely. He writes on a sheet of paper that is continuously divided. For any two real numbers x and y varying between 0 and 1, there is a point (x, y) on the paper that can be either marked by the pencil or left unmarked. Drawing the Royce Map is a supertask. It consists of ω many tasks. Each task is finitely complex, and all tasks have the same complexity. Figure 2.1 shows the first four tasks in the construction of the Royce Map. Zeus draws the complete Royce Map by following these three rules:

1. <u>Initial Rule</u>. The initial map M_0 = a square with a cross drawn in it.
2. <u>Successor Rule</u>. The successor map M_{n+1} is the previous map M_n plus a cross drawn in the lower right square of M_n. Zeus can draw the map M_{n+1} in half the time he takes to draw the map M_n. So Zeus has drawn M_{n+1} by the Zeno moment Z_{n+1}.
3. <u>Limit Rule</u>. The limit map M_ω is the superimposition of all the finite maps. Zeus has drawn the Royce Map M_ω at the limit Zeno moment $Z_\omega = 1$. Following Dedekind, we say a structure is infinitely complex (*infinitary*) iff it has a proper part that can be put into a 1-1 correspondence with the whole (that is, isomorphic to the whole). Any lower right square of the Royce Map is isomorphic with the whole.

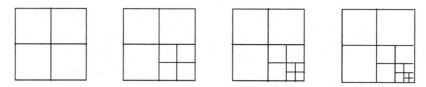

Fig. 2.1. The first four iterations of a Roycean self-nested map.

2.3.2 Drawing the Hilbert Paper

Our second supertask is the construction of the *Hilbert Paper*. The Hilbert Paper is a finitely sized square piece of paper on which every natural number is written in base 1 notation (as a stroke series). Writing down all the natural numbers on the Hilbert Paper is a supertask. It consists of ω many tasks. Although each task is only finitely complex, each successive task is more complex than its predecessor (the complexity goes up linearly). The n-th finite Hilbert Paper has the numbers 1 to n written on it. The Hilbert Paper itself is the limit of the progression of finitary Hilbert Papers. The construction of all the Hilbert Papers is given by the three rules below and is illustrated in Figure 2.2. The rules are:

1. <u>Initial Rule</u>. The initial Hilbert Paper H_0 = a piece of paper divided in half vertically and horizontally with a single stroke | in the upper left quarter.
2. <u>Successor Rule</u>. The successor Hilbert Paper $H_{n+1} = H_n$ + Zeus divides the right column in half vertically and divides the bottom row in half horizontally; Zeus copies the bottom row of strokes into the next lower

row and adds one stroke on the right. Zeus can draw the successor paper H_{n+1} in half the time he takes to draw the paper H_n. So Zeus has drawn H_{n+1} by the Zeno moment Z_{n+1}.

3. <u>Limit Rule</u>. The limit Hilbert Paper H_ω = the superimposition of all the H_n with n finite. Zeus has drawn the limit paper H_ω at the limit Zeno moment 1. The Hilbert Paper is the limit paper. The Hilbert Paper is infinitely complex: any square in the lower right-hand corner has exactly the same structure as the whole Hilbert Paper.

The rows and columns of the Hilbert Paper form a *Zeno Matrix*. A Zeno Matrix is a piece of (continuous) paper that is divided up into ω many columns and rows. The first row takes up $\frac{1}{2}$ of the paper, the next row takes up the next $\frac{1}{4}$ of the paper, and so on. The first column takes up $\frac{1}{2}$ of the paper, the next column takes up the next $\frac{1}{4}$ of the paper, and so on. For any n and m, there is a cell on the paper at row n and column m. The Hilbert Paper is a Zeno Matrix with all cells in the lower left triangle filled in with 1s.

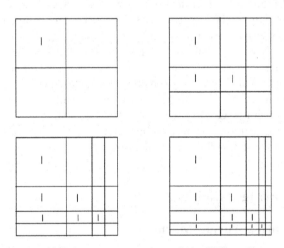

Fig. 2.2. A few iterations toward the Hilbert Paper.

2.3.3 Computing on Hilbert Papers

Zeus loves to compute. His writing tablet is made of special sheets of paper. Each sheet is divided into infinitely many rows. The top row is $\frac{1}{2}$ the sheet, the next row takes up the next $\frac{1}{4}$ of the sheet, and so it goes. Each sheet is divided into two columns. The left column is a copy of the Hilbert Paper. So the natural numbers are inscribed on the left column, starting with |, then ||, then |||, and so on. Each number in any row in the left column is associated with an empty cell in the same row in the right column.

Zeus wants to determine the locations of the primes in the natural numbers. For any n, it is a finitely complex task to determine whether n is prime or not. Of course, the complexity of these tasks increases without bound as n increases without bound. But that doesn't bother Zeus. Since Zeus is a super-agent, he can do any finitely complex task in any finite interval of time. He can do any task of complexity less than ω in any time interval greater than $\frac{1}{\omega}$. For any n, and for any finite time, Zeus can determine if n is prime.

Zeus is ready to compute. At time 0, every right column in every row is blank. At time $t = 0$, Zeus puts his pen on the square in the initial row and right column of his tablet. Within $\frac{1}{2}$ second, he does two tasks. First, he looks at the number written in the left column of that row (the number 1) and records the fact that it is not prime by writing a 0 in the right column of that row. Second, he moves his pen down one row. His pen is now over the square in the right column of the second row. Within $\frac{1}{4}$ second, he does two tasks. First, he looks at the number in the left column of that row (the number 2) and records the fact that it is prime by writing a 1 in the right column of that row. Second, he moves his pen down one row. His pen is now over the square in the right column of the third row. By the nth Zeno moment in the unit time interval, Zeus has either written 0 or 1 in the right column of the nth row. At the ωth Zeno moment 1, Zeus has written 0 or 1 in the right column of every row. Hence, at time 1, for every row n, the right column of n is 0 if n is not prime and is 1 if n is prime. Zeus has thus located every prime number. For any even number p, it is a finitary task to determine whether or not p is the sum of two primes. Goldbach's Conjecture says that every even number is the sum of two primes. By performing another supertask in the next unit of time, Zeus can test Goldbach's Conjecture.

2.4 Accelerating Machines

2.4.1 Accelerating Turing Machines

A conventional Turing machine (a CTM) is a digital computer with an unbounded memory. Many good descriptions of CTMs are available (e.g., [Wei76, Hop84]). We won't describe CTMs here. We show how to extend a CTM so that it can accelerate. We thus describe an *accelerating Turing machine* (an ATM). An ATM can do supertasks [Cop98b, Dav00, HL00].

An ATM has two main parts: a head and a tape. The tape of an ATM is only finitely long. It has some unit length. It is a line segment running from 0 to 1. The tape is divided into ω many cells. Each cell can hold either a 0 or a 1. The initial cell, 0, occupies the interval 0 to $\frac{1}{2}$ without including the endpoint at $\frac{1}{2}$. More precisely, cell 0 occupies the interval $[0, \frac{1}{2})$. The next cell, 1, occupies the interval $[\frac{1}{2}, \frac{3}{4})$. Each cell $n+1$ occupies an interval half as long as its predecessor. The boundaries of the cells are thus the Zeno points in the interval $[0, 1]$. Such a tape is therefore a *Zeno Tape*.

The head of an ATM moves across the tape. The head can read the content of any cell and can write a character on a cell. The head has a finite set S of possible states. It is always actually in some state from S. The head operates according to a fixed list of transition rules. Each transition rule is an instruction to the head of this form: if you're in state A and you read character B, then write character C, make a motion D, and change to state E. The states in a rule are from S. The characters are from the character set {0, 1}. The set of motions is {left, stay put, right}. The head has a rule for each (state, character) pair. The size of the head varies as it moves. As the head moves right, it shrinks to half its size. As it moves left, it expands to twice its previous size. If the head moves to either boundary of the tape (to 0 or 1), it shrinks to an infinitesimal size. It shrinks to the size of a point.

An ATM runs on an accelerating clock. An ATM performs its first operation in $\frac{1}{2}$ second. It performs its next operation in $\frac{1}{4}$ second. It performs each next operation in half the time it took to perform its previous operation. Its operations thus fill the Zeno moments in the interval $[0, 1]$. At time 1, the ATM has performed ω many operations. We can precisely describe the behavior of an ATM by three rules:

1. Initial Rule. The initial tape T_0 is inscribed with the input to the ATM. The clock is at time 0. The head is over cell 0. It is in state 0.
2. Successor Rule. For every tape T_n, there is a successor tape T_{n+1}. The successor tape T_{n+1} is defined by applying some transition rule. The head reads the value of the cell beneath it and looks at its state. It finds a rule whose antecedent matches its current (state, character) pair. It then applies that rule to write a character into the cell, make a motion, and change into a new state. The head accelerates. It makes each next transition twice as fast. Each successor tape is computed twice as fast. An ATM has computed tape T_{n+1} by the Zeno moment Z_{n+1}.
3. Limit Rule. Either the progression of tapes T_n for n finite converges to a limit tape T_ω or else it does not.[2] If it converges, then the limit configuration of the ATM is the limit tape with the head at its limit position. Thus if the progression of tapes converges, the head is located either at some finitely indexed cell or at the endpoint 1. If the progression of tapes does not converge, then the limit configuration of the ATM is the completely unmarked tape with the head positioned exactly over the

---

[2] We think of convergence in terms of increasing resemblance. The idea is that as $n \to \omega$, the *difference* between the tape T_n and the limit tape becomes arbitrarily small. We think of each tape as encoding a real number and the difference between tapes as the difference between real numbers. Hence convergence for a sequence of tapes is defined using the familiar Weierstrass theory of limits. Another kind of convergence is set-theoretic. An infinite series of set-theoretic structures can converge to a set-theoretic limit. Set-theoretic limits are defined in terms of infinite unions: $\bigcup_{n<\omega} S_n$. For example, the set-theoretic limit of the von Neumann ordinals {}, {{}}, {{}{{}}}, and so on is the von Neumann ω.

point 0. Thus, if the progression of tapes does not converge, the head is not on any cell at all.

2.4.2 Examples and Powers of Accelerating Turing Machines

We describe an ATM that converges and an ATM that does not. The convergent ATM starts with a blank tape (all cells unmarked). It starts in state 0. It always acts according to this rule: it writes a 1, it moves right, and it stays in state 0. At the nth clock tick, it has filled the first n cells with 1s. At the limit clock tick (at time 1), the head is on cell ω and the tape is entirely filled with 1s. The ATM has thus converged. The ATM that does not converge (that diverges) also starts with a blank tape and in state 0. It always acts according to two rules. The first rule says: if you are over a cell with value 0 and you are in state 0, then change the value of the cell to 1, stay put, and go into state 1. The second rule says: if you are over a cell with value 1 and you are in state 1, then change the value of the cell to 0, stay put, and go into state 0. This ATM *oscillates*. It always stays over cell 0. It marks the cell, it unmarks the cell, it marks the cell, it unmarks the cell, and so it goes. This ATM is the equivalent of the *Thompson lamp* [Tho54]. This ATM does not converge to any state at the limit time 1. Hence, at time 1, its head is on point 0 and its tape is blank.

An ATM can solve problems that cannot be solved by any CTM. Copeland [Cop98a] has shown that a universal ATM (a universal CTM that accelerates) can solve the Halting Problem for CTMs. It can thus fill in the *Halting Table* for CTMs. The Halting Table is recorded on a piece of paper divided into a Zeno Matrix. For any n and m, there is a cell on the paper at row n and column m. There is an ATM that can fill in each cell at row n and column n with 0 if the nth CTM does not halt on input m and with 1 if the nth CTM does halt on input m. A universal ATM can use the Halting Table to compute all the Rado numbers [BJ89, ch.4].

2.5 Intellects and Games

2.5.1 Infinite State Machines

Although Turing machines (both conventional and accelerating) are interesting in many ways, they are also rather dull. They don't interact. If an ATM realizes a mind, it is a solipsistic mind. But it is plausible that intelligence requires interaction with another agent either directly or through an environment [RN95, Mae95], for if perception and action are genuine, then another agent is necessary. We therefore move beyond Turing machines to consider infinitary machines that interact.

An *infinite state machine* (ISM) has a set I of possible inputs, a set S of possible states, and a set O of possible outputs. Its input and output sets may be finite or infinite. Its state set must be infinite. We think of the input, output, and state sets as sets of ordinals. An ISM has a function F that maps its current (input, state) pair onto its next state and a function G that maps its current (input, state) pair onto its next output. So the tuple (I, S, O, F, G) specifies a species of ISM. Of course, ISMs can accelerate.

We can think of the ordinals in the input set I as corresponding to the possible configurations of an input device. If we think of these input configurations in cognitive terms, they are the possible *perceptions* of the ISM. The ordinals in the output set O correspond to the configurations of an output device. These are the possible *actions* of the ISM. The states in S are the possible internal mental states (*ideas*) of the ISM. An ISM has an operation cycle. It consumes an input, it changes its state by applying F, and it produces an output by applying G. We can interpret the operation cycle psychologically as involving a perception, a calculation, and an action. We have discussed the psychological aspects of infinite minds elsewhere [Ste03], and so we do not discuss them here.

Since ISMs have inputs and outputs, they can be coupled together. One way to couple two (or more) ISMs together is to link them to a common structure. This common structure is their shared environment. And a nice way to model the interactions of two (or more) agents is to have them play a game. Many ethical, social, and political concepts can be analyzed in game-theoretic terms.[3] Of course, ISMs will only be interested in playing infinitely complex games. There is much literature on infinitary games.[4]

2.5.2 Infinitary Board Games

An *m, n, k-game* is a game in which two players (black and white) take turns placing marks of their own colors on the points of an m by n grid. You win iff you get k marks of your color in a line. For example, tic-tac-toe is a 3,3,3-game. Freestyle gomoku is a 19,19,5-game. Other m, n, k-games include Pente and Connect6. Finitary m, n, k-games are of no interest to superminds. We can extend m, n, k-games to the infinite by allowing the grid to be infinite (with grid points indexed by pairs of integers). We can easily compress a grid whose points are indexed by pairs of integers into a finite area. The compression is by Zeno compression on each direction of the x and y axes. Each next step away from the origin is twice as small as the previous step. The resulting *Zeno Grid* has its origin at (0, 0) and its limit edges at points with x or y coordinates $+1$ or -1.

We mechanize an infinitary m, n, k-game by extending the mechanization of a finitary m, n, k-game (e.g. tic-tac-toe). For any infinitary m, n, k-game,

---

[3] There is much literature associated with the analysis of ethical, social, and political concepts in game-theoretic terms. Axelrod [Axe84] and Danielson [Dan92] develop ethical theories in the context of games played by machines. For a preliminary discussion of infinitary value theory, see [Sor94].

[4] For some examples, see [GS53, GJM78, Fre84, Jec84, CL90, Sch93, HS02].

each player has at least an eye, a brain, and a hand. The eye surveys the board. The eye is an infinitary array of sensors with the same structure as the Zeno Grid. It is an infinitary retina positioned over and looking at the game board. Each configuration of the board corresponds to a number in I. The eye sends this number to the brain. The brain computes the next move according to the player's strategy. This strategy is encoded in the functions F and G. The brain uses F to change its mental state. It uses G to generate its output. Its output is sent to its hand. The hand is a device that can mark a point on the Zeno Grid. The output instruction tells the hand which point to mark. For instance, an output number can encode a pair of numbers (i, j). If the hand gets output instruction (i, j), then it moves to the ith row and jth column and puts its mark on the grid point with those coordinates. Since the hand must be able to move from any point to any other point in finite time, it has to accelerate.

Suppose that Zeus and Hera are ISMs playing some infinitary m, n, k-game. Each player has to move in one clock tick, and the clock accelerates. Hera goes first. She moves in the first $\frac{1}{2}$ second. Zeus moves in the next $\frac{1}{4}$ second. And so it goes. Of course, this simplistic scheme doesn't enable us to select a winner. We need some way to determine when a player wins. We could let each player decide when he or she wins. But that might introduce conflict. So we add a *referee* who checks the board after each move. We can call this referee *Apollo*. Apollo is also an ISM. According to this scheme, each move is divided into two parts: a player operates, and the referee checks for a winner. So we can think of Zeus and Hera playing various infinitary m, n, k-games, carefully watched by Apollo. Other board games (such as chess) can also be extended to the infinite (see [Pic95]).

2.5.3 Infinitary Number Selection Games

An infinitary number selection game involves two players (Zeus and Hera) who construct an infinitely long sequence of numbers. They take turns selecting numbers from a fixed set and adding their choices to the sequence. Suppose the set of numbers is just the set of decimal digits (see [Ham82, p. 189]). It is the set $\{0, \ldots 9\}$. The game is played on a Zeno Tape. Hera and Zeus take turns reading from and writing on the tape. The first few plays in an infinitary number selection game might go like this: Hera writes 3 in tape cell 0 in the first $\frac{1}{2}$ second; Zeus writes 4 in cell 1 in the next $\frac{1}{4}$ second; Hera writes 9 in cell 2 in the next $\frac{1}{8}$ second; and so on. This game makes a sequence that starts with 349.

Each player is an ISM. Each player consists of a controller, an input device, and an output device. The input and output devices always rest over some position on the tape. We can think of these devices very simply as combined into a single read/write head that rests over some position on the tape just like the read/write head of an ATM. The controller is an infinitely complex CPU. It has an infinitary memory and can perform any of its basic operations in any finite nonzero time. As an ISM, the logic of the controller is defined by the tuple (I, S, O, F, G). Its input set I is {blank, 0, . . . 9}. The blank is used to start the game. Its state set S is the set of all finitely long digit sequences. Its output set O is {0, . . . 9}. The functions F and G are stored in a Zeno Matrix in the controller. The matrix that stores F and G is the long-term memory of the player. The short-term memory of each player includes the variables used to track the player's current configuration. The program that regulates the behavior of the players is given below.[5]

As the clock accelerates to the limit moment 1, the players complete an infinitely long sequence $<d_0, d_1, d_2, d_3 . . .>$ on the tape. Since each d_i is from the set {0, . . . 9}, we may think of the tape as the decimal expansion of the real number $0.d_0d_1d_2d_3 . . .$ that lies between 0 and 1. To make this into a game, we need to add some definition of winning. A player wins by hitting a real number. Before the game begins, the referee (*Uranos*) partitions the set of real numbers in [0, 1] into two sets, H and Z. Every real in [0, 1] is either in H or in Z but not in both. At the end of the game, Uranos checks whether the tape defines a real in H or Z. If it is in H, Hera wins. If it is in Z, Zeus wins.

At the end of an infinite series of moves (at the limit time 1), the referee Uranos checks whether the sequence on the tape is in H or Z. Of course, he only needs to check whether it is in H. If it is not, then it is in Z by default. The set H may be finite, countable, or uncountable. Let C be the cardinality of the real number continuum. The set H is stored in an array with C slots. The addresses of this array thus correspond to a well-ordering of an uncountably infinite set.[6] This array is compressed into a tape of finite unit length. Each cell on this tape holds a series of ω many digits. It is a supertask to determine

---

[5] Each player in the infinite number selection game has a data structure M (its memory). M is a Zeno Matrix with four columns labeled (input, current state, next state F, output G). For the sake of starting the game, M has an initial row whose input column is blank. Every row in M has the form (n, k, kno, o). That is, the next state is the current state plus the input plus the output. Each player has a variable p that points at a row in M. The players are the First Player (player number 1) and the Second Player (player number 2). The tape is initially filled entirely with blanks. Player 1 starts with his or her head over cell 0, and player 2 starts with his or her head over cell 1. Each player runs the following algorithm: state = blank; the head is positioned over cell with address (player number 1); the index p into M is initially 0; for i accelerating from 0 to ω do {in = read the content of the cell under your head; advance p until M[p, input] is in and M[p, current state] = state; state = M[p, F]; out = M[p, G]; advance head; write out on the cell under your head; wait one clock tick for the other player; advance your tape head to catch up with the other player}.

[6] We are working within the standard set theory known as ZFC. The Axiom of Choice in ZFC entails that every set can be well-ordered. Hence there is a well-ordering of every uncountable set. For example, there is a well-ordering of the real numbers. And yet no such well-ordering of the reals is known. We thus enter terra incognita.

whether the sequence defined by Zeus and Hera is located in slot n of the array that stores H. For full iteration over H, Uranos must be able to perform uncountably many supertasks in finite time. Uranos is a machine that is far more powerful than either Hera or Zeus. Uranos works with spatio-temporal continua that are far richer than the continua used by Hera and Zeus. It is not entirely clear how to define these continua. Since they are richer than the real number line, they are nonstandard. Perhaps Uranos is working with continua that approximate Peirce's inexhaustible continua [Pei65, 3, pp. 563–570] or that approximate Conway's surreal number line [Con01].

A somewhat more complex version of this game allows the players to select any natural number at each turn [Nee04]. We can think of these natural numbers as encoding various kinds of information. A natural number (expressed in base 2) is a bit string. It can be thought of as a file that describes an image (e.g., a JPG file). We can think of the read head of each player as an eye that can recognize any of ω many images. We can think of the write head of each player as a hand that can paint any of ω many images. Thus, when a player writes a number on the tape, he or she is painting a picture. And when a player reads a number from the tape, he or she is perceiving a picture. We might thus think of the whole sequence written on the tape as a movie. The sets H and Z define two kinds or styles of movies. Hera prefers those in H, while Zeus prefers those in Z.

2.5.4 Infinitary Athletic Contests

Although so far we've only talked about games for supernerds (infinitary board games and number games), we can define games for superathletes. Consider infinitary tennis. We define it as a generalization of ordinary finitary tennis. Finitary tennis is played in a finite volume of space-time (a tennis court). A court has two sides. We can think of each side as a unit cube. Finitary tennis is a two-player game. We can refer to the players as Hera and Zeus. Each player has a finitely sized racket. Each player occupies one side of the tennis court and can move freely in his or her unit cube. Tennis is played with a finitely sized ball. The players use their rackets to hit a finitely sized ball back and forth. We assume some familiarity with finitary tennis. We won't go into it in any more detail.

We start our definition of infinitary tennis by defining it at level 1. It is much like finitary tennis. In finitary tennis, the size of the ball is fixed. Since the size of the ball is fixed, we can divide each side of the tennis court into cubical cells. Each cell is exactly large enough to contain the ball. This division also divides the floor of the court into finitely sized square cells. For tennis at level 1, the ball always passes through (and only through) cubical cells. It thus lands on any bounce in some square cell on the floor of the court. In tennis at level 1, each player has a racket of normal finitary size. This racket is a disk whose diameter is larger than that of the ball. Each player has to move through his or her unit cube to hit the ball. Each player has more or less skill in getting to the ball and in hitting it back in such a way that it will land in the opposing player's court. Tennis at level 2 is much like tennis at level 1. The difference is just this: each cube in the court is divided in half on each axis to make eight smaller subcubes. The ball shrinks to fit into these smaller cubes. The rackets shrink proportionally. The players remain the same size. They are trying to hit a smaller ball with a smaller racket. Tennis at level 3 is defined analogously. Each cube is again cut in half on each axis to make eight even smaller cubes. The ball and rackets shrink again. We can iterate through tennis at level 4, level 5, and so on to level ω. At level ω, the players are playing with a ball that is the size of a point and rackets also the size of a point.

An easy version of infinitary tennis is played by moving from level n to level $n + 1$ each time the ball passes over the net. A harder version allows the ball to either shrink or expand monotonically from any size to any other size as it moves across the court. Each volley in infinitary tennis (whether easy or hard) takes place in a unit time. Hera serves the ball in $\frac{1}{2}$ second. If Zeus returns it, the return takes only $\frac{1}{4}$ second; if Hera returns it, the return takes only $\frac{1}{8}$ second. And so it goes until someone fails to return the ball or returns it in an illegal way (so it lands out of bounds). If the volley goes to the limit, then the volley is counted for neither player. Playing infinitary tennis requires a body with infinitely precise perception, cognition, and volition. An infinitary tennis player has to have eyes with infinitary resolution. He or she has to have a brain that can compute the trajectories of arbitrarily small and arbitrarily fast objects. Its brain has to be able to accelerate. It has to have a motor system that can move in infinitely precise ways. Its muscles have to be able to accelerate. It has to have infinitely fine hand-eye coordination. An infinitary tennis player has to have an infinitary body. We can easily use analogous techniques to define infinitely precise versions of other games: infinitary handball, soccer, pool, and so on.

2.6 Infinitely Complex Bodies

A mind is an agent that interacts with an environment. The interaction is a loop involving perception, cognition, and action. A mind is more than merely a calculator or a brain. It has parts that enable it to perceive and to act. A mind is thus a whole body. An infinitary mind has to have an infinitary body. It has to have a body able to perform perceptual, cognitive, and volitional supertasks. It has to have a body able to at least perform operations with arbitrarily high finite precision (e.g., if it can hit a ball of some size moving at some speed, then it can hit a ball that is twice as small moving twice as fast). We describe an infinitary humanoid body here. Nonhumanoid infinitary bodies are also possible.

As with any body, the infinitary body starts with a single cell (its zygote). The zygote encodes a growth plan that builds the infinitary body by means of an endless series of iterations. An infinitary body can only grow in a universe in which space, time, and matter are continuously divisible. The initial iteration of the growth plan takes $\frac{1}{2}$ unit of time. Each successor iteration happens twice as fast as its predecessor, so the body grows through infinitely many iterations in one time unit. The growth plan of the infinitary body is based on the generation of body forms (phenotypes) by L-systems [PL90]. It would be fun to present the infinite growth plan with greater biological realism, but to save space our presentation is merely schematic.[7]

The growth plan defines an initial iteration. On this first iteration, the body grows by ordinary cellular division into a central trunk with a head. Each offspring cell has the same size as its parent. Hence the initial iteration fills out a finite volume. For simplicity, let the trunk just be a cylinder and the head a sphere. The trunk is the initial limb of the body. It has two *growth sites* at the top (for its arms) and two growth sites at the bottom (for its legs). After the initial iteration, the growth plan drives the body through endlessly many successor iterations. We discuss successor iterations for the limbs, eyes, and brain.[8] The successor iterations converge to an infinite form in the limit. The limit form is infinitely complex. Infinite organs support infinite forms of perception, cognition, and action.

The growth plan defines an endless series of successor iterations for the limbs. The limbs that exist at the start of the nth iteration are the parent limbs. Parent limbs have growth sites. Each growth site generates an offspring limb. Each offspring limb has a bottom and a top. The bottom is attached to its parent by a joint. The top has twice as many growth sites as its parent. Each offspring limb is half as long and half as thick as its parent limb. The trunk grows two arms (each half as long and half as thick as the trunk). Each arm sprouts four fingers (each half as long and half as thick as the arm). Each finger sprouts eight subfingers. The trunk also grows two legs (each half as long and half as thick as the trunk). Each leg grows four toes. Each toe grows eight subtoes. Each nth limb has the form of a branching binary tree with n levels and 2^n limb tips, see [Mor88, pp. 102–108]. The series of finitely complex

---

[7] The growth plan of the human body is recursive: the rules in the growth plan are repeatedly applied to their own outputs. Since the growth plan is recursive, it generates a body with a fractal structure [GRW90, BLW94]. Our human bodies are generated by iterating the growth plan only a few times. The result is a fractal structure with only a few levels of depth (a fractal bush). But the growth plan can be iterated any number of times. More iterations increases the fractal depth of the body. The growth plan can be iterated to infinity, thus making an infinitely deep fractal body.

[8] We have defined idealizations only for the eyes, limbs, and brain. Idealizations of other organs are easily defined. These idealizations both universalize and infinitely amplify the powers of the organs. For example, the respiratory, digestive, and circulatory systems have the function of supplying the body with energy. These organs are universalized so the ideal body can obtain energy from any source in its universe.

limbs converges in the limit to an infinitely complex limb with as many levels as natural numbers and as many tips as real numbers. These limbs can do infinitely complex motor tasks.

The growth plan defines an endless series of successor iterations for the eyes. The initial eye closely resembles a normal mature human eye. On each successor iteration, each photocell in the retina divides in an ideal way into two daughter photocells. Each daughter photocell is twice as small, fast, reliable, and efficient as its mother. So each next retina is twice as dense and twice as computationally powerful as the previous retina. The lens of each eye is progressively more perfect. Normal human eyes are sensitive to a limited part of the optical spectrum. But the idealization of the function of the eye implies a universalization of its function. It implies a widening of its sensitivity until it covers the entire spectrum of radiant energy in its universe. The series of finitely complex retinas converges in the limit to an infinitely complex retina. The infinitary eye has an infinitely dense retina (between any two photocells, there is another photocell). The infinitary eye can see an infinitely detailed object in a single glance. For instance, it can see Royce's perfect map of England in England in a single glance [Roy99, pp. 506–507]. The infinitary eye can perform infinitely complex perceptual tasks.

The growth plan defines an endless series of successor iterations for the brain and nervous system. The initial brain closely resembles a normal mature human brain. On each successor iteration, the next brain is derived from the previous brain by dividing every neuron and doubling its connections. Each offspring neuron is twice as small, fast, reliable, and efficient as its parent. As the brain grows by ideal division, so the nervous system grows. A branching pattern of nerves follows the branching pattern of limbs. The nerves that control the next level of limbs are twice as small, fast, reliable, and efficient. Hence each next level of limbs is more precisely controlled. The series of finitely complex brains converges in the limit to an infinitary brain. An infinitary brain is a dense neural network (between any two neurons, there is another neuron wired to both of them). An infinitary brain has the computational power of an accelerating universal Turing machine [Cop98b, Ste03]. It can perform infinitely complex cognitive tasks.

2.7 Conclusion

We have informally discussed a variety of infinitely complex machines and minds. On the one hand, we might wonder whether any infinitary minds exist in our universe. On the other hand, we might wonder whether our universe exists in an infinitary mind. An infinitary mind can simulate any finitary process. For instance, it can exactly simulate or realize a finitary physical universe. A finitary universe has finitary space, finitary time, and finitary matter (there is some fixed finite upper bound on the number of bits of information that can be stored in any finite volume of space-time). Such universes may contain finitary living, thinking things (e.g., finitary persons). An infinitary mind can simulate all possible finitary universes in exact detail in any finite time.[9]

Some writers have argued that our universe is only finitely complex (see [Fre91, Fin95, Ste98]). So, if infinitary minds exist, they can easily run simulations of our universe. Bostrom [Bos03] argues that this possibility must be taken seriously. Of course, theists have long argued that our universe is the product of an intelligent creator (an infinitary mind). Some theists have argued (roughly) that everything must have an explanation; that since our universe is something, it must have an explanation; and that the best explanation for the existence of our universe is an intelligent creator. Skeptics have objected that if everything must have an explanation, then the intelligent creator must have an explanation. And if the best explanation for our universe is an intelligent creator C_1, then by analogy the best explanation for the existence of an intelligent creator is an even more intelligent supercreator C_2. But then C_2 is best explained by C_3, and so it goes. The result is an endless regression of creators. Such a regression is possible.[10] Since one kind of creation is simulation (as when an author imagines a character—see [Mor88, pp. 122–124]), the endless series of creators can be thought of as an endless hierarchy of simulators. It is easy to describe an endless hierarchy of simulators:

1. Initial Rule. An initial universe is a computation that is not simulating any other universe. It is like a novel in which no character is writing another novel (and by *novel* we mean a novel that completely and exactly describes an entire universe). There is at least one initial computation (namely, our universe C_0). There may be many other initial computations (other initial universes).

2. Successor Rule. Every computation is a virtual machine running on a more powerful computation. For every computation C_n, there exists a more powerful computer C_{n+1} that runs C_n as a virtual machine. C_{n+1} simulates C_n. This is like saying that every novel is written by a character (a virtual author) in another novel. We thus have an endless series of virtual authors writing novels within novels.

---

[9] Since there are only ω many finitary universes, an infinitary mind can build a database in its memory of all finitary universes. This database is the finitary part of Leibniz's Palace of the Fates [Lei10, pp. 414–417].

[10] Bostrom [Bos03, pp. 253–254] writes: "Virtual machines can be stacked: it's possible to simulate a machine simulating another machine, and so on, in arbitrarily many steps of iteration. . . . Reality may thus contain many levels. . . . Although all the elements of such a system can be naturalistic, even physical, it is possible to draw some loose analogies with religious conceptions of the world. . . . Further rumination on these themes could climax in a *naturalistic theogony* that would study the structure of this hierarchy."

3. <u>Limit Rule</u>. For every endless series of computers simulating computers, there exists a more powerful computer that simulates that entire series. The limit computer is more powerful than every computer in the series of which it is a limit. The first limit computer is C_ω. Following our literary analogy, C_ω writes a novel in which (1) some character writes a novel and (2) every novel written by a character contains a character who writes a novel. And C_ω is a character in yet another novel $C_{\omega+1}$.

We can gain even more precision by defining a chain of simulators as a function from the whole ZFC ordinal number line to simulations. One might conclude that every chain that spans the whole ZFC ordinal number line is the result of a simulation by an Absolute Mind whose power is proportional to the proper class of ordinals.[11] Obviously, we have not provided any argument for this endless series of nested simulations. And it is far from clear that any serious argument can be given for such a series. But if such a series does exist, then it is truly a case of intelligent computing everywhere. Our universe would be a thought in an infinitary mind, and that infinitary mind would itself be a thought in an even greater infinitary mind, and so on. If a scheme like this were true, it would be a computational version of the classical idealism of Berkeley and Royce. And if every possible universe is a member of a chain of nested simulations that converges to an Absolute Mind, then we would really have a case of intelligent computing *everywhere*.

References

[Ach05]   W. Achtner. Infinity in science and religion. *Neue Zeitschrift für System-atische Theologie und Religionsphilosophie*, 47:392–411, 2005.

[Axe84]   R. Axelrod. *The Evolution of Cooperation*. Basic Books, New York, 1984.

[BJ89]   G. Boolos and R. Jeffrey. *Computability and Logic*. Cambridge University Press, New York, 1989.

[BLW94]   J. Bassingthwaighte, L. Liebovitch, and B. West. *Fractal Physiology*. Oxford University Press, New York, 1994.

[Bos03]   N. Bostrom. Are you living in a computer simulation? *Philosophical Quarterly*, 53(211):243–255, 2003.

[CL90]   K. Ciesielski and R. Laver. A game of D. Gale in which one of the players has limited memory. *Periodica Mathematica Hungarica*, 22(2):153–158, 1990.

---

[11] An absolutely infinite mind (with power proportional to a proper class) would be the mind of God (see [Tal85]). But how would such a mind be defined? We cannot use any logical or mathematical techniques since proper classes cannot enter into more complex structures. It does not seem likely that there is any machine or mind with complexity proportional to a proper class. On the contrary, set-theoretic reflection principles suggest that anything that looks like an absolutely infinite machine or mind is really only an object at some nonabsolute level of the set-theoretic hierarchy.

[Con01]   J. Conway. *On Numbers and Games*. Natick, MA, A. K. Peters Lt., 2nd edition, 2001.

[Cop98a] B.J. Copeland. Even turing machines can compute uncomputable functions. In C. Calude, J. Casti, and M. Dinneen, editors, *Unconventional Models of Computation*, pages 150–164. Springer-Verlag, New York, 1998.

[Cop98b] B.J. Copeland. Super turing-machines. *Complexity*, 4(1):30–32, 1998.

[Dan92]   P. Danielson. *Artificial Morality: Virtuous Robots for Virtual Games*. Routledge, New York, 1992.

[Dav00]   E.B. Davies. Building infinite machines. *British Journal for the Philosophy of Science*, 52(4):671–682, 2000.

[Doy91]   J. Doyle. The foundations of psychology: a logico-computational inquiry into the concept of mind. In R. Cummins and J. Pollock, editors, *Philosophy and AI: Essays at the Interface*, pages 39–78. MIT Press, Cambridge, MA, 1991.

[Dra74]   F. Drake. *Set Theory: An Introduction to Large Cardinals*. American Elsevier, New York, 1974.

[EN93]   J. Earman and J. Norton. Forever is a day: supertasks in Pitowsky and Malament-Hogarth spacetimes. *Philosophy of Science*, 60:22–42, 1993.

[Fin95]   D. Finkelstein. Finite physics. In R. Herken, editor, *The Universal Turing Machine: A Half-Century Survey*, pages 323–347. Springer-Verlag, New York, 1995.

[Fre84]   C. Freiling. Banach games. *Journal of Symbolic Logic*, 49(2):343–375, 1984.

[Fre91]   E. Fredkin. Digital mechanics: an informational process based on reversible universal cellular automata. In H. Gutowitz, editor, *Cellular Automata: Theory and Experiment*, pages 254–270. MIT Press, Cambridge, MA, 1991.

[GJM78]   F. Galvin, T. Jech, and M. Magidor. An ideal game. *Journal of Symbolic Logic*, 43(2):284–292, 1978.

[Gru69]   A. Grunbaum. Can an infinitude of operations be performed in a finite time? *British Journal of the Philosophy of Science*, 20(3):203–218, 1969.

[GRW90]   A. Goldberger, D. Rigney, and B. West. Chaos and fractals in human physiology. *Scientific American*, 262(2):42–49, 1990.

[GS53]   D. Gale and F.M. Stewart. Infinite games with perfect information. In H. Kuhn and A. Tucker, editors, *Contributions to the Theory of Games*, volume 28, pages 245–266. Princeton University Press, Princeton, NJ, 1953.

[Ham82]   A. Hamilton. *Numbers, Sets, and Axioms: The Apparatus of Mathematics*. Cambridge University Press, New York, 1982.

[HL00]   J.D. Hamkins and A. Lewis. Infinite time turing machines. *Journal of Symbolic Logic*, 65(2):567–604, 2000.

[Hop84]   J. Hopcroft. Turing machines. *Scientific American*, 250(5):86–107, 1984.

[HS02]   S. Huddleston and J. Shurman. Transfinite chomp. In R. Nowakowski, editor, *More Games of No Chance*. Cambridge University Press, New York, 2002.

[Jec84]   T. Jech. More game-theoretic properties of Boolean algebras. *Annals of Pure and Applied Logic*, 26:11–29, 1984.

[KA97]   T. Koetsier and V. Allis. Assaying supertasks. *Logique et Analyse*, 159:291–313, 1997.

[Leb93]   J. Leblanc. Infinity in theology and mathematics. *Religious Studies*, 29(1):51–62, 1993.

[Lei10]   G.W. Leibniz. *Theodicy*. 1710. Trans. E. M. Huggard. Open Court, Peru, IL, (1996).

[Mae95]   P. Maes. Modeling adaptive autonomous agents. In C. Langton, editor, *Artificial Life: An Overview*, pages 135–162. MIT Press, Cambridge, MA, 1995.

[Mor88]   H. Moravec. *Mind Children: The Future of Robot and Human Intelligence*. Harvard University Press, Cambridge, MA, 1988.

[Nee04]   I. Neeman. *The Determinacy of Long Games*. Walter de Gruyer, New York, 2004.

[Pei65]   C.S. Peirce. In C. Hartshorne and P. Weiss, editors, *Collected Papers of Charles Sanders Peirce*. Harvard University Press, Cambridge, MA, 1965.

[Pic95]   C. Pickover. *Keys to Infinity*. John Wiley & Sons, New York, 1995.

[PL90]   P. Prusinkiewicz and A. Lindenmayer. *The Algorithmic Beauty of Plants*. Springer-Verlag, New York, 1990.

[RN95]   S. Russell and P. Norvig. *Artificial Intelligence: A Modern Approach*. Prentice-Hall, Englewood Cliffs, NJ, 1995.

[Roy99]   J. Royce. *The World and the Individual*. The Macmillan Company, New York, 1899. First Series. Supplementary Essay.

[Sch93]   M. Scheepers. Variations on a game of Gale (i): Coding strategies. *Journal of Symbolic Logic*, 58(3):1035–1043, 1993.

[Sor94]   R. Sorensen. Infinite decision theory. In J. Jordan, editor, *Gambling on God*, pages 139–159. Rowman & Littlefield, London, 1994.

[Ste98]   E. Steinhart. Digital metaphysics. In T. Bynum and J. Moor, editors, *The Digital Phoenix: How Computers Are Changing Philosophy*, pages 117–134. Academic Press, San Diego and London, 1998.

[Ste03]   E. Steinhart. Supermachines and superminds. *Minds and Machines*, 13:155–186, 2003.

[Tal85]   C. Taliaferro. Divine cognitive power. *International Journal for Philosophy of Religion*, 18:133–140, 1985.

[Tho54]   J. Thomson. Tasks and supertasks. *Analysis*, 15:1–13, 1954.

[Wei76]   J. Weizenbaum. *Computer Power and Human Reason: From Judgment to Calculation*. W.H. Freeman and Co., New York, 1976.

[Wey63]   H. Weyl. *Philosophy of Mathematics and Natural Science*. Atheneum, New York, 1963. Original work in German, 1927.

3

The Nonclassical Mind: Cognitive Science and Nonclassical Computing

Colin G. Johnson

Computing Laboratory, University of Kent, Canterbury, Kent CT2 7NF, England,
C.G.Johnson@kent.ac.uk

Summary. This chapter explores the ideas of *nonclassical computation* (computing where one or more traditional assumptions about what defines computation have been dropped) in the context of cognitive science. A framework that classifies nonclassical computing concepts is discussed, and the potential impact of each of these concepts on issues of cognition, mind, and affect is analzsed.

3.1 Introduction

Computational modeling of mental activity is one of the core activities in cognitive science. This is grounded in a *computational functionalist* view of mind. That is, the substrate in which mind is realized is irrelevant to being able to produce mentality, and a computer is a sufficient substrate in which to be able to carry out that realization. In recent years, a discipline of *nonclassical computing* has emerged. This aims to reappraise the foundations of computing, and discover what happens when we break in turn each of the assumptions that we make about what a computer is and how it functions. In particular, we would like to understand whether the system that remains when the assumption is removed can still be meaningfully understood as being a computer and if it can solve computational problems that are difficult or impossible for traditional computers.

In this chapter, we examine what the consequences of nonclassical computing might be for cognitive science. If the notion of *computation* can be stretched, what does this imply for the *computational* side of computational functionalism? To do this, we take the taxonomy of classical computing assumptions devised by Stepney et al. [SBC+05] and look at each part of this taxonomy in turn. The chapter is structured as follows, Section 3.2 gives more detail on the background to computational functionalism and nonclassical computation, and Section 3.3 gives a taxonomy of the assumptions within classical computation that can be relaxed or removed to create nonclassical computing systems. The remaining substantive sections take one class of assumption from classical computing and examine the implications for cognitive science of nonclassical computers that break those kinds of assumptions. Finally, there is a brief conclusion and some questions for further thought.

3.2 Computational Functionalism and Nonclassical Computing

One of the key ideas in cognitive science is the use of computational metaphors and models in understanding the mind. The justification for this is a set of assumptions that we will term *computational functionalism*.

This consists of two parts. The first part is the *functionalist* assumption. This is the notion that a mind equivalent in capability to a human (or animal) mind can be created in any medium that is sufficient to allow *processes* of the kind found within the brain to happen. Essentially, the mind results from the processes in the brain rather than from the stuff of which the brain is made. This assumption has been well studied (see [Blo96] and [Lev04] for overviews). An important implication of this is that a mind having the same capabilities as a human or animal mind could, in theory, be realized on an alternative, non-neural substrate.

The second assumption is the *computational* assumption (sometimes called *machine-state functionalism*). This states that a computer is a sufficient medium for the realization of the activity that is realized in neurallysubstrated minds [Put75]. This assumption has received less critical attention than the core functionalist assumption.

In order to take this computationalist stance toward mind, we need to have some notion of what a computer is. Traditionally, the definition of computation is given by giving an abstract, mathematical definition of a sufficient computing device (a Turing machine or equivalent), then treating as a computer any physical device that is capable of processing information in a way that is (behaviorally) indistinguishable from that of a Turing machine. This is sometimes referred to as the *classical* notion of computation.

In recent years, a new approach to the foundations of computation has been created. This is called *nonclassical, postclassical* or *reality-based* computing [SBC$^+$05, SBC$^+$06]. This seeks to ground the notion of computation by assessing the computational properties of physical systems in the world rather than beginning with a notion of a computational machine.

This stance has its origins in a 1982 paper by Feynman [Fey82]. In this paper, he discusses physical phenomena that are not efficiently realizable on (traditional) computing machines. The example given is drawn from quantum mechanics. Feynman notes that there are some quantum processes that cannot be efficiently simulated on traditional computers. Then, significantly, he inverts this argument—if there are processes that cannot be simulated efficiently, then we can use these processes to *build* new kinds of computers that are, at least in that limited domain, capable of doing more than traditional computers:

> *Now I explicitly go to the question of how we can simulate with a computer—a universal automaton or something—the quantum mechanical effects. ... The full description of the quantum mechanics for a large system with R particles is given by a function $\psi(x_1, x_2, \ldots, x_R, t)$, which we call the amplitude to find the particles $x_1, x_2, \ldots, x_R$, and therefore, because it has too many variables, it* cannot *be simulated with a normal computer with a number of elements proportional to R or proportional to N. We had the same troubles with the probability in classical physics. And therefore, the problem is, how can we simulate the quantum mechanics? There are two ways we can go about it. We can give up on our rule about what the computer was, we can say: Let the computer itself be built out of quantum mechanical elements which obey quantum mechanical laws.*

Nonclassical computing generalizes this to other systems. Instead of defining computation "up front", we examine things in the world for properties that could lead them to be useful as computational devices. This is important for cognitive science because if such alternative computational capabilities exist in the world, it is likely that they will have been adopted by evolutionary processes as part of the "toolkit" of structures that could come together to create mind.

The remainder of this chapter explores the consequences of such reality-based computation for the study of mind. If we look at the assumptions that underlie classical computation (and, by consequence, cognitive science), what happens if we break these assumptions?

3.3 A Taxonomy of Assumptions for Nonclassical Computation

In order to carry out this program of work, we first need to understand what assumptions underpin classical computation. For this purpose, we will use the taxonomy developed by Stepney et al. [SBC+05]. This breaks down the classical computing assumptions into six categories:

The Turing Paradigm: The assumptions that are made in specifying the Turing machine as a canonical model of computation. In particular, the idea that a computer consists of processing discrete states that can be freely read and copied, that resources are freely available to extend the tape or carry out some process, and that the choice of substrate is an implementation detail rather than an important feature. More abstractly, the idea of the *universal computer* that can be applied to all tasks is implicit in this set of assumptions.

The von Neumann Paradigm: The assumptions that every computing machine contains a single core computational unit and that information is brought to this unit for computation.

The Output Paradigm: The assumptions that suggest that a computational process has a well-defined output and that what is interesting or productive about a computer is this output rather than what happens during the computation.

The Algorithmic Paradigm: The assumption that a computer executes a well-defined process, bounded in time, with input and output clearly understood. Also the idea that a computer is a deterministic (nonrandom) device.

The Refinement Paradigm: The assumption that solving a problem on the computer consists of turning some description of what a problem is into how to solve it and the assumption that such a description exists, exists before the attempt to solve the problem starts, and does not change during this process.

The Computer-as-Artifact Paradigm: The assumption that a computer is a device of fixed extent that cannot extend itself and that does not interfere with the problem being solved during the solution. Also, the notion that solving a particular problem involves finding a way of processing that problem on a given computer system rather than searching for something in the physical world that already does the computational process of interest.

The remainder of this chapter examines each of these paradigms in turn and considers the implications for cognitive science of breaking each of them.

3.4 Breaking the Turing Paradigm

The Turing paradigm is, at its broadest, the idea that computation is best defined by giving an abstract mathematical description of what a "computation" is and then showing that real-world computations are equivalent to that description. More narrowly, this is the *Church-Turing thesis*, which asserts that a Turing machine (see, e.g., [HMU01]) is capable of acting as a universal computation device. By contrast, we can start from a set of physical activities in the world, all of which appear to be doing something that we can term "computation", and ask what is common to them (and not found in things or processes that are not computations). In this section, we explore both the consequences of going beyond the Turing machine model as a model and more generally the consequences of computing embedded in the world.

3.4.1 More than Turing Machines: Analog, Quantum and Diffusive

One assumption that is part of the Turing paradigm is that representations of state in computer systems are discrete. This discreteness occurs at two levels: systems have a discrete set of *containers* for information (in the Turing machine model, there are discrete spaces on the tape to receive symbols), and those containers can contain one of a finite alphabet of symbols.

A system that can represent an analog symbol of unbounded resolution could potentially act in a different fashion. For example, Siegelmann [Sie98] has shown that neural networks with analog weights are more powerful than those with digital weights (in the sense that there are processes that can be carried out efficiently with the analog weights that cannot be carried out efficiently with integer or floating-point weights).

Another assumption is that symbols can be independently modified without interfering with other symbols and that multiple states can exist simultaneously. Quantum systems have been controversially [Put95] hypothesized by Penrose [Pen89, Pen95] as a way of carrying out cognitive processes that cannot be realized on a traditional neural structure. However, it has been argued [Teg00] that the difference in timescales between the quantum and neural processes makes this infeasible.

A final assumption is that the modeling of neurons and their connections alone is sufficient to reproduce cognition in a connectionist model. The traditional model of connectionist networks used in cognitive science abstracts from brain physiology at the level of the discrete neuron. However, recent models such as the GasNets model, devised for robot control and related problems [HSJO98, SdHS01], include the nonlocal effects of neurotransmitters such as nitrous oxide, where the molecules are small enough to diffuse throughout the brain. This provides a level of nonsynaptic communication within the brain.

3.4.2 Exploiting Nonstandard Features During Learning

One aspect of embedding computing in the real world and then using a learning system to adapt that computational system to its environment is that the learning process might exploit features of the medium in which it is embedded rather than just features of the computing system that is embedded in the medium.

An example of this is illustrated in Thompson's work [Tho98] on the evolution of digital circuits. The aim of this work is to evolve circuits within field programmable gate arrays (FPGAs), which are programmable logic devices that can be configured to a particular digital circuit via a program. Evolution can be carried out on these by evolving programs on a conventional computer, using a variant of genetic programming [Koz92, BNKF98], and testing fitness by downloading the programs to the FPGA and testing them on the chip.

During one of these experiments [TL99], an unusual behavior was observed. The circuit worked very well during evolution, but when tested on a second FPGA chip, the circuit failed to work at all. Upon closer inspection, it was noted that the evolved circuit was relying on some analog property of the original digital circuit. As the FPGAs are not designed to behave consistently at the analog level (just to be equivalent in terms of the digital process that they carry out), the evolved circuit could not be transferred to the second chip successfully.

Might we see equivalent phenomena during neural learning in the brain? Might learning exploit particular nonneural aspects of brain physiology in order to provide a different kind of computation from that which is easy or possible to implement in neurons? Or is a physiological system such as the brain changing too much in the off-substrate areas to make this kind of thing possible?

3.5 Breaking the von Neumann Paradigm

The assumption here considers a central sequential processing unit that fetches program code and data to it and writes its output to an addressed space.

3.5.1 Concurrency and Parallelism in Cognition

This is one of the more established nonclassical computing notions in cognitive science. It has long been argued that the brain implements computation in a parallel fashion, and neural networks work in an inherently parallel way.

One recent argument [PST+05] about concurrency in computer systems is that we should stop regarding concurrency as a special kind of computing and instead regard serial operation as being unusual. This is of particular relevance in building models and simulations of real-world phenomena on the computer—a concurrent system (or a programming language where concurrency is the default) allows us to model such a system by reproducing the real-world concurrency. This raises questions for cognitive science about whether the concurrency in the brain is there in order to model the many concurrent actions in the real world.

Another way in which to break these assumptions is to consider systems where the data remain in its location and the computational device moves over the data, modifying the data or the device (or both) to produce an output rather than the processing unit remaining in one place and bringing data to it; for example, reaction-diffusion computers [Ada01a] that move through a physical representation of a problem (such as a fluid diffusing through a maze [ADMR03]). There do not appear to be any immediate applications of these concepts in understanding cognition beyond trivial examples such as viewing the flow of neural activity through fixed-position neurons.

3.6 Breaking the Output Paradigm

The output paradigm is the set of assumptions that the output from a process is the only way of getting information out of a computational process and that we have to wait until the program has finished its execution before we can get a meaningful answer.

3.6.1 Algorithms and Interruptibility

One assumption that is made in many computer learning systems, including many that are designed to emulate human or animal learning, is that we can run a carefully designed schedule of learning trials leading to a final learned system.

However, in many learning situations that are embedded in the world, the process of learning is regularly interrupted. The time required for a learning process to work to completion is variable. Given that this will have been the case throughout the evolution of these learning systems themselves, it is likely that the kinds of learning algorithms that will evolve will be able at any time to carry out an action that makes maximal use of what has been learned up to the point of interruption.

Such algorithms have been termed *anytime algorithms* [Zil96, BD89] in computing. An anytime algorithm is one that can be disrupted at any point in its calculation and is able to report an intermediate result that makes use of some or all of the calculation that has occurred up to that point. These have been applied for example in planning systems [BD89] and robotics [ZR93]. Some commonly used bio-inspired learning algorithms have this property. For example, a neural network trained using an algorithm such as backpropagation adjusts its weights when each example is presented. Therefore it would be possible to run an example "for real" after an arbitrary number of training runs, and the network would report an answer based on all of the training runs to date.

3.6.2 Physical Observations and Trajectories

In order for a computation to be carried out on a computer, the physical state of the machine must change and energy must be taken into the system. These changes are usually seen as unimportant consequences of the physical grounding of computation. However, in a number of specialized areas, these physical characteristics are important. One example is in the design of software for low-energy embedded devices such as environmental monitoring or satellite systems [Tah04]. Another example can be found in the concept of *power analysis* attacks in computer security [CJRR03]. This is the idea that an attacker could get some information about the process going on inside a device (such as a smartcard) by analyzing the power usage of the device in response to various inputs and correlating this power usage profile with profiles from known computations. Overall, we can ask what we can learn by observing physical properties of a computational device while it is computing and how a computational device with multiple components might communicate between those components other than with explicit outputs.

How might this be of significance in cognitive science? In carrying out mental processes, the brain makes varying demands on the body—for example, certain processes may require more blood flow to the brain. Might some components of the brain monitor these demands (perhaps indirectly via the monitoring of other processes in the body) and adjust aspects of mental function appropriately? Might this represent a possible mechanism for the evolution of certain kinds of emotional processes? The mechanism would be that a certain mental process might monitor other mental processes not directly but by monitoring the demand that the brain is making on the body and learn the correlations between those demands and relevant mental responses. In certain circumstances, this might prove more efficient than communicating directly with other brain-based processes.

3.7 Breaking the Algorithmic Paradigm

The assumptions here are that programs take an input and then compute some output, ignoring the remainder of the world while the computation is taking place, and that randomness and noise are problems to be avoided.

3.7.1 Interactivity

Wegner [Weg97] has argued that the major shift in computer technology from the 1970s to the 1990s has been that computer systems have moved from being algorithmic systems (with a fixed idea of when a particular computation starts and stops and with no cumulative memory or history of the computation) to being interactive systems, which run for long periods of time, have many interactions over that time, and learn or accumulate information as they run that influences future interactions.

His core argument is that interactive systems can achieve more than algorithmic systems—interaction cannot be reduced to algorithms. This is formalized [Weg98] by the development of a model of an "interaction machine" consisting of a Turing machine with the addition of input and output actions that allow the external environment to influence the computation while it runs. It can be shown that interaction machines, and other such formalisms for interactive systems [Mil93], cannot be reduced to a Turing machine model.

One example of particular interest in cognitive science is interactive systems that "outsource" some of their cognition to systems in the outside world. A (somewhat artificial) example of this is given by Wegner [Weg97] in the context of computer chess. This is illustrated in Figure 3.1. An *interactive agent*, largely ignorant of chess, plays against two master-level players. The agent lets one of the master players (say player A) play first, then copies that move on the other board. The agent then waits for player B to make a move and then copies that as its response to player A. This process then continues back and forth. In such a system, the interactive "player" will typically win half of its games; by contrast, a noninteractive player with minimal chess experience will lose both games.

Master A   Master B

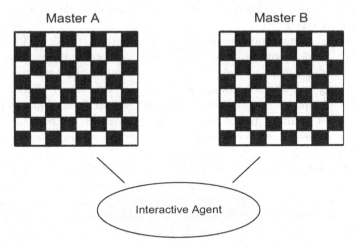

Fig. 3.1. Wegner's Interactive Chess-Playing Agent (after [Weg97]).

Do humans delegate cognitive capacity out "into the world" in this way? Clearly we do this with memory—for example through making notes, looking up references in books, or using an Internet search (which has, for some people, become almost an automated volitional action!). Clearly, we also use devices to carry out cognitive processes that are too complicated or take too long to do on-substrate, such as the use of a calculator. A less obvious example of this phenomenon is flipping a coin, which delegates the task of generating a random event, something that we cannot readily do mentally, to an external device. Does the brain's "outsourcing" of cognition go beyond working with simple cognitive devices?

3.8 Breaking the Refinement Paradigm

The assumption here is that programs are created by a process of refinement from a clearly defined specification, via a sequence of intermediate stages, to a concrete program. By contrast, many natural systems demonstrate emergent properties [PS05] that are not "refinable" from an attempt to solve a particular well-specified problem.

3.8.1 Data-Driven Systems

Traditional computer programs are *specification-defined*. That is, the best way of describing the desired behavior of the program is to give a specification of that behavior, that is, a description of *what* the system should do. Then, the process of computer programming consists of translating that specification into a working program by an informal or formal process of *refinement*, where descriptions of *what* the system should do are replaced by descriptions of *how* the system should do it.

By contrast, some problems are best defined by data [PG95, PY97, Par97], for example, a program designed for letter or word recognition. In order to describe what is meant by a letter "a", for example, the best approach is to give a large number of examples of such a letter rather than giving a description of what is and isn't an "a". Along similar lines, some properties that we might want to realize on a computer system are best defined by the system interacting with a human user—for example, properties concerned with aesthetic judgments.

Algorithms for learning in neural networks typically work by calculating errors based on examples. This is a typically data-defined way of working—take data, calculate errors, and update the model based upon those errors. However, high-level cognition is able to operate on specification-driven problems. A significant issue in cognitive science is how to reconcile these two theories. Are systems for learning specification-driven problems able to be built from a generic neural architecture (for example, Lebière and Anderson [LA93] show how a variant on the ACT-R symbolic architecture can be built on a connectionist substrate)? By contrast, dual-process theories [Eva03] suggest that evolutionarily old parts of the brain are focused on learning from examples, while structured thinking of the kind required to solve specification-driven problems is a newcomer on an evolutionary timescale and has its own distinct neural architecture.

3.9 Breaking the Computer-as-Artifact Paradigm

The assumption here is that computation is performed by specific computational artifacts built for the purpose (whereas many natural objects "just do" some kind of computation as part of their normal existence) and that these artifacts remain unchanged throughout the computation.

3.9.1 Delegation

In traditional computing, it is assumed that a single kind of general-purpose computing device is available. As anything that can be computed can be computed by such a device, there is no need to use different kinds of physical devices to solve different kinds of problems. This is in contrast to most other kinds of problem-solving technologies, where different physical devices are used for different stages of a problem rather than a single generic device being "programmed" for the different stages of the problem. This is a contrast with other engineering disciplines, where machines are built from a number of different materials rather than a single material that can be molded to the relevant task. However, in recent years, a number of computational devices have been created that exploit features of particular material substrates to carry out particular computations in an efficient manner [Ada01a, Ada01b]. For example, Adamatzky has demonstrated chemistry-based computers that exploit reaction-diffusion systems to calculate Voronoï diagrams [DAR+04] or to find paths through complex environments by exploring many paths simultaneously [ADMR03].

Now consider the practical application of a nonclassical computing technology such as quantum computing or computing with a liquid medium. It is likely that in preparing a problem for solution on such a computer, a number of (conventional) computational steps would have to be carried out before the nonclassical computer could be applied and other computational steps carried out afterward. For example, in the application of Shor's algorithm for factoring numbers on a quantum computer [Sho94], a pair of numbers need to be provided as a starting point for the algorithm, and, following the quantum processing, algorithms to extract the period of a sequence and calculate greatest common divisors need to be applied.

Therefore, when we talk about "nonclassical" computing, we are rarely talking about entire problems that can be solved solely using a nonclassical computer. Instead, the classical computer is *delegating* certain aspects of its computation to a special-purpose nonclassical computation engine.

We can imagine that the mind might act in a similar way by delegating tasks to special-purpose structures in the brain or body that deal with tasks in a nonneural fashion. One example is provided by the *somatic markers* hypothesized by Damasio [Dam94, DDL06]. In this theory, it is suggested that the mind "uses" the bodily state to facilitate rapid computation of certain situations (i.e., that the mental process is realized through a mixture of neurally substrated processing and bodily state). This is carried out by neural processes that trigger nonneural changes in body state, which are subsequently reperceived by the neural substrate, in particular drawing attention toward some salient feature of the external world that might otherwise be missed.

As an example, consider the falling sensation felt in the belly when reaching a cliff-edge unexpectedly or the feeling of nausea felt when witnessing a violent act. In both of these cases, the feeling is generated by some complex perceptual process in the brain and is subsequently reperceived (by a different brain component) for rapid action. The neurally substrated mind has delegated the task of dealing with emergency situations to the body state and proprioceptive systems.

In such scenarios, the task of dealing with attention shift has been delegated to the somatic system. However, much of the remainder of the computation is carried out using the main neural substrate. This is reminiscent of the various ways in which nonclassical computation uses specific, nongeneric computing devices to carry out a particular aspect of a computation (a quantum factoring engine or a reaction-diffusion route finder).

3.9.2 Porous Boundaries

Somatic markers extend the "computation" that goes on in the mind beyond the neural substrate into the body. However, need we stop here? One important theme in nonclassical computing is the extension of computing beyond the immediate computing artifact, perhaps including computations that are "unbounded" in the sense that we cannot decide before beginning the computation exactly which information will be needed to carry it out.

A similar idea has been explored in the biological context by Dawkins [Daw82] in the concept of the *extended phenotype*. The core of this idea is that the phenotypic effect of a gene can extend beyond the body of the organism in which it is found:

> *An animal's behaviour tends to maximize the survival of the genes 'for' that behaviour, whether or not those genes happen to be in the body of the particular animal performing it.*

As a simple example, the genes of a male bird that influence it to mate preferentially with female birds with blue feathers can be viewed as having a phenotypic effect within the body of the female bird. Another example is the dams and subsequent lakes built by beavers.

Can we see examples of this extension process in cognition? One example could be somatic markers that extend beyond the body [Joh05]. We have described somatic markers as effects of the mind on the body that are subsequently perceived by the proprioceptive system and subsequently acted upon by the mind. An *extended somatic marker* is some change that is carried out in the world outside the body by a process that is not currently the focus of attention and is subsequently reperceived and acted on in an attentive way. For example, might inattentive scribbling on a piece of paper when anxious be a marker of that anxiety, later to be perceived and acted upon visually? Such a mechanism might have evolved or been learned from the somatic marker mechanism, exploiting a different perceptual route.

3.10 Conclusions and Questions

In this chapter we have taken a model of nonclassical computation that consists of outlining the various assumptions of classical computing and asking what happens to computing when each of them is removed. These ideas have then been applied to questions about cognition and mentality.

A theme that recurs multiple times in this discussion is that of specialization and delegation: does (some component of) the mind make use of specialized structures (within the brain, within the body, or out in the world) to do particular tasks that cannot be readily done by the neural substrate? This dovetails well with many of the questions asked in nonclassical computing, which move away from the notion of a universal computer and instead ask questions about the computational capabilities of particular kinds of materials and machines on particular kinds of problems.

References

[Ada01a] A. Adamatzky. *Computing in Nonlinear Media and Automata Collectives*. Institute of Physics Publishing, Bristol, 2001.
[Ada01b] Andrew Adamatzky. Computing in nonlinear media: Make waves, study collisions. In J. Kelemen and P. Sosík, editors, *ECAL*, volume 2159 of *Lecture Notes in Computer Science*, pages 1–11. Springer, Berlin, 2001.
[ADMR03] A. Adamatzky, B. De Lacy Costello, C. Melhuish, and N. Ratcliffe. Experimental reaction-diffusion chemical processors for robot path planning. *Journal of Intelligent and Robotic Systems*, 37:233–249, 2003.
[BD89] M. Boddy and T. Dean. Solving time dependent planning problems. In *Proceedings of the 11th International Joint Conference on Artificial Intelligence*, pages 979–984, Detroit, MI, 1989. Morgan Kaufmann, San Francisco.
[Blo96] N. Block. Functionalism. In D.M. Borchert, editor, *The Encyclopaedia of Philosophy: Supplement*. Macmillan, London, 1996.
[BNKF98] W. Banzhaf, P. Nordin, R.E. Keller, and F.D. Francone. *Genetic Programming: An Introduction*. Morgan Kaufmann, San Francisco, 1998.
[CJRR03] S. Chari, C.S. Jutla, J.R. Rao, and P. Rohatgi. Power analysis: attacks and countermeasures. In A. McIver and C. Morgan, editors, *Programming Methodology*, pages 415–439. Springer, New York, 2003.
[Dam94] A.R. Damasio. *Descartes' Error: Emotion, Reason and the Human Brain*. Gosset/Putnam Press, New York, 1994.
[DAR+04] B. De Lacy Costello, A. Adamatzky, N. Ratcliffe, A.L. Zanin, A.W. Liehr, and H.G. Purwins. The formation of Voronoi diagrams in chemical and physical systems: experimental findings and theoretical models. *International Journal of Bifurcation and Chaos*, 14(7):2187–2210, 2004.
[Daw82] R. Dawkins. *The Extended Phenotype*. Oxford University Press, Oxford, 1982.
[DDL06] B.D. Dunn, T. Dalgleish, and A. Lawrence. The somatic marker hypothesis: a critical evaluation. *Neuroscience and Biobehavioural Reviews*, 30(2):239–271, 2006.
[Eva03] J.St.B.T. Evans. In two minds: dual process accounts of reasoning. *Trends in Cognitive Sciences*, 7:454–459, 2003.
[Fey82] R.P. Feynman. Simulating physics with computers. *International Journal of Theoretical Physics*, 21:467–488, 1982.
[HMU01] J. Hopcroft, R. Motwani, and J. Ullman. *Introduction to Automata Theory, Languages and Computation*. Addison-Wesley, Reading, MA, 2nd edition, 2001.
[HSJO98] P. Husbands, T. Smith, N. Jakobi, and M. O'Shea. Better living through chemistry: evolving gasnets for robot control. *Connection Science*, 10(4):185–210, 1998.
[Joh05] C.J. Johnson. Does a functioning mind need a functioning body? In D.N. Davis, editor, *Visions of Mind*, pages 307–321. Idea Group Publishing, Hershey, PA, 2005.

[Koz92]   J.R. Koza. *Genetic Programming: On the Programming of Computers by Means of Natural Selection.* Series in Complex Adaptive Systems. MIT Press, Cambridge, MA, 1992.

[LA93]   C. Lebiere and J.R. Anderson. A connectionist implementation of the ACT-R production system. In *Proceedings of the 15th Annual Conference of the Cognitive Science Society*, pages 635–640. Lawrence Erlbaum Associates, Hillsdale, NJ, 1993.

[Lev04]   J. Levin. Functionalism. In E. Zalta, editor, *The Stanford Encyclopedia of Philosophy.* 2004. Available at http://plato.stanford.edu/archives/fall2004/entries/functionalism/.

[Mil93]   R. Milner. Elements of interaction. *Communications of the ACM*, 36(1):78–89, 1993.

[Par97]   D. Partridge. The case for inductive programming. *IEEE Computer*, 30(1):36–41, January 1997.

[Pen89]   R. Penrose. *The Emperor's New Mind: Concerning Computers, Minds, and the Laws of Physics.* Oxford University Press, Oxford, 1989.

[Pen95]   R. Penrose. *Shadows of the Mind.* Vintage, London, 1995.

[PG95]   D. Partridge and A. Galton. The specification of "specification". *Minds and Machines*, 5(2):243–255, 1995.

[PS05]   F. Polack and S. Stepney. Emergent properties do not refine. In *REFINE 2005 Workshop*, volume 137 of Electronic Notes in Theoretical Computer Science, pages 163–181, Guildford, UK, April 2005. Elsevier, Amsterdam.

[PST+05]   F. Polack, S. Stepney, H. Turner, P. Welch, and F. Barnes. An architecture for modelling emergence in CA-like systems. In M.S. Capcarrere, A.A. Freitas, P.J. Bentley, C.G. Johnson, and J. Timmis, editors, *Advances in Artificial Life, 8th European Conference on Artificial Life (ECAL 2005)*, volume 3630 of *Lecture Notes in Computer Science*, pages 427–436. Springer, Berlin, 2005.

[Put75]   H. Putnam. *Mind, Language, and Reality.* Cambridge University Press, Cambridge, 1975.

[Put95]   H. Putnam. Book review: Shadows of the mind. *Bulletin of the American Mathematical Society*, 32(3):370–373, 1995.

[PY97]   D. Partridge and W.B. Yates. Data-defined problems and multiversion neuralnet systems. *Journal of Intelligent Systems*, 7(1–2):19–32, 1997.

[SBC+05]   S. Stepney, S.L. Braunstein, J.A. Clark, A. Tyrrell, A. Adamatzky, R.E. Smith, T. Addis, C.G. Johnson, J. Timmis, P. Welch, R. Milner, and D. Partridge. Journeys in non-classical computation I: a grand challenge for computing research. *International Journal of Parallel, Emergent and Distributed Systems*, 20(1):5–19, April 2005.

[SBC+06]   S. Stepney, S.L. Braunstein, J.A. Clark, A. Tyrrell, A. Adamatzky, R.E. Smith, T. Addis, C.G. Johnson, J. Timmis, P. Welch, R. Milner, and D. Partridge. Journeys in non-classical computation II: initial journeys and waypoints. *International Journal of Parallel, Emergent and Distributed Systems*, 21(2):97–125, April 2006.

[SdHS01]   C.L.R. Santos, P.P.B. de Oliveira, P. Husbands, and C.R. Souza. Three case studies on the GasNets model in discrete domains. *International Journal of Neural Systems*, 11(3):295–304, 2001.

[Sho94]   P.W. Shor. Polynomial-time algorithms for prime factorization and discrete logarithms on a quantum computer. In S. Goldwasser, editor,

Proceedings of the 35th Annual Symposium on the Foundations of Computer Science, pages 20–22. IEEE Computer Society Press, New York, 1994.

[Sie98]   H.T. Siegelmann. *Neural Networks and Analog Computation: Beyond the Turing Limit*. Birkhäuser, Boston, 1998.

[Tah04]   W. Taha. Resource-aware programming. In Z. Wu, M. Guo, C. Chen, and J. Bu, editors, *Proceedings of the 2004 International Conference on Embedded Software and Systems*, volume 3605 of *Lecture Notes in Computer Science*, pages 38–43, Hangzhou, China, December 2004. Springer, Berlin.

[Teg00]   M. Tegmark. The importance of quantum decoherence in brain processes. *Physical Review E*, 61:4194–4206, 2000.

[Tho98]   A. Thompson. *Hardware Evolution: Automatic Design of Electronic Circuits in Reconfigurable Hardware by Artificial Evolution*. Distinguished dissertation series. Springer-Verlag, New York, 1998.

[TL99]   A. Thompson and P. Layzell. Analysis of unconventional evolved electronics. *Communications of the ACM*, 42(4):71–79, April 1999.

[Weg97]   P. Wegner. Why interaction is more powerful than algorithms. *Communications of the ACM*, 40(5):80–91, May 1997.

[Weg98]   P. Wegner. Interactive foundations of computing. *Theoretical Computer Science*, 192(2):315–351, 1998.

[Zil96]   S. Zilberstein. Using anytime algorithms in intelligent systems. *AI Magazine*, 17(3):73–83, 1996.

[ZR93]   S. Zilberstein and S.J. Russell. Anytime sensing, planning and action: a practical model for robot control. In *Proceedings of the 13th International Joint Conference on Artificial Intelligence*, pages 1402–1407, Chambóry, France, 28. August—3. September 1993. Morgan Kaufmann, San Francisco.

4

A Computing Model Combining Artificial Neural Networks and Petri Nets

Alfons Schuster

School of Computing and Mathematics, Faculty of Engineering, University of Ulster, Shore Road, Newtownabbey, Co. Antrim BT37 0QB, Northern Ireland, a.schuster@ulster.ac.uk

Summary. We propose a new machine-learning algorithm. The approach combines artificial neural network style learning and Petri net style modeling in a single technique. We call this technique "tokenized artificial neural networks". We apply the technique on a basic perceptron-type network and present results from experimental investigations as well as a proof for the proposed technique.

4.1 Introduction

Although artificial neural networks (ANNs) and Petri nets both enjoy great esteem within the machine-learning and network modeling communities neither technique is without problems. For example, artificial neural networks are successful machine-learning applications, but their total lack of any explanation facilities makes them a black-box technique. Petri nets, on the other hand, are a successful modeling technique, but so far the theory does not consider machine learning. The work presented in this chapter combines ANN-style learning and Petri net style modeling in a single technique. We call this technique tokenized artificial neural networks (TANNs). We demonstrate the approach on a very basic model. This model bears similarity to the well-known perceptron. Despite this similarity our approach has its unique character, making it significantly different from the traditional working of a perceptron. We believe that our approach can be useful for scientists in several fields, including biologists, chemists, physicists, computer scientists, and artificial intelligence practitioners, for example.

Section 4.2 provides a brief introduction to ANNs and Petri nets. The section also highlights those similarities and differences between Petri nets and ANNs that are important for our study. Section 4.3 introduces TANNs and also describes a TANN learning algorithm. Section 4.4 demonstrates the usefulness of our approach on a basic problem. Section 4.5 and Section 4.6 provide conclusions and a summary, respectively. Appendix A provides a proof demonstrating the correctness (in terms of convergence) of the TANN approach.

4.2 Petri Nets and ANNs

Figure 4.1 highlights similarities between ANNs and Petri nets. The Petri net illustrated in Figure 4.1 consists of an input place P_1, one output place P_2, one transition T_1, two arcs connecting the two places and the transition, and one token (black dot in place P_1).

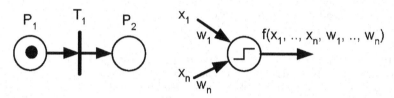

Fig. 4.1. Similarities between Petri nets and ANNs.

The design rules for Petri nets are relatively straightforward. An arc always connects a place to a transition and vice versa. An arc never connects a place directly to another place or a transition directly to another transition. There is also no upper limit to the number of arcs that can connect to a place or a transition. Petri nets use so-called tokens to indicate which places are active. For example, place P_1 in Figure 4.1 is an active place because there is one token in the place. Place P_2 is not active because there are no tokens in this place. An active place may contain more than one token. The rules for operating a Petri net are equally simple. A transition fires if all of its incoming places are active. When a transition fires, two things happen: all of its incoming places lose a token, and all of its outgoing places gain a token. In Figure 4.1 transition T_1 fires because all of its incoming places are active (there is a token in P_1). If transition T_1 fires, then place P_1 loses its token and place P_2 gains a token. Petri nets are particularly useful for the general specification of event-driven systems. For instance, P_1 in Figure 4.1 could represent a push-button and P_2 a projector. If the projector is initially off (no token in P_1), then pushing the button (placing a token into P_1) is an event that executes the behavior described earlier, where P_2 gains a token (projector is on) and P_1 loses its token again (push-button is released). Alternatively, the ANN in Figure 4.1 consists of one node (neuron), a number of inputs (x_1 to x_n), weights (w_1 to w_n), and one output. This output is generated by a particular learning algorithm, represented by the function f in the figure. It is important to understand that it is possible for an ANN to learn or simulate the behavior demonstrated in the push-buttton/projector example mentioned before. ANNs and Petri nets, their application, and potential are well-documented by the vast literature existing for these fields. We therefore direct the reader to a small number of selected resources we consider appropriate to represent these fields [MMR97, Ros58, Pet62, Pet81].

4.2.1 Similarities and Differences between Petri Nets and ANNs

From Figure 4.1, initial similarities are apparent. Nodes in ANNs are symbolically similar to places in Petri nets. ANNs and Petri nets both have connections in the form of arcs. In an ANN, these arcs carry weights. In a Petri net, arcs carry no weights. Both techniques compute, where they apply some processing to inputs to produce some output. In the case of an ANN, this computing involves the processing of numerical inputs and weights. In a Petri net, the mechanism is implemented via tokens and the firing rules mentioned earlier. Despite these similarities, there are also fundamental differences. ANNs can learn, and, at least so far, Petri nets can't. From a machine-learning perspective, ANNs are a black-box technique. The knowledge is encoded as a weight vector configuration, and this configuration provides no explanations for a reasoner. Petri nets, on the other hand, provide means for an explanation. For example, it is quite clear what happens in the push-button/projector scenario.

Our interest is to use the similarities we have identified to produce a hybrid between ANNs and Petri nets, called TANNs, that can be used for both system modeling (the domain of Petri nets) and learning (the domain of ANNs).

4.3 Tokenized Artificial Networks (TANNs)

Figure 4.2 delves straight into this topic by presenting a simple TANN.

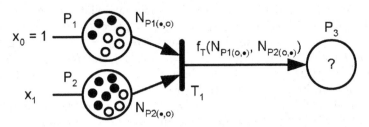

Fig. 4.2. Illustration of an example TANN.

This TANN consists of three places (P_1, P_2, and P_3) and one transition (T_1). Place P_1 holds four white tokens and three black tokens, and place P_2 holds three white tokens and six black tokens. Places P_1 and P_2 are *input places*. Each of these input places has exactly one output. The output for P_1 is $N_{P_1(\circ,\bullet)}$, and for P_2 it is $N_{P_2(\circ,\bullet)}$. These two outputs serve as inputs to transition T_1. Transition T_1 has one output. This output is connected to place P_3. Place P_3 is a *terminal place* and has no output. The question mark in place P_3 indicates that the number of tokens in this place is undetermined at the moment. Figure 4.2 also illustrates two possible input values (x_0 and x_1). One of them, x_0, is a bias, set to 1, whereas x_1 is a data value from an object. This object is applied to the network for classification. The following sections define this process in more detail.

Place outputs, which are equivalent to individual transition inputs, are calculated as

$$N_{P_x(\circ,\bullet)} = (n_{P_x(\circ)}, m_{P_x(\bullet)}), \qquad (4.1)$$

where $n_{P_x(\circ)}$ is the number of white tokens in place P_x and $m_{P_x(\bullet)}$ the number of black tokens in the same place. Basically, a transition receives all tokens from its incoming places.

Next, we define the output generated by a transition when an object (with value x) is presented to the network. This output shall be one single token, colored either black or white. This token is received by place P_3. Transition outputs for any particular transition T are calculated as follows:

$$f_{T(x)} = f(N_{P_1(\circ,\bullet)}, \dots, N_{P_k(\circ,\bullet)}) \qquad (4.2)$$

$$= \begin{cases} Class2 = 1_\bullet \text{ if } x \geq \dfrac{\sum_{i=1}^{k} n_{P_i(\circ)}}{\sum_{i=1}^{k} n_{P_i(\bullet)}} = r \\ Class1 = 1_\circ \text{ otherwise.} \end{cases}$$

Basically, f_T computes the ratio r between all white tokens and all black tokens arriving at a transition. If the value x for an object is larger than this ratio, then the object is classified into *Class 2*, and P_3 receives one black token ($1_\bullet$). Otherwise the object is classified into *Class 1*, and P_3 receives one white token ($1_\circ$).

EXAMPLE 1: In Figure 4.2 place P_1 holds four white tokens ($n_{P_1(\circ)} = 4$) and three black tokens ($m_{P_1(\bullet)} = 3$), and place P_2 holds three white tokens ($n_{P_2(\circ)} = 3$) and six black tokens ($m_{P_2(\bullet)} = 6$). Applying these values in Equation (4.1) yields $N_{P_1(\circ,\bullet)} = (4_\circ, 3_\bullet)$ and $N_{P_2(\circ,\bullet)} = (3_\circ, 6_\bullet)$. Consequently, there are $4 + 3 = 7$ white tokens and $3 + 6 = 9$ black tokens arriving at transition T_1. The ratio r produced by these values is $\frac{7}{9} = 0.78$. The color of the token received by place P_3 depends on the value x (x_1 in Figure 4.2) inputted to the network and this ratio r. For example, an object with a value of $x = 0.9$ would be classified into *Class 2*, in which case place P_3 receives a black token.

Although forthcoming sections are going to define this process in more detail, what we might be able to do with such a network seems to take shape now. The process illustrated in Figure 4.2 and formalized by equations (4.1) and (4.2) is very similar to an ANN. For example, input places are similar to input nodes (neurons), the transition (firing) mechanism is similar to a transfer function in an ANN, and a terminal place is similar to an output node (neuron) in an ANN. The missing component that integrates these similarities into a functional unit is a learning algorithm.

4.3.1 TANN Learning Algorithm

Figure 4.3 illustrates the problem we want to solve. Figure 4.3 illustrates an arbitrary real-valued x-axis on which a number of different objects need to be classified into one of two classes, *Class 1* (white squares) or *Class 2* (black diamonds). From the viewpoint of a classification task, Figure 4.3 illustrates a simple one-dimensional, linearly separable task.

Fig. 4.3. Example of the classification task.

In an ANN context, such a task can be solved by a single neuron with two inputs (one of them being a bias) and one output by using the so-called perceptron learning algorithm, for example [MMR97, Ros58]. This chapter does not describe the technicalities of the perceptron learning algorithm, but we want to note that the problem-solving strategy employed by this algorithm is quite similar to the strategy employed by the algorithm we present here. In the case of a TANN, the problem illustrated in Figure 4.3 can be solved by the network illustrated in Figure 4.4.

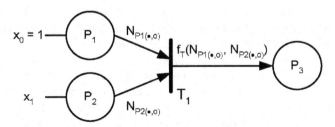

Fig. 4.4. TANN for classification task in Figure 4.3.

Although the content of Figure 4.4 should be clear from our previous explanations, three comments should be made. First, initially there are no tokens in any of the three places. Second, Figure 4.4 illustrates an input vector $\mathbf{i} = (x_0, x_1)$. This input vector typically represents an object for classification in a particular domain. The x_0 component of the vector is a bias and is set to 1. And third, the network in Figure 4.4 classifies an object on the basis of the color of the token received by place P_3.

As was mentioned before, the learning algorithm for the network in Figure 4.4 works similar to the well-known perceptron learning algorithm.

For example, the algorithm starts with a random token allocation to the input places P_1 and P_2. The terminal place P_3 does not receive tokens in this initial allocation. An initial token allocation can be represented by the vector $\mathbf{t}$, for example. The algorithm then produces outputs for places P_1 and P_2 according to equation (4.1). Then, equation (4.2) is applied in order to determine the class for the current object and the token for place P_3. The overall aim is to correctly classify all objects presented to the network. If an object is misclassified, then the algorithm alters the initial token allocation on places P_1 and P_2 in a number of successive defined steps. This process continues until either all objects are classified correctly or a predefined number of iterations is reached. Figure 4.5 illustrates the algorithm in pseudo-code.

Algorithm: TANN;
Start with a randomly chosen token allocation vector $\mathbf{t_0}$;
Let $k = 1$;
while there are input vectors that are misclassified by $\mathbf{t}_{k-1}$ **do**
    Let $\mathbf{i}_j$ be a misclassified input vector;
    Update the token allocation vector to $\mathbf{t_k} = \mathbf{t}_{k-1} \pm \Delta \mathbf{t_k}$;
    Increment k;
end-while;

Fig. 4.5. Pseudo-code for TANN learning algorithm.

In order to explain the learning algorithm in more detail, we use the example given earlier where we had objects from *Class 1* and *Class 2*. In the case of a perceptron, we could use outputs such that a value of 1 represents an object of *Class 1* and a value of -1 an object of *Class 2*. In a tokenized network, classification is based on token color. For our example, we define the relationship between objects, classes, and tokens as follows: for an object of *Class 1*, the desired output shall be $1_\circ$; and for an object of *Class 2*, the desired output shall be $1_\bullet$. If an object is classified correctly, then the network remains unchanged. If the desired output is different from the actual output generated by the network, then the current token allocation vector $\mathbf{t}$ needs to be changed accordingly. In terms of classification, two types of errors can occur.

Error 1: The input vector $\mathbf{i}$ belongs to *Class 1*, for which the desired TANN output is $1_\circ$ but the actual network output is $1_\bullet$.

Error 2: The input vector $\mathbf{i}$ belongs to *Class 2*, for which the desired TANN output is $1_\bullet$ but the actual network output is $1_\circ$.

A TANN overcomes both types of errors through a defined update of the token allocation vector $\mathbf{t}$. In both cases, this update results in a new token allocation vector $\mathbf{t}'$ such that $\mathbf{t}' = \mathbf{t} + \Delta \mathbf{t}$. The motive behind the update procedure is to change the ratio r in equation (4.2). This can be achieved by changing the number of black tokens and white tokens in places P_1 and P_2 in a coordinated way. One initial definition assumes that in the case of an error, the learning algorithm only changes one type of token in the token allocation vector (i.e., either the number of white tokens or the number of black tokens in the token allocation vector). For example, in the case of Error 1 where the desired network output is $1_\circ$ but the actual output is $1_\bullet$, the algorithm would alter (increase) the number of white tokens in each input place in a defined way. On the other hand, for Error 2, where the situation is reversed, the algorithm only alters (increases) the number of black tokens in each input place. In order to achieve this goal, we need to clarify and define a few more concepts. We start with the definition of a token allocation vector. A token allocation vector $\mathbf{t}$ for a network is defined as

$$\mathbf{t} = \begin{pmatrix} t_{P_1}(n_{P_1,\circ}, m_{P_1,\bullet}) \\ \vdots \\ t_{P_k}(n_{P_k,\circ}, m_{P_k,\bullet}) \end{pmatrix}, \tag{4.3}$$

where n is the number of white tokens and m the number of black tokens in a particular place $(P_1 \ldots P_k)$. Basically, every element in the token allocation vector $\mathbf{t}$ represents a place, including information about the number of white tokens and the number of black tokens in that place.

EXAMPLE 2: The token allocation vector for the network illustrated in Figure 4.2 would be

$$\mathbf{t} = \begin{pmatrix} t_{P_1}(4_\circ, 3_\bullet) \\ t_{P_2}(3_\circ, 6_\bullet) \end{pmatrix}.$$

The definition of a token allocation vector in place, we now define the relationship between an input vector $\mathbf{i}$ and a token allocation vector $\mathbf{t}$, as well as the influence this relationship has on the final output produced by the network. The ratio r introduced by equation (4.2) plays a central role in this relationship because it divides the two classes in the classification task. For simplicity, here we express this ratio by the fraction $\frac{a_\circ}{b_\bullet}$, where $a_\circ$ is the number of white tokens and $b_\bullet$ the number of black tokens arriving at a transition. We now take the ratio we produced for the network in Figure 4.2 in Example 1. This ratio was $r = \frac{a_\circ}{b_\bullet} = \frac{7}{9} = 0.78$. Let this ratio represent the initial random token allocation to the network. So, no learning has been undertaken yet. Imagine now that training begins with a *Class 1* object having an input value of $x = 0.90$, say. In this case, the value of the object is larger than the dividing point r ($0.90 > 0.78$), and so the output generated by equation (4.2) is *Class 2* and one black token ($1_\bullet$) for place P_3. Clearly, this represents a misclassification. The learning algorithm needs to overcome this problem. It does so by updating the token allocation vector $\mathbf{t}$ (the number of tokens in places P_1 and P_2) and hence the ratio r in a controlled way. In order to understand this process, we assume the following conditions. First, there exists a token allocation vector $\mathbf{t}$. This token allocation vector $\mathbf{t}$ could be the initial random token allocation vector or a token allocation vector produced by the learning algorithm after this initial assignment. Second, an input vector **i** representing an object for classification is presented to the network. Third, the outcome of the update is a new token allocation vector **t**′. This new token allocation vector exists temporarily and is used for the classification of an object using equation (4.1) and equation (4.2). With these assumptions established, we define a token allocation vector update as

$$\mathbf{t}' = \mathbf{t} + \Delta\mathbf{t} = \mathbf{t} + \eta \cdot 1_{color}, \qquad (4.4)$$

where **t** is the current token allocation vector, **t**′ the new, updated token allocation vector, and η a positive constant called the learning rate. The expression 1_{color} in the equation stands for either one black token or one white token. The color for this token depends on the error made by the classifier. This was explained earlier.

EXAMPLE 3: In Example 2, an object of *Class 1* was incorrectly classified into *Class 2* because the value $x = 0.90$ for this object is larger than the dividing point $r = 0.78$. In order to overcome this problem, the ratio r needs to be updated to a higher value. Earlier, r was defined as the ratio $\frac{a_\circ}{b_\bullet}$ between the number of white tokens and black tokens. Obviously, if the number of white tokens increases, then the value for r gets larger too, which is what we want. Given a learning rate set to $\eta = 1$, equation (4.4) produces the new token allocation vector:

$$\mathbf{t}' = \begin{pmatrix} t_{P_1}(4_\circ, 3_\bullet) \\ t_{P_2}(3_\circ, 6_\bullet) \end{pmatrix} + 1 \begin{pmatrix} 1_\circ \\ 1_\circ \end{pmatrix}$$

$$= \begin{pmatrix} t_{P_1}((4_\circ + 1_\circ), 3_\bullet) \\ t_{P_2}((3_\circ + 1_\circ), 6_\bullet) \end{pmatrix} = \begin{pmatrix} t_{P_1}(5_\circ, 3_\bullet) \\ t_{P_2}(4_\circ, 6_\bullet) \end{pmatrix}.$$

The example shows that the number of black tokens remains unchanged. Only the number of white tokens changes. How does this change affect the classification outcome? The new ratio we obtain from this update is $r = \frac{a_\circ}{b_\bullet} = \frac{(5+4)_\circ}{(3+6)_\bullet} = \frac{(9)_\circ}{(9)_\bullet} = 1.0$. Now the ratio r is larger than the value $x = 0.90$ of the object. According to equation (4.2), the object is now allocated to *Class 2*, and place P_3 receives a black token $(1_\bullet)$. This is the correct outcome.

4.4 Experimental Testing and Results

In an experimental investigation, we produced a computer program, using the Delphi programming language, for the modeling of a TANN for the one-dimensional, linearly separable classification task illustrated in Figure 4.3. Initially the program generates two input places, one transition, and one output place (see Figure 4.4). The input places are then seeded with a random number n of white tokens and black tokens. A typical setting would be $1 \leq n \leq 20$.

The program then defines an interval, for example, the interval $0 \leq x \leq 100$. This interval represents the x-axis in Figure 4.3. The program then generates a random number d within this interval (e.g., $d = 65$) and produces a specific number (e.g., 5) of random numbers to the left of point d (e.g., 6, 11, 15, 44, 51) as well as to the right of point d (e.g., 68, 71, 88, 91, 95). The program allocates the color white to the numbers to the left of point d and the color black to the numbers to the right of point d. Basically, this process produces a Figure 4.3 scenario, where two different types of objects are placed on an x-axis. These objects are linearly separable.

The TANN is a classifier. If the TANN is provided with the value of the location of an object on the x-axis, then the TANN should determine whether the object belongs to *Class 1* (white token) or to *Class 2* (black token). The initial token allocation to the input places was a random allocation. The TANN produced by this initial allocation therefore may provide a solution to the problem but more likely it may not. In the first case, the TANN does not change its setup. In the second case, the learning strategy defined in the previous sections and illustrated in Figure 4.5 executes. The algorithm runs until either all objects are classified correctly or a predefined number of iterations (e.g., 500 in our study) is reached.

Our study generated 1000 different datasets. Each dataset contained ten data items, five data items belonging to *Class 1* and five belonging to *Class 2*. For testing we applied k-fold cross-validation with a setting of k equal to the number of data items in a dataset ($k = 10$). This is called leave-one-out cross-validation. In leave-one-out cross-validation, a network is trained k times. Each time a different data item from the same dataset is left out from training. After training, this data item is applied to the network for classification. As mentioned before, our study generated 1000 datasets, each containing 10 data items. This gives a total number of $1000 \cdot 10 = 10,000$ individual tests. In one application, 90.10% of 10,000 tests were successful. We have conducted many more tests in our study, and the 90.10% is a typical outcome.

Examination of those tests that were not successful identified a common pattern. In order to understand the pattern imagine a dataset with six data items, three from *Class 1* (e.g., 4, 9, 14) and three from *Class 2* (e.g., 20, 25, 28). Suppose the *Class 1* data item with the value 14 is left out in the network training process. That is, the network is trained on the remaining five data items only. Now imagine the training process produces a division point between the two classes, say at $r = 11$. This division point separates the five data items used in the training process. Data items 4 and 9 are to the left of the division point (11), and data items 20, 25, and 28 are all to the right of this point. But data item 14, which was left out in the training phase, is not on the correct side of the division point. It should be on the left side of the division point and not on its right side. Clearly, this type of misclassification is not due to a malfunction of the algorithm. The data item was simply not included in the training process. Further investigation into this problem has shown that *all* misclassifications encountered are due to this problem. Our study therefore concludes that the algorithm had a 100% success rate on all other data items. This is an encouraging result in our view.

We also investigated nonlinearly separable scenarios; for example, scenarios where we place one or more *Class 1* objects in-between two *Class 2* objects. In these tests, we experienced the typical problems (e.g., application may run infinitely) and solutions (e.g., use of a predefined number of iterations as a stop criterion, variations in learning rate, a priori specified misclassification rate) known for perceptrons. The ANN literature has dealt with these issues, extensively and so we do not further elaborate on them here [MMR97, pp. 46–52].

Another observation emerging from our work is that TANN design involves as much trial and error as the design of traditional ANN applications. For example, so far there are no definite rules determining the learning rate, the number of iterations, or the initial number of black and white tokens in a place. Equation (4.4) is another source for potential modifications. In its current form, the update in the equation is based on only one type of token; either the number of black tokens is increased or the number of white tokens is increased. Another solution to the problem would be to increase one type of token and also decrease the other type of token. This feature as well as others are currently being investigated.

Finally, we are aware of course that our experimental study requires a more rigorous proof. Appendix A provides this proof.

4.5 Discussion and Potential of the TANN Approach

Although there is a lot of material available on ANNs and Petri nets, according to our knowledge so far the two fields have not been combined in the way demonstrated in this chapter. We are aware, of course, of the simplicity of the current model, which is similar to that of a perceptron. There are reasons, however, why this does not necessarily degrade our work. First, scientific testing and progress often begins with simple models. For example, Rosenblatt's perceptron and Widrow's "Adaline" model are fundamental contributions to the development of ANNs [Ros58, Wid59]; the simplest Petri net with a single place, one transition, and one token is an equally powerful idea. Second, our main aim here is to present a novel type of algorithm that combines two previously separated fields. We feel that we have achieved this goal. In our eyes, the TANN approach is a unique and meaningful contribution to the field. We also feel that our work is relevant to several other fields. We need to be careful, however. For example, imagine a Petri net place representing a vehicle (e.g., a bus), a transition representing a bus stop, and a token representing a person. Then, a person entering the bus at that stop can be represented by placing a token into the place (bus). Although there is nothing wrong with this, there is no particular reason at this stage for associating the bus/person scenario with a fundamentally intelligent process or behavior. On the other hand, a complex transport network (e.g., that of Shanghai city in China) may develop the emergent feature "rush hour". Rush hour may be seen as a particular state of the system, the quieting down of the system as a reaction to this state, and the whole process as a highly dynamic and complex system. The point is that we may need to look at systems where we feel that intelligence or intelligent behaviour is an inherent or emerging part of the system. There are many such systems, they can be natural or artificial, and they are typically large, highly dynamic, and extremely complex. For simplicity, this section briefly mentions a few of those areas we consider particularly interesting.

For example, the previous rush hour scenario leads us immediately to swarm intelligence systems and applications. These systems are usually extremely complex, highly dynamic, consist of discrete entities, and show emergent properties, including intelligent behavior and problem solving. Swarm intelligence is already a popular field in artificial intelligence (AI) and soft computing [Eng06]. In our eyes, the TANN approach has some appeal for researchers in the field, as it combines modeling of discrete entities and learning. Another quite recent field is the field of artificial immune systems. Artificial immune systems are inspired and use problem-solving strategies found in biology for solving engineering problems [DT03]. For example, a biological system under attack by a virus may apply existing mechanisms or develop novel mechanisms for counteracting the virus. In the case of development of new strategies, the biological system may be attributed with the ability to learn. Artificial immune systems in a way model this aspect as well as many other aspects via computational techniques. For the reasons expressed earlier, we feel that the TANN approach may be of some interest for the artificial immune systems community. For example, a particular type of token may represent the virus, and other parts may represent components of a biological system working and developing new strategies against this virus.

Artificial immune systems may lead us to bioinformatics, a field that combines and orchestrates efforts in molecular biology and computing. In our time, bioinformatics has already transformed into a rich application area for AI [KN05]. For example, bioinformatics and AI are involved with analysis of genetic regulatory pathways, which is crucial for a thorough understanding of biological processes such as gene regulation and cancer development; micro-array gene expression analysis, which is important for drug development and medical treatment; gene sequencing, which has similar goals; protein folding, the transition from genes to complex three-dimensional structures; or the modeling of cellular processes. The latter seems to be particularly interesting to us. There are huge efforts in producing solutions for the modeling of the complex processes that are going on in cells, such as the processes of transporting materials in and out of cells, the diffusion of molecules through cell membranes, or the process of cell division [KK95]. The TANN approach appears to be related to these processes, as the cell-biology processes mentioned before can be seen as basic computations involving inputs, some processing, and outputs. The processes also usually involve discrete entities such as atoms, molecules, and DNA nucleotides, for example. TANNs cover these features but also introduce the learning dimension. This could be interesting for biologists and AI practitioners.

In the field of neuroinformatics, which combines the fields of neuroscience and informatics, we have a similar situation [AG01]. In a way, neuroinformatics logically complements bioinformatics. Bioinformatics includes data and tools from different biological levels of organization. In an upward fashion, these levels may be molecules, genes, more complex cell formations, organs, and, on the highest level, complex higher organisms, including human beings. Neuroinformatics complements this chain in a natural way by investigating the cognitive functions inherent in such organisms. The phrase "from molecules to cognition" therefore is sometimes used to summarize the field. Although neuroinformatics is not easy to define, most definitions involve the terms informatics, neuroscience, and computational neuroscience. Neuroscience is concerned with the study of the fundamental principles that explain how biological nervous systems, most notably the human brain, work. The field also aims to acquire an understanding of behavioral constructs such as attention, learning, memory, emotion, or cognition. Computational neuroscience supports neuroscientists by providing computational techniques, resources and metaphors for the modeling, simulation, experimentation, and investigation of neural structures, their functioning, and neural relationships. Neuroinformatics, like bioinformatics, is permeated with AI. The field is characterized by a constant flux of novel modeling approaches for the complex processes happening in biological brains. Our approach relates quite well to some of the challenging problems just mentioned. For example, the approach may provide a model for discrete entities on a molecular level; it may relate particularly well to the learning dimension associated with biological brains, which is a key area in neuroinformatics.

The final potential candidates from a biology perspective shall be the relatively young fields of artificial synthetic life and synthetic biology. Briefly, these fields aim for the creation of new life forms from nonliving chemicals in the lab [Hol05]. Long-range goals include the design and fabrication of biological components, systems, and artificial cells that do not already exist in the natural world from nonliving raw material and programming them with the desired chemical functionality. The field also envisages the redesign and fabrication of existing biological systems [RCD$^+$04]. Artificial synthetic life and synthetic biology are taken quite seriously, and there are strong beliefs by many practitioners that artificial cells will eventually be created. For example, Craig Venter, who was instrumental in sequencing the human genome, is involved in the field. Another fundamental research aim of artificial synthetic life is the discovery of the "minimal genome", the smallest set of genes needed to support a simple living cell [Ain03]. From an AI and TANN perspective, these ambitions are all extremely interesting. The creation of intelligent, human-like entities is a fundamental ambition of AI. The modeling in these projects may involve some intelligent processing on a molecular level, which establishes a link to our approach again.

Another area where we feel our approach may have some value is in "smart homes" (also known as ambient or intelligent homes) and the related disciplines of ambient intelligence, pervasive computing, and ubiquitous computing [AN06]. Intelligent homes are equipped with a large number of "smart" sensors, microelectronic devices, wireless gadgets, and computers [CM04]. Typically, these devices communicate via RFID (radio frequency identification) technology. In such a home, computing could be blended invisibly into everyday tasks in an intelligent way. For example, homeowners may use intelligent bags that alarm users in case they are about to forget a wallet or car keys. Other systems may adjust or prepare a home for particular events such as a garden party or a relaxed evening. Intelligent homes also bear great potential for health care. Twenty-four hour, noninvasive tracking of the well-being of people in their own homes may revolutionize the practice of medicine, and a health-related infrastructure in the home may allow effective preventative medicine, helping doctors to monitor health, exercise, and nutrition and to identify problems before they become critical. The TANN approach may fit into this picture. The approach allows the modeling of individual entities (bags, car keys, persons, etc.) and their complex interactions. On top of this, the approach also provides an integrated learning component, which is a fundamental, and so far extremely challenging, area in the field of smart homes. Related to smart homes, we also consider autonomic computing relevant. The field involves hugely complex systems that are autonomously controlled, self-organized, radically distributed, technology-independent, and scale-free [Mur04]. Autonomic computing uses the autonomic nervous system as a key analogy for creating distributed networks that are largely self-managing, self-diagnostic, transparent to users, and able to adapt to new situations when new resources are available.

Particle physics and cosmology may also be discussed in the context of our work. For example, the basic idea of the photoelectric effect is that when light shines on a metal surface, the surface emits electrons in a manner inexplicable in terms of the wave nature of light. Einstein explained this behavior by assuming that the energy transferred between the incoming radiation and the outgoing electrons is delivered in discrete packets, or quanta, called photons. From the TANN perspective, there are several relationships. A surface can be a place, photons and electrons can be tokens, etc. Actually, the idea of using Petri nets and state transition diagrams for modeling particle interaction is not so new. The inventor of Petri nets, Carl Adam Petri, made this suggestion earlier [Pet62, Pet82]. The difference between this earlier work and our study is that the TANN approach goes beyond this earlier work by adding the dimension of learning to this model. It is possible to extend this view from a micro to a macro environment. For example, there are views that our universe represents a computer shuffling information in a cosmic program whose output is time, space, particles, and us—humans. Black holes appear naturally in this universal computer as subroutines in the program, sucking in matter and information, hiding it from the rest of the universe, but eventually evaporating their output [LJ04]. Intelligence is, of course, part of these discussions. The interesting aspect of this is that many processes deal with discrete entities, and as we know, in the TANN approach, a token and a place can be anything, from a person to a whole universe. The final aspect we consider in a related context is that between the TANN approach and questions related to information theory and the quantization of information. Over the last couple of years, the concept of information has attained more and more attention within the science community [Bae01, SR00]. Speculations include the quantization of information. For example, Zeilinger suggested that elementary systems (e.g., the spin of an electron) representing the truth value of one proposition carry just one bit of information [Zei99]. Maybe in a TANN a token and a place could be used for similar purposes. A token could hold a unit of information, and a place could be a container for information. Then again, from information it is only a small step to thinking, learning, mind, and intelligence. It is evident now that it is possible to direct this discussion into the widest philosophical debate. This is not our intention. Our sole intention here is to introduce the TANN approach to a wider audience. Members of this audience may find the approach relevant to a particular field. Such interest may lead to more sophisticated implementations and models of the basic, but nevertheless meaningful, model presented here.

4.6 Summary

Our aim was to introduce a novel computing model called TANN. The model combines features from ANNs and Petri nets in an innovative way. We described the formalism for a TANN and successfully tested our approach in various experimental investigations. We also provided a proof demonstrating the correctness (in terms of convergence) of the algorithm presented. Our work identifies various interesting relationships between the TANN approach and other disciplines in engineering and science. Analysis of the approach presented and other developments in the area of ANNs and Petri nets indicate various directions for further research. Extension of the current approach for the modeling of more complex systems (e.g., multilayer systems) is one possibility. Although our experience in the field suggests that an extension of the current model to more complex networks should be possible with relative ease, we emphasize that the work presented here aims to demonstrate the general principle of the TANN approach on a simple model.

Appendix A

We show that the TANN learning algorithm presented in previous sections always converges toward a solution. Figure 4.6 illustrates objects for two linearly separable classes. *Class 1* objects are represented by white squares and *Class 2* objects by black diamonds. We assume that any value for a data item (object) presented to a TANN can be expressed by a rational number $\frac{a}{b}$. For example, the value 0.24 can be represented as $\frac{24}{100}$. We also assume that $a, b \in [0, 1]$, $a \le b$, and $b \ne 0$.

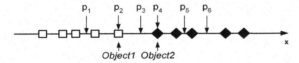

Fig. 4.6. Possible locations for a division point after a token assignment. The first assignment (r_0) involves a random procedure.

The ratio r introduced by equation (4.2) is derived from the number of black and white tokens assigned to a network. Conceptually, the ratio r can be viewed as a division point on the x-axis in Figure 4.6. The first token assignment to a network r_0 is undertaken in a random fashion. Positions p_1 to p_6 in Figure 4.6 capture cases that can emerge from an initial token assignment. We look at position p_3 and position p_4 in Figure 4.6. In position p_3, the division point falls between the x values of *Object 1* and *Object 2*, and in position p_4 the division point equals the value x of *Object 2*. In these two cases, the division point separates the two classes correctly (equation (4.2)), and no error correction is needed. On the other hand, in case p_1, case p_2, case p_5, and case p_6, the division point does not separate the two classes correctly. In p_1 the division point is to the left of *Object 1*, p_2 equals the value x of *Object 1*, and in p_5 and p_6 the division point is to the right of *Object 2*. Note that case p_2 is a special case of case p_1 and that case p_5 is similar to case p_6. Note also that case p_1 is similar (symmetric) to cases p_5 and p_6. Finally, please note that forthcoming sections always assume a learning rate $\eta = 1$ in equation (4.4).

Lemma 1: Whenever the division point is equal to or smaller than the x value of *Object 1*, then the TANN algorithm always moves the division point farther to the right.

Proof

Let $p_1 = \frac{a}{b}$. The division point is to the left of *Object 1*. Equation (4.4) then produces $p' = \frac{a+1}{b}$. Clearly, $p_1 = \frac{a}{b} < p' = \frac{a+1}{b}$. $\square$

Lemma 2: Whenever the division point is larger than the x value of *Object 2*, then the TANN algorithm always moves the division point farther to the left.

Proof

Let $p_6 = \frac{a}{b}$. The division point is to the right of *Object 2*. Equation (4.4) then produces $p' = \frac{a}{b+1}$. Clearly, $p' = \frac{a}{b+1} < p_6 = \frac{a}{b}$. $\square$

Lemma 3: A division point that has moved in n updates from a point p located to the left of *Object 1* to a point p' located to the right of *Object 2* and then, after m updates back to a point p'' located to the left of *Object 1* again, always ends up to the right of the point last visited on the left of *Object 1*, that is, $p < p''$. For example, in Figure 4.6, assume division point p_1 moving to p_5 and then back towards a point p'' located to the left of *Object 1* again. Then $p_1 < p''$.

Proof

Let $p_1 = \frac{a}{b}$ and $p_5 = \frac{a+n}{b}$, where $n > 1$. Also let $p'' = \frac{a+n}{b+m}$ be a division point located to the left of *Object 1*, where $m > 1$. Clearly, $p_1 = \frac{a}{b} < p_5 = \frac{a+n}{b}$, and also $p'' = \frac{a+n}{b+m} < p_5 = \frac{a+n}{b}$.

We show that $p_1 = \frac{a}{b} < p'' = \frac{a+n}{b+m}$. We recognize that $a < (a + n)$ and $b < (b + m)$. The substitution $c = (a + n)$ and $d = (b + m)$ leads to $\frac{a}{b} < \frac{c}{d}$. We show that $\forall a \forall b \forall c \forall d((a < c$ and $b < d) \rightarrow \frac{a}{b} < \frac{c}{d})$. Let $a, b, c,$ and d be arbitrary, and assume $a < c$ and $b < d$. We show that $\frac{a}{b} < \frac{c}{d}$. We apply proof by contradiction on $\frac{a}{b} \geq \frac{c}{d}$. The setting $a = 2 < c = 8$ and $b = 4 < d = 10$ leads to the contradiction $\frac{2}{4} = 0.5 \not\geq \frac{8}{10} = 0.8$. $\square$

We are now able to prove the convergence of the TANN learning algorithm.

Theorem: The TANN learning algorithm always converges toward a solution.

Proof

Lemma 1 has shown that whenever a division point is equal to or smaller than the x value of *Object 1*, then the TANN algorithm always moves the division point farther to the right. Lemma 2 has shown that whenever a division point is larger than the x value of *Object 2*, then the algorithm always moves the division point farther to the left. Lemma 2 also indicates that it is always possible to get the division point to the left of *Object 1*. Lemma 1 and Lemma 2 show that the basic behavior expected by the algorithm is correct. Lemma 3 has shown that a division point that has moved back and forth from a location to the left of *Object 1* to a location to the right of *Object 2* and back to a location to the left of *Object 1* again always ends up to the right of the division point last generated on the left of *Object 1*. Lemma 3 covers cases where the division point kind of oscillates toward a solution. The overall characteristic of the TANN learning algorithm demonstrates a behavior where a division point converges incrementally toward a solution. $\square$

References

[AG01]   M.A. Arbib and J.S. Grethe, editors. *Computing the Brain: A Guide to Neuroinformatics*. Academic Press, New York, 2001.

[Ain03]   C. Ainsworth. The facts of life. *New Scientist*, 178:28–31, May 2003.

[AN06]   J.C. Augusto and C.D. Nugent, editors. *Designing Smart Homes—The Role of Artificial Intelligence*, volume 4008 of *Lecture Notes in Artificial Intelligence*. Springer-Verlag, Berlin, 2006.

[Bae01]   H.C. Baeyer. In the beginning was the bit. *New Scientist*, 2278:26–30, February 2001.

[CM04]   D.E. Culler and H. Mulder. Smart sensors to network the world. *Scientific American*, 290:53–59, June 2004.

[DT03]   L.N. De Castro and J. Timmis. Artificial immune systems as a novel soft computing paradigm. *Soft Computing*, 7(8):526–544, 2003.

[Eng06]   A.P. Engelbrecht. *Fundamentals of Computational Swarm Intelligence*. John Wiley & Sons, New York, 2006.

[Hol05]   B. Holmes. Alive. *New Scientist*, 185:29–33, February 2005.

[KK95]   L.J. Kleinsmith and V.M. Kish. *Principles of Cell and Molecular Biology*. Harper Collins College Publishers, New York, 2nd edition, 1995.

[KN05]   E. Keedwell and A. Narayanan. *Intelligent Bioinformatics: The Application of Artificial Intelligence Techniques to Bioinformatics Problems*. John Wiley & Sons, New York, 2005.

[LJ04]   S. Lloyd and Y. Jack. Black hole computers. *Scientific American*, 291:30–39, November 2004.

[MMR97]   K. Mehrotra, C. Mohan, and S. Ranka. *Elements of Artificial Neural Networks*. MIT Press, Cambridge and London, 1997.

[Mur04]   R. Murch. *Autonomic Computing*. IBM Press, Yorktown Heights, NY, 2004.

[Pet62]   C.A. Petri. Kommunikation mit automaten, 1962. Schriften des IIM Nr. 2, Institut fur Instrumentelle Mathematik, Bonn.

[Pet81]   J.L. Peterson. *Petri Net Theory and the Modelling of Systems*. Prentice-Hall, Englewood Cliffs, NJ, 1981.

[Pet82]   C.A. Petri. State-transition structures in physics and in computation. *International Journal of Theoretical Physics*, 21(12):979–992, 1982.

[RCD+04]   S. Rasmussen, L. Chen, D. Deamer, D.C. Krakauer, N.H. Packard, P.F. Stadler, and M.A. Bedau. Transitions from nonliving to living matter. *Science*, 303:963–965, February 2004.

[Ros58]   F. Rosenblatt. The perceptron, a probabilistic model of information storage and organization in the brain. *Psychological Review*, 62:386–408, 1958.

[SR00]   A.M. Steane and E.G. Rieffel. Beyond bits: the future of quantum information processing. *Computer*, 33(1):38–45, January 2000.

[Wid59]   B. Widrow. Adaptive sample-data systems—a statistical theory of adaptation. *WESCON Convention Record: Part 4*, pages 74–85, 1959.

[Zei99]   A. Zeilinger. A foundational principle for quantum mechanics. *Foundations of Physics*, 29(4):631–643, April 1999.

Part II

Artificial Intelligence, Quantum Mechanics,
and the Mind

Quantum Mechanics and Artificial Intelligence

Subhash Kak

Department of Electrical & Computer Engineering, Louisiana State University,
Baton Rouge, LA 70803-5901, kak@ee.lsu.edu

Summary. This chapter presents the case that quantum mechanical machines will be needed for AI (artificial intelligence) to match biological intelligence. We begin with an overview of quantum mechanics and describe some of its paradoxes related to nonlocality and instantaneous reduction of the wave function. The case is made that the nonlocality of quantum mechanics and the probabilistic state reduction upon measurement make the theory noncomputable in the classical sense. Some parallels between quantum processing and the workings of the human mind are sketched. Biological systems at the physical level as well as the brain are characterized by reorganization in response to stimulus, which is clearly seen in the changing of the strength of interconnection between neurons, indicating that biological learning is very different from classical machine learning. But reorganization by itself cannot be the reason behind the power of biological intelligence, and therefore we examine the recently proposed quantum computing models for their computing power. We provide an overview of their functioning and we also critique them from the point of view of their realizability. We argue that practical quantum machines will have to be conceived differently from those presently being researched.

5.1 Introduction

The computer scientist must understand the nature of biological intelligence to help him build machines that are able to match, and perhaps surpass, this intelligence. These machines will be physical, and their information-processing capacity has to conform to the constraints of physical law [Lan96]. But current theory appears to be incapable of describing the workings of the human mind on the computer paradigm [Pen89, Pen94, Kak04]. According to the psychologist Ronald Melzack [Mel89], "there is a profusion of little theories—theories of vision, pain, behaviour-modification, and so forth—but no broad unifying concepts. ... Cognitive psychology has recently been proclaimed as the revolutionary concept which will lead us away from the sterility of behaviourism ... but there have been no important conceptual advances. We are adrift, without the anchor of neuropsychological theory, in a sea of facts—and practically drowning in them. We desperately need new concepts, new approaches." The failure of cognitive psychology and AI theory may be based on the limitations of the underlying physical laws. Since quantum logic, the foundational basis of physical reality, is more powerful than classical logic, on which current computing models are based, one may imagine that the limitations of current models of artificial intelligence arise from the limitations of their logic.

To look at intelligence from the perspective of computability, AI is comput- able by definition, but that doesn't appear to be true of biological intelligence, for a variety of reasons that will be discussed later in this chapter. If biological intelligence is computable, machines should eventually match it, but if it is not computable, then machines will fall short at certain tasks. The noncomputability of biological intelligence may be due either to its holistic nature [Kak96, Kak00] or the "freedom" of action that characterizes life [Mel89], or it may reflect a basic property of reality [Boh80, Pen89]. One may wish to see higher intelligence as a new noncomputable property that emerges out of the physical ground that is, in principle, completely describable. This "explanation" has been expressed sometimes as the principle that higher cognitive abilities are a consequence of the increased complexity of neuronal structures and interconnections. This complexity in biological systems is so immense that it is computationally infeasible to falsify this principle, and due to this unfalsifiability, any further discussion of this point is useless.

In this chapter, we address the question of computability of physical reality, arguing that the nonlocality and superposition of quantum mechanics make for a noncomputable system. We will also argue that similar noncomputability is at the basis of life [DGK76, Lib89, BL98] and animal behavior [Her85, Kak00], and therefore classical AI will remain limited compared with natural intelligence. Since the ingredient that is missing in current models of AI is quantum mechanics, we suggest that it may be essential to obtain artificial intelligence more powerful than currently available, but we show that recently proposed quantum computation models are not physically realistic and there- fore are not likely to represent the technology to deliver on this promise.

5.2 Quantum Superpositions

The quantum perspective is a radical departure from the classical or objective view of reality, where we speak of particles and their precise motions or of objects with definite attributes. Quantum evolution proceeds as a superposi- tion of many characteristics that reduces to just one upon observation. According to one interpretation, the quantum view splits the world into two: one of the process and the other of the observation. We cannot speak of a preconceived notion of reality; it is upon interaction with the apparatus that characteristics of the system are revealed. The classic Young's two-slit experiment serves as a background to illustrate these ideas [Fey88, Pen05]. In this experiment, light from a source must go through two slits to a screen. If it is allowed to pass through one slit at a time, we see a bright spot directly in line with the slit on the screen, with decreasing intensity away from it. Using classical reasoning, the existence of two slits should lead to two such bright regions. But, we find alternating bands of high and low intensity. If light were waves, then new waves would start out from the slits, and where the peak of one wave is coincident with the peak of the other, the two waves would add and reinforce (constructive interference), giving rise to a bright fringe, and where a peak of one wave was coincident with the trough of the other, the two waves would cancel (destructive interference), giving a dark fringe.

This may be seen also in a Mach-Zehnder interferometer (Figure 5.1), where the photon, emitted at the lower left corner, seemingly splits into two parts as it strikes a half-silvered mirror, and these parts recombine at the second half-silvered mirror in the upper right corner, effectively interfering constructively in detector D_1 (clicks) and destructively in detector D_2 (no clicks).

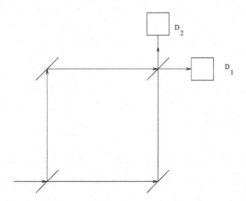

Fig. 5.1. The Mach-Zehnder interferometer.

The particle nature of light is established by the photoelectric effect. When light is projected on a metal surface, electrons are emitted, but the energy of these electrons is proportional not to the intensity of the incident light but rather its frequency. We may see the incident light as a stream of particles where the energy of each photon is given by $\hbar\nu$, where $\hbar$ is the Planck constant and ν is the frequency associated with the light. We can visualize an electron absorbing a photon, and if its total energy exceeds the threshold for escaping the surface of the metal, it will be emitted with an energy that is the excess of the escape energy. This is precisely what happens in experiments.

When the double-slit or the Mach-Zehnder interferometer experiments are viewed in relation to the particle nature of light, one may assume that somehow each photon is spread out like a little wavepacket, and these wavepackets interfere constructively or destructively. But the interference persists even when the light intensity is so low that the photons are produced one at a time in sequence. This forces us to acknowledge that somehow each photon is able to travel through both the paths simultaneously, and the classical notion of what constitutes an entity is not true.

The wave-particle duality is true not only for light but for all matter. Interference findings have been observed for electrons and neutrons also. Since we accept that these are massive objects, we must agree that particles somehow spread through both the slits to undergo self-interference.

In the classical description, given two points A and B in the path of a particle, and given all forces acting on the particle in its path as well as its previous interactions, one can determine the exact trajectory between A and B. But in a quantum description, localization of a particle at specific points in its path is impossible. Even if one assumes that two points in the path have been determined, all one can do is indicate a large bundle of paths, each with its own probability, that could potentially be the trajectory of the particle.

One may wish to track this strange behavior and check how the particle travels through both the slits in Young's experiment. But when experiments are set up to see which of the slits the particle may have travelled through, the interference effects vanish, and the behavior actually becomes particle-like. Likewise, when one attempts to find which of the two branches of the Mach-Zehnder interferometer the photon actually moved, the difference in the interference in the two detectors vanishes and both of them have clicks, indicating that specific photons are taking the path through one branch or the other. *If the photon is not watched, it travels through both paths; when it is watched, it travels through only one!*

5.2.1 Polarized Photons

Let us examine this strange behavior through the anomalous polarization property of photons. Light may be viewed as electromagnetic waves of a certain band of frequencies. For plane light waves, the oscillations of the electric vectors are confined in one dimension and the propagation of plane light is in the z-direction. In vertically polarized light, the electric vector is confined to oscillate only in the x-direction and in horizontally polarized light, this vector oscillates only in the y-direction. Polarizing filters are polymers that allow light that is polarized in a specific direction to go through but reduce the intensity for polarizations of other directions according to equation (5.1)

$$I = I_0 \cos^2 \phi \tag{5.1}$$

where ϕ is the angle between the polarization of the incident wave and that of the filter, I_0 is the intensity of the incident light, and I is the intensity of the transmitted light.

Polarized photons may have polarizations at various angles. The 45^0 photon may be considered as a superposition of photons polarized horizontally and vertically. A calcite crystal separates vertical and horizontal photons into different streams [Fey88]. When passed through the calcite crystal again, the vertical and the horizontal photons remain unchanged. When a stream of 45^0 polarized photons is incident on a calcite crystal, the intensities at the horizontal and vertical ports of the calcite crystal are the same. But one cannot assume that half of the 45^0 photons are vertically polarized and half are horizontally polarized. When passed through a calcite crystal that is rotated through 45^0, all of the photons will pass through a single port. The only conclusion open to us is that a 45^0 photon is simultaneously also at 0^0 and 90^0. If one tries to determine which path of the calcite crystal a specific 45^0 polarized photon travelled through, the photon is reduced to one of the constituent components, showing again that the act of observation elicits a particle-like behavior from the photons.

5.3 Quantum Rules

The polarization behavior of photons justifies viewing the quantum state or wave function as the weighted sum of the possibilities associated with the system. A weight represents a "probability amplitude", and its magnitude squared represents the probability of obtaining that possibility. The weights are complex numbers, which makes it impossible to see quantum theory as a mere probabilistic theory. The complex numbers tell us that the *underlying* structure of reality has an extra dimension that is not accessible to machine measurement.

The basis of the standard interpretation of quantum mechanics consists of the following statements [NC00]:

1. The state of a system is completely described by its wave function or quantum state $|\psi\rangle$. This state itself may be seen as a sum of basis states $|\psi\rangle = \sum_i a_i|\psi_i\rangle$, and the basis may be chosen in a variety of ways.
2. The a_i are the probability amplitudes associated with a basis state. Upon measurement, the system is reduced to the basis state $|\psi_i\rangle$ with probability $|a_i|^2$.
3. Observable quantities are represented by mathematical operators. For example, the energy of the system is determined by applying the Hamiltonian operator, $\hat{H}$, to the wave function.
4. The wave function of a system obeys a continuous equation of motion, the Schrödinger equation.

The time-dependent Schrödinger equation is given by equation (5.2)

$$i\hbar\frac{\partial}{\partial t}|\psi_t\rangle = \hat{H}|\psi_t\rangle. \tag{5.2}$$

Integrating this equation, we obtain equation (5.3)

$$|\psi_t\rangle = e^{-i\hat{H}t/\hbar}|\psi_0\rangle, \tag{5.3}$$

where $|\psi_0\rangle$ is the state vector at some initial time $t = 0$, and $|\psi\rangle$ represents the state vector at a later time t.

The exponential term is called the time-evolution operator and is usually given by the symbol $\hat{U}$. So we can write

$$|\psi_t\rangle = \hat{U}|\psi_0\rangle, \quad \hat{U} = e^{-i\hat{H}t/\hbar}. \tag{5.4}$$

The time-evolution operator can be simplified by using the Euler series expansion of the exponential function. The operator $\hat{U}$ is a unitary operator, which means that its conjugate transpose is equal to its inverse. If the state is a binary vector, as represented in the case of photons by their polarization or in electrons by their spin, then for a vector of n components, the unitary operator will be a $2^n \times 2^n$ matrix.

The process of measurement is described by the action of an appropriate operator on the state. A measurement sends the system into a new state. In general, the process of observation brings about a discontinuous change implying the *reduction of the wave packet*. Significantly, the time evolution of a quantum system is continuous and deterministic, and this equation cannot explain the discontinuous jumps that take place upon measurement.

Since the dynamical variables are expressed in terms of probabilities, if an experiment were repeated several times, one would be able to predict the outcome of the measurements in a probabilistic sense only.

The wave function for a particle may be symmetrical or antisymmetrical. Particles with symmetrical wave functions are bosons, and those with antisymmetrical wave functions are fermions. Bosons have integer angular momentum, while fermions have angular momentum in odd multiples of one-half. Photons are bosons, as are the mesons. On the other hand, electrons, protons, neutrons, muons, and neutrons are fermions. Several bosons can be in the same state. As the number of bosons in a particular state increases, the probability that more will enter that state also increases. Fermions behave differently, with the probability of finding two identical fermions in the same state being zero. The rule that the presence of a fermion in a state excludes all other identical fermions is the exclusion principle.

Our inability to determine what happens during the interaction of the quantum system and the apparatus may be viewed as a consequence of the veiling of reality by means of a fundamental uncertainty [Boh80].

The uncertainty may be seen from the point of view of the observation disturbing the system. Thus, when we measure the temperature of a hot liquid by inserting a thermometer, heat flows from the liquid to the thermometer until their temperatures are equal. The liquid cools somewhat to this common temperature, and the thermometer reading therefore measures the disturbed system. In large systems, the effect of the measurement can be made so small as to be negligible. This is not so in the microworld, where the uncertainty is more basic. Whereas in the classical picture one can always talk about the precise position, momentum, or some other attribute even before a measurement, one cannot do so in the quantum world unless the system has been prepared in a specific state.

The state of the system (the wave function) varies with time. If the wave function is known at some initial instant, then from the very meaning of the concept of complete description of a state, it is in principle determined at every succeeding instant. The sum of the probabilities of all possible values of the coordinates of the system must, by definition, be equal to unity (the normalization condition for wave functions). All quantities calculated by means of the wave function and having a direct physical meaning have a form in which ψ is multiplied by ψ^*. This means that the normalized wave function is determined only to within a constant phase factor.

If the states do not interact, their joint wave function can be represented as the product of the individual wave functions. Since a system consisting of two particles very far apart moving toward each other would have these particles interact with each other eventually, the condition above causes computational difficulties in the analysis of complex quantum systems.

5.4 Paradoxes, Realism, and Positivism

The state function seems to evolve in two different ways. First, it evolves in time according to Schrödinger's equation. Second, it changes discontinuously according to probability laws if a measurement is carried out on the system. While the state function evolves in a causal manner so long as no measurement is made on it, the process of measurement requires a definite choice to be made regarding the wave function, defining a puzzling duality seen clearly in the following paradox. Consider a closed room consisting of an experimenter studying the motion of an electron with the help of an apparatus. One may associate with the room a wave function that would evolve with time. Given the initial wave function, one would, without ambiguity, determine it for all time. This wave function, however, is a product of the wave functions of the experimenter, the apparatus, and the electron, and we know that upon his measurement the experimenter within the room would modify the wave function of the electron. If the experimenter within the room communicated his observation to us later, we would need to revise our earlier results as well. This, however, leads to a contradiction since a Schrödinger type equation should have completely described the evolution of the room wave function.

This difficulty was pointed out by Schrödinger himself in a scenario that is now known as the cat paradox [Sch58]. Consider a closed chamber containing a cat and a small amount of a radioactive substance, the probability of decay per minute of one atom of which is exactly 0.5; the decay, if it occurs, activates a Geiger counter and closes a circuit that electrocutes the cat. The entire system can be represented by a wave function that is a superposition of two waves, one denoting the state "cat alive" and the other the state "cat dead". At the end of the experiment, when the chamber is opened, the cat is thrown into a definite alive or dead state only through the act of observation. According to quantum mechanics, one cannot speak of the cat as being either dead or alive before the act of observation when surely the cat must have been in one of these two states even before the chamber was opened. In another version of this paradox, due to Wigner, the cat is replaced by the experimenter's friend. This is to circumvent the objection that the cat might not possess full awareness of its own existence. Then the question arises as to whether the experimenter's friend is alive or dead before the act of observation because being "dead-alive" is definitely meaningless.

Wigner and some others believe that the only way to get out of the paradoxes above is to assume that the wave function of the object is reduced due to its interaction with the "consciousness" of the experimenter. And since the dynamics of "consciousness" are not known, the problem of the room with an experimenter inside it lies beyond the pale of quantum mechanics and present-day physics. This viewpoint has symmetry: matter affects consciousness, therefore, consciousness must also affect matter. Wigner's view assigns to sentient beings a central role in the organization of the universe. But this view is not accepted by many theorists since such reduction occurs even if there is only an instrument (and not a sentient observer) present in the system that can, potentially, interact with the wave function.

A quite different resolution of Schrödinger's cat paradox is provided by the many-worlds interpretation of quantum mechanics proposed in 1957 by Hugh Everett. According to this interpretation, the wave function represents objective reality. This is in contrast to the usual understanding of the wave function, where it defines a sum of potentialities and a computational procedure. According to Everett's view, the states of the wave function represent the description of the system in the many universes that coexist with ours. An act of observation does not cause the wave function to collapse but merely shows up one of the actualities. Each moment, the universe splits into countless near copies of itself, and the electron through a slit reaches different positions on the screen in the copies, so that the distribution is according to what the wave function predicts. This view circumvents our paradoxes of measurement. Schrödinger's cat would, in the many-worlds interpretation, be dead in some worlds and alive in others. But this interpretation is so removed from a commonsensical view of reality that it need not be taken seriously.

But how should the task of creating scientific theories be approached? According to the view called *positivism*, speculations that are intrinsically unverifiable are not scientific. In the more restrictive position called *logical positivism*, it is contended that a scientific statement must be a formally logical and verifiable statement. On the other hand, *realism* is the position that there exists a reality that is independent of the observer and the instruments used to make observations. What is the distinction between positivism and realism? A realist will assert that there is an independent reality that is probed through observation and experiment. A positivist accepts that there are elements of an empirical reality that are probed in this way, but that is not quite the same as the realist view. According to the positivist view, the realist position involves a logical contradiction. Since we have no way of observing an observer-independent reality, we cannot verify that such a reality exists. We have no means of acquiring knowledge of the physical world except through observation and experiment, and so the reality we probe is, of necessity, dependent on the observer for its existence. The positivist argues that as we cannot verify the existence of an observer-independent reality, such a reality is metaphysical and therefore quite without meaning. The logical contradiction implied in the realist's view is sidestepped only by an appeal to faith.

A quantum particle exhibits properties we associate with waves and particles. Its behavior appears to be determined by the kind of instrument used to probe its properties. One kind of instrument will tell us that the quantum particle is a wave. Another will tell us that it is a particle. All we can know is the *empirical* reality—sometimes the quantum particle is a wave, and sometimes it is a particle. It is not meaningful to specify, without mentioning the context, what the objective reality of a quantum particle is.

Objectivity itself can be associated with degree. One may speak of *weak* objectivity in the sense that it is the same for all observers, whereas *strong* objectivity is independent of observers. The positivist is content with weak objectivity. For the realist, the aim of a theory is to describe an independent reality, to describe the world as *is*, in the sense of strong objectivity.

Both positivists and realists use deductive logic and the criteria of verifiability and simplicity in the development of their theories. Both will strive for the ideal of objectivity in the way they apply these methods and criteria. However, for the positivist, the theory is merely an instrument that can be used to interrelate observed facts and make new predictions. It does no more than describe elements of an empirical reality that depend on the observer and the measuring device for their existence.

The difference between positivism and realism also informs AI. The mainstream view is to look only at intelligence in an operational sense (for example, whether a machine can perform a task as well as a human) and ignore philosophical questions related to mind and awareness. The flip side to this view is to explain human intelligence in machine terms. These positions appear like that of positivism, unlike the realist position, which is to define intelligence by itself. It is interesting that while the realist position has much appeal to the physicist, it has much less appeal to the computer scientist.

5.5 The Copenhagen Interpretation

The complementary interpretation of quantum mechanics, proposed by Bohr in 1927, elevates duality, such as that between waves and particles for matter, to a fundamental attribute of the physical reality. According to Bohr, mutually exclusive aspects are part of a comprehensive description. For light, it is the wave aspect that corresponds with the classical description and the concept of a photon is symbolic, required to express the exchange of energy and momentum between matter and radiation, while for electrons and protons the situation is the reverse.

We can speak of quantum phenomena only using classical concepts. The effect of an event occurring at the level of the individual quantum particle must somehow be amplified or otherwise turned into a macroscopic signal so that we can perceive and measure it. The Copenhagen interpretation rests on the paradox that its description is in terms of idealized classical concepts, emphasizing that we can never fully *know* quantum concepts, in accord with the positivist view.

In spite of its inner consistency, the Copenhagen interpretation leaves us with several questions. If reality is only what is observed, and if quantum physics is universal, who or what does the observing? The positivists would say that this question is outside the scope of science. Nevertheless, one wonders if reality can only be conceived in terms of consciousness and subjectivism.

Bohr emphasized the applicability of quantum theory to macroscopic objects to guarantee that measurements at the atomic scale were consistent with the uncertainty principle. But doing so brings in difficulties such as the Schrödinger cat measurement problem. It also calls into question the dichotomy of the classical and quantum worlds, which is fundamental to the Copenhagen interpretation.

The correlations inherent in quantum mechanics cannot be interpreted in classical terms. This situation may be compared to the case where we have two roommates who share a wardrobe. If they had a total of just two shirts of different colors, red and blue, then it would be easy to see why knowing that one of them was wearing the red shirt, one would immediately know that the other was wearing the blue shirt. However, if the number of shirts in their wardrobe was very large, with both the colors in equal abundance, and they lived thousands of miles away, one would be justifiably astonished if they wore shirts of different colors each time this was checked. Since the characteristic of the object manifests itself only when it is observed, the inescapable conclusion is that the correlations are long-range and they propagate instantaneously!

One may explain the paradox inherent in this by adopting the positivist attitude toward measurement, whereby the question of whether the particle has spin before the measurement becomes meaningless. If one wishes to retain the essence of the reality criterion, it becomes imperative to give up the assumption of locality. This implies that one should be prepared to accept that certain influences can travel faster than the speed of light, so that the measurement on one particle can influence the measurement on another particle even if it is far removed.

5.6 Web of Reality

In Young's interference experiment, we found that if we try to check the path light takes, it adopts one of the two paths by ceasing to be a wave, and the interference effect vanishes. One may ask what would happen if one examined the photons well after the passage through the slits had already occurred. Photons travel too fast for such an experiment to be conducted in a laboratory setting. But Wheeler [Whe82] suggested doing this experiment on an astronomical scale, conjuring up a dramatic scenario that has consequences for what one can say about what *already* happened in the earliest days of the universe, long before there was any life on Earth.

Wheeler pointed out that astronomers could perform the delayed-choice experiment on light from quasars that has passed through a galaxy or other massive object that acts as a gravitational lens, splitting the light from the quasar and refocusing it in the direction of the distant observer.

The results show that light travels by anticipating whether the path would be blocked or open, and the integrity of either particle or wave picture is maintained. The astronomer's choice of how to observe photons from the quasar determines whether each photon took both paths or just one path around the gravitational lens in its journey which commenced billions of years ago. When they left the quasar to pass through the beam splitter, the photons made a choice that would satisfy the conditions of an experiment to be performed by unborn beings on a still nonexistent planet. There is no fallacy here for the positivist, in whose view the photon has no physical form before the astronomer's observation.

If one insists on using classical logic, then one must acknowledge that choices made now can influence the past. Put differently, what we consider to be a choice in the present was already decided billions of years ago. The photon, "knowing" that a measurement of its path would be made at some future date, chose to travel as a particle and not as a wave.

In the classical picture of physics, any complex object is seen in terms of elementary constituent parts. The universe itself is a giant machine, and our individual personalities, thoughts, actions, and emotions are to be traced back to one or more material causes. In contrast, quantum physics discards classical causality and determinism. Our conscious choices appear to make a difference as far as outcomes of experiments are concerned. Effects seem to propagate instantaneously, even over large distances, and the past and the present seem to be part of a web [Boh80]. The behavior of objects varies with the experimental arrangement, making it possible to measure it in the absence of interaction. Using informal terminology, one could assert that the photon possessed *knowledge* of the system before it set out on its path.

Although the positivist position requires that we ask no questions beyond the ones related to the specific measurement situation and therefore not ask if a photon took a definite path on its way to the screen, one may still wonder if an objective reality exists, even if it is not directly accessible to us.

Classical physics, which informs our common sense, is based on idealized concepts. In our intuition, things exist permanently, and we imagine systems to be in perfect isolation from the rest of the universe. In truth, the notion of an object as a collection of things does not exist. Reality is not mere *being*; it is unceasing change, a *becoming*.

In a situation of continual change, it is an idealization to speak of definite form. Zeno's arrow paradox captures the heart of the problem in relation to motion, which actually exists even in classical reasoning. If physical objects exist discretely at a sequence of discrete instants of time, and if no motion occurs in an instant, then we must conclude that the arrow has no motion at any given instant. If there is no physical difference between a moving and a nonmoving arrow, then how does the arrow know from one instant to the next if it is moving? In other words, how is causality transmitted forward in time through a sequence of instants in each of which motion does not exist?

If we see the entire physical world as a purely spatial expanse, existing in and progressing through a sequence of instants, then how can a quality that exists only over a range of instants be causally conveyed? In short, we cannot understand motion if it is seen in relation to an absolute definition of objects.

Thus not only in quantum theory but also in classical theory, we have problems understanding motion. Since quantum theory deals with transitions at the most elementary level, logical difficulties, which are hidden by the use of idealized notions in classical physics, come to the fore. The experiments of wave-particle duality inform us that these difficulties cannot be wished away.

5.7 Neural Computation

Theoretical models of neural computation are based on classical logic. Their connection with biological reality is the artificial neuron (a simple threshold device model of the real neuron), which is taken to have numerous interconnections with adjacent neurons. Although these models are quite good in learning patterns in terms of interconnection strengths, they do so in extremely constrained environments. Furthermore, they are no more effective than statistical learning systems and therefore can do no better than other rule-based AI systems. Neither are they able to explain many questions of biological memory [Nei82]. They also cannot address the problem of the humunculus, related to how the activity inside the neurons is recognized, because if one were to postulate special neurons that do it, then the question of what recognizes the activity of the special neurons arises. This leads to an endless hierarchy of specialized neurons [Kak96].

Intelligent behavior in animals is associated with continuing self-organization of the animal in response to the changing environment. This occurs at several levels, including at the level of neuronal interconnection in the brain [Kak96]. The reduction of the wave function due to the interaction with the observer may also be seen as a self-organizing response. True self-organization of the structure is beyond the capability of neural computation models, although one might erroneously believe that the training of weights in the learning of patterns constitutes such self-organization.

At the structural level, then, classical machines (and we include neural networks amongst them) are unable to match the physical complexity (for example, in terms of self-organization) of biological systems. But this doesn't warrant the conclusion that this is the main reason why they don't perform as well as biological systems at certain tasks. For example, the problem of the humunculus remains unresolved even in a self-organizing neural network.

At the behavioral level, there are other riddles related to natural categorization that do not admit straightforward logical explanations [Her85, Kak00]. This may be due to the fact that the nature of biological computation is different from the Turing machine model, but we do not know if non-Turing, nonquantum computation models other than the seemingly more powerful quantum neural computation model exist [Kak96].

The manner in which the human mind operates also has many counter-intuitive aspects [DGK76, Lib89]. The inner reality of the individual is not a simple mapping of the outer through the agency of the senses. Rather, it is created by the mediating mind. Expectation, therefore, is an important element in the working of the human senses and the mind. We are forced to look at human cognition in a holistic sense.

There are also proposals on quantum neural computing, models where a neural framework is considered together with quantum theory. Penrose and Hameroff [Pen94] have suggested that quantum processes can exist in the tubulins (subunit proteins) of the cytoskeletal microtubules, and these are eventually reduced by the gravitational field. They claim that at a level intermediate between the quantum and the classical, the distribution of matter and energy of the superposed states becomes gravitationally significant and the state collapses into a single state. But this model solves nothing since it replaces a classical machine with another one that has randomness and nonlocality built into it. In my own view, it is more plausible that the neural system is the apparatus that reduces a quantum field that is not necessarily established by the biological system [Kak96, Kak04]. But we do not possess sound experimental evidence to develop this view further at this stage.

5.8 Quantum Computing Models

In recent years, quantum computing models have been proposed, motivated not by AI but by the promise to solve standard engineering problems much faster than can be done by classical machines. Specifically, the quantum Fourier transform can be computed in $O(\log n)$ steps rather than the $O(n \log n)$ steps of the fast Fourier transform (FFT), and this can be used to factorize composite numbers much faster than by using the best classical algorithm. Since the security of certain popular ciphers is based on the difficulty of factorization of numbers, this has led to much interest in these quantum algorithms. Another example is the random database search problem where the best classical algorithm is basically a search through the list and will, on average, require $n/2$ steps. A quantum algorithm has been found that can solve the same problem in only $O(\sqrt{n})$ operations. Clearly, if n is very large, the savings can be enormous, although not as dramatic as in the solution of the quantum Fourier transform. But its capacity to solve certain problems faster than any classical machine does not, by itself, establish that quantum computing is at the basis of natural intelligence.

The power of quantum computing comes from superpositions, so that an exponential number of problems can be solved in principle at the same time. But there is the complication that only one of the solutions can be accessed upon measurement, which makes the search for effective quantum algorithms in the standard paradigm a challenging task. Another quantum resource is that of entanglement, for which no classical analogue exists. Pairs of entangled qubits can, in principle, have remarkable applications: two bits of classical information may be exchanged with the two parties using an existing entangled pair while transferring only one qubit by means of the protocol of dense coding, and an unknown quantum state may be teleported to another location by using an entangled pair of qubits and classical bits so long as the entangled qubits do not have any associated phase uncertainty between them [NC00]. When we go from single and entangled pairs of particles to groups of particles, as in various methods of quantum computing, the question of the physical realizability of the mathematical model becomes more problematic [Kak06b]. For example, the circuit model of quantum computing [NC00] leaves out problems of state preparation [Kak99], gate realizability [Kak06a], particle statistics [Kak01] (indistinguishability of quantum particles of the same quantum state), and effective error correction [Kak03]. It is assumed that once the qubits, each placed into a superposition of $|0\rangle$ and $|1\rangle$ by using an appropriate rotation operator, are loaded individually on the n-cell register, Hamiltonians for the subsequent evolution of the set of n-qubits will somehow be found. The physical implementability of the unitary matrices is not addressed.

The quantum Turing machine and the quantum cellular automata models are equivalent to the circuit model and therefore face the same difficulties. These models, inspired by the philosophically extravagant many-worlds interpretation of quantum mechanics, assign specific information to the qubits, postulating gates that implement the unitary transformation representing the solution to the computational problem.

The quantum circuit model converts the physical problem to a circuit-theoretic form, but it does not map all the physical constraints required by the laws of quantum mechanics. It gives specific labels to different lines of the circuit and does not consider the question of the indistinguishability of particles in quantum mechanics. This indistinguishability may require constraints in addition to the ones that are usually assumed when considering implementation. It should be remembered that quantum mechanics is an abstraction of reality but is not equivalent to that reality [Per95]. Quantum computing models use selected elements of this abstraction in a manner that may preclude successful physical implementation. If a quantum computing model is not physically implementable, then it should be called a quasi-quantum model.

The quantum computing model is an example of a Hamiltonian system. Several years ago, Rolf Landauer cautioned [Lan96] against the Hamiltonian approach to computation. In contrast to digital computers where data are reset, a Hamiltonian system cannot correct local errors. Quantum error-correcting codes have been proposed, but they can only correct certain large errors without correcting small errors. Even in theory, these codes work only to correct bitflips and phaseflips, which is a vanishingly small fraction of all the phase errors that can occur in the quantum state. Besides successful error correction, coding requires that the error be within bounds, whereas the uncertainty with regard to phase makes that assumption invalid. The question of decoherence of quantum states is another problem afflicting quantum computation [NC00].

There is also the question of the fundamental limitations of the standard quantum computing paradigm. Its unitary evolution is unable to perform basic nonlinear mappings. For an unknown state ψ, a general unitary matrix U does not exist that will take $|\psi_0\rangle$ to $|\psi_t\rangle$ or vice versa. In other words, an unknown state can neither be copied nor deleted. These operations are nonlinear and are beyond the capacity of a unitary transformation. By carrying the input data alongside, one can convert a one-way mapping to a reversible mapping, but that would involve an exponential growth of overhead in any substantial computation and therefore this possibility cannot be taken seriously for real computational tasks. As unitary transformations, quantum algorithms would still be useful in certain problems, but this usefulness would be similar to that of optical computing. Since unitary mappings are rotations on a sphere (of high dimensionality), one can only hope to compute periodicity information or properties that can be related to this information.

Now I list some interrelated issues related to the quantum circuit model. I first review the problems of creating an appropriate pure state to get the computation started and then consider the question of quantum statistics in the context of such a state. The thesis of this is that "quantum computing" models use the mathematical apparatus of quantum theory but do not appear to incorporate all of its restrictions. If this thesis is correct, then one may ask if other mathematical models of distinct computing power exist.

5.9 On the Realizability of the Circuit Model

The circuit model of quantum computing provides a schematic realization of the unitary matrix that represents the computation in terms of its submatrices.

It is implicit that when such transformations are applied to the qubits on the register, the evolution will correspond to the quantum evolution given by the Schrödinger equation. This is correct but for the fact that the circuit model takes the qubits to be unique and distinguishable from each other, a condition that maps into the uniqueness of the wires in the quantum circuit. But quantum objects cannot be distinguished amongst each other before measurement. From a practical point of view, it imposes severe constraints on the labels that are ascribed to qubits. This could mean that the unitary matrices for certain gates may not be physically realizable. The circuit model may then be seen as an implementation not of quantum physics but of unitary transformations.

In the circuit model, the register is loaded with data one qubit at a time, where these qubits are independent of each other. Now Hadamard transformation is applied to each qubit. From a practical point of view, due to the imprecision in the implementation of the transformations, this will create a compound pure state with uncertain weights.

In several proposed implementations, the individual qubits themselves are not in a pure state. One must remember that a pure state must yield a predictable outcome in *a specified maximal test*, and no such test may be conceptualized for the qubits on the quantum register in certain practical systems.

5.9.1 Unknown Phase

The state function of a quantum system is defined on the complex plane, whereas observations can only be real. This means that the state function may not be completely known even if the state is prepared because of the uncertainty associated with the state preparation process itself. In such a situation, one cannot hope to characterize this reality with such precision as to carry out a specific computation using a single quantum state.

In general, there may be an unknowable phase associated with the qubits [Kak99] making it impossible to rotate this qubit through a precise angle. For convenience, assume that the operator

$$M = \frac{1}{\sqrt{2}} \begin{bmatrix} 1 & 1 \\ 1 & -1 \end{bmatrix} \tag{5.5}$$

is implementable. When applied to the qubit $\frac{1}{\sqrt{2}}(|0\rangle + |1\rangle)$, it will lead to the pure state $|0\rangle$. But since the qubit should realistically be seen to be $\frac{1}{\sqrt{2}}(e^{i\theta_1}|0\rangle + e^{i\theta_2}|1\rangle)$ (because of the imprecision in the gate), an operation by M will take the qubit only to

$$\frac{(e^{i\theta_1} + e^{i\theta_2})}{2}|0\rangle + \frac{(e^{i\theta_1} - e^{i\theta_2})}{2}|1\rangle. \tag{5.6}$$

The probability of obtaining a $|0\rangle$ will now be $\frac{1}{2}[1 + \cos(\theta_1 - \theta_2)]$, whereas the probability of obtaining a $|1\rangle$ will be $\frac{1}{2}[1 - \cos(\theta_1 - \theta_2)]$. The probabilities for the basis observables are not exactly $\frac{1}{2}$, and they depend on the starting *unknown* θ values. Thus, the qubit can end up anywhere on the unit circle. As an example, consider $\theta_2 = 0$, $\theta_1 = \pi/2$; the probabilities of $|0\rangle$ and $|1\rangle$ will remain $\frac{1}{2}$ even after the unitary transformation has been applied.

This may also be seen from the point of view of information. A computation is a mapping from an initial sequence to the solution sequence, where both these sequences may be considered to be binary. In classical computing, small noise added to the initial sequence bits is filtered out using techniques of discretization. But in quantum computing, we face the impossibility of distinguishing between amplitudes with the multiplier $e^{i\theta}$.

If the quantum register cannot be properly initialized, the algorithms will not work as desired.

5.9.2 Error Correction

A realistic model of computing must address the problem of random errors. In the circuit model, small errors would creep in during state preparation and in the implementation of the gate operations that constitute the unitary transformations.

Error correction, intuitively and in classical theory, implies that if

$$y = x + n,$$

where x is the discrete code word, n is analog noise, and y is the analog noisy code word, one can recover x *completely and fully* so long as the analog noise function n is less than a certain threshold. If it exceeds this threshold, then there is also full correction so long as this does not happen more than a certain number of times (the Hamming distance for which the code is designed) at the places where the analog signal y is sampled.

The hallmark of classical error-correcting codes is *the correction of all possible small analog errors* and many others that exceed the thresholds associated with the code alphabet. This full correction of all possible small analog errors is beyond the capability of the proposed quantum error-correcting codes.

This definition of error correction in classical theory is not merely a matter of convention. In the communication process, the errors are analog, and therefore all possible small errors must be corrected by error-correcting codes. To someone who looks at classical error-correction theory as an outsider, it may appear that one only needs to fix bit flips. In reality, small analog errors, occurring on all the bits, are first removed by using clamping and hard-limiting.

Since the definition of a qubit includes an arbitrary phase, it is necessary to consider errors from the perspective of the quantum state and not just from that of final measurement. Just as in the classical theory it is implicitly accepted that all possible small analog errors have already been corrected by means of an appropriate thresholding operation, we must define correction of small analog phase errors as a requirement for quantum error-correction. This is something that the proposed quantum error-correction schemes are unable to do [Kak03].

5.9.3 Statistics

Classical particles are distinct, whereas quantum particles are indistinguishable if they are part of the same quantum state. Thus it becomes impossible for us to distinguish between 01 and 10 or between 001, 010, and 100 *before* the measurement is made. But the circuit model considers each particle to carry unique information, albeit in a superposition.

The model does not consider boson/fermion statistics [Kak01] that prevent the identification of a qubit with any specific atom or particle within the system. This, in turn, should make it impossible to distinguish between the different wires of the circuit, but in the model each wire is uniquely labeled.

5.9.4 Realization of Quantum Gates

Consider now the problem of gate complexity in quantum systems. Control of the gate, which is a physical device, is performed by modifying some classical variable that is subject to error. Since one cannot assume infinite precision in any control system, the implication of varying accuracy amongst different gates becomes an important problem. It can be shown that in certain arrangements a stuck fault cannot be reversed down the circuit stream using a single qubit operator, for it converted a pure state into a mixed state. It is essential that the entropy rate associated with the quantum circuit be smaller than what can be implemented by the information capacity of the controller [Kak06a].

If quantum gates, which are perfectly reliable, cannot be built, then one cannot generate pairs of particles of specific entanglement at will, making it impossible to effectively implement the simplest operations that are characteristic of quantum information science such as teleportation and dense coding. The challenge of implementing more complex gates is much greater.

5.9.5 Hierarchy of Computation Models

There may be a hierarchy of models of varying computational power that lie between classical and quantum paradigms. We know that the quantum circuit model and others that are equivalent to it have computational power greater than that of classical computers. But can we find other models, still not fully quantum, that will be even more powerful? For example, it has been argued that if the initial state were highly mixed, one could under certain conditions obtain more efficient solutions to some problems compared with classical techniques. This suggests that a hierarchy might very well exist. Imposing further constraints such as indistinguishability of the particles may lead to computing power less than that of the quantum circuit model. This question should be of interest to computer science theorists.

5.9.6 On Useful Quantum Computing Models

Although the common quantum circuit model is not realistic, we should not be pessimistic about the plan to devise quantum computers. Physical processes in the microworld unfold according to quantum mechanics, and this is enough for us to seek a paradigm for computation that satisfies all the rules of quantum mechanics. One would expect that in this paradigm some problems will be solved faster than by the fastest classical computer by virtue of the parallelism of quantum states.

For example, it is believed that the protein-folding problem is NP-complete [BL98], yet nature performs the folding of a 100 amino acid long sequence in a second or so (which using a classical machine should take an astronomical amount of time), and it is plausible that this is due to the quantum basis of the underlying chemical process. Furthermore, the use of a quantum apparatus offers an exponential edge over the classical apparatus [Kak98], providing us with assurance that useful models of quantum computing do exist.

A realistic model of quantum computing must ensure that the question of preparation of pure states and that of boson/fermion statistics for a quantum state are not ignored. It would also require a realistic method of error correction.

5.10 Concluding Remarks

This chapter has provided an overview of quantum theory and its paradoxes to highlight the nonlocal aspects of its logic. It has also provided a summary of reasons why current quantum computing models are not practically implementable and therefore, in themselves, they are unlikely to lead to more powerful computing machines that have a greater capacity to solve AI problems than classical machines. But more easily implementable quantum models of considerable computing power may yet be discovered.

Although the computing paradigm underlies cognitive theories, the case can be made that this paradigm is unable to simulate intelligent agents. It is also remarkable that the computing paradigm is unable to simulate the paradoxical aspects of quantum mechanics, as in instantaneous propagation of effects, or in the simulation of the evolution of the wave function, where the probability amplitudes can be negative or complex. But this in itself does not imply an identity between a quantum process and either biological intelligence or consciousness. If consciousness is an adaptive quantum principle, it requires the organization of the conscious structure to be in a complementary relationship with the environment. The organization changes continually in terms of synaptic strengths and connections [Gaz95, PK96]. But the logic behind the reorganization is not understood by current theory.

My view is different from those who see classical machines evolving through a process where ultimately they will also be endowed with higher intelligence and self-awareness. In other words, I don't see life itself reduced completely to the machine paradigm. If quantum mechanics doesn't prove to be adequate to describe this evolution in some manner that is not clear now, then one would have to wait for the discovery of a hitherto unknown principle.

The fact that quantum mechanics and gravitation are not consistent with each other has led many to believe that ultimately quantum theory itself will have to be modified [Pen05]. The other possibility is that a unified underlying theory does not exist [Kak07].

To conclusively establish that quantum processing is at the basis of higher natural intelligence would require new findings grounded in neurophysiology as well as further investigations into the nature of animal behavior.

References

[BL98]   B. Berger and T. Leighton. Protein folding in the hydrophilic-hydrophobic (HP) model is NP-complete. *Journal of Computational Biology*, 5(1):27–40, 1998.

[Boh80]   D. Bohm. *Holeness and the Implicate Order*. W. Routledge & Kegan Paul, London, 1980.

[DGK76]   L. Deecke, B. Grötzinger, and H.H. Kornhuber. Voluntary finger movements in man: cerebral potentials and theory. *Biological Cybernetics*, 23:99–110, 1976.

[Fey88]   R.P. Feynman. *QED: The Strange Theory of Light and Matter*. Princeton University Press, Princeton, NY, 1988.

[Gaz95]   M.S. Gazzaniga, editor. *The Cognitive Neurosciences*. The MIT Press, Cambridge, MA, 1995.

[Her85]   R.J. Herrnstein. Riddles of natural categorization. *Philosophical Transactions of the Royal Society of London, B*, 308:129–144, 1985.

[Kak96]   S. Kak. The three languages of the brain: quantum, reorganizational, and associative. In K. Pribram and J. King, editors, *Learning as Self-Organization*, pages 185–219. Lawrence Erlbaum Associates, Mahwah, NJ, 1996.

[Kak98]   S. Kak. Quantum information in a distributed apparatus. *Foundations of Physics*, 28:1005–1012, 1998.

[Kak99]   S. Kak. The initialization problem in quantum computing. *Foundations of Physics*, 29:267–279, 1999.

[Kak00]   S. Kak. Active agents, intelligence, and quantum computing. *Information Sciences*, 128:1–17, 2000.

[Kak01]   S. Kak. Statistical constraints on state preparation for a quantum computer. *Pramana*, 57:683–688, 2001.

[Kak03]   S. Kak. General qubit errors cannot be corrected. *Information Sciences*, 152:195–202, 2003.

[Kak04]   S. Kak. *The Architecture of Knowledge: Quantum Mechanics, Neuroscience, Computers, and Consciousness*. CSC, Delhi, 2004.

[Kak06a] S. Kak. Information complexity of quantum gates. *International Journal of Theoretical Physics*, 45:933–941, 2006.

[Kak06b] S. Kak. On the realizability of quantum computers. *ACM Ubiquity*, 7(11):1–9, 2006.

[Kak07]   S. Kak. Quantum information and entropy. *International Journal of Theoretical Physics*, 46(4):860–876, 2007.

[Lan96]   R. Landauer. The physical nature of information. *Physics Letters A*, 217:188, 1996.

[Lib89]   B. Libet. Conscious subjective experience vs. unconscious mental functions: a theory of the cerebral process involved. In M.J. Cotterill, editor, *Models of Brain Function*, pages 35–43. Cambridge University Press, Cambridge, 1989.

[Mel89]   R. Melzack. Phantom limbs, the self and the brain. *Canadian Psychology*, 30:1–16, 1989.

[NC00]   M.A. Nielsen and I.L. Chuang. *Quantum Computation and Quantum Information*. Cambridge University Press, Cambridge, 2000.

[Nei82]   U. Neisser. *Memory Observed*. W.H. Freeman, San Francisco, 1982.

[Pen89]   R. Penrose. *The Emperor's New Mind*. Oxford University Press, London, 1989.

[Pen94]   R. Penrose. *Shadows of the Mind*. Oxford University Press, London, 1994.

[Pen05]   R. Penrose. *The Road to Reality*. Alfred A. Knopf, New York, 2005.

[Per95]   A. Peres. *Quantum Theory: Concepts and Methods*. Kluwer Academic, Dordrecht, 1995.

[PK96]   K. Pribram and J. King, editors. *Learning as Self-Organization*. Lawrence Erlbaum Associates, Mahwah, NJ, 1996.

[Sch58]   E. Schrödinger. *Mind and Matter*. Cambridge University Press, Cambridge, 1958.

[Whe82]   J.A. Wheeler. The computer and the universe. *International Journal of Theoretical Physics*, 21:557–572, 1982.

6

Quantum Mechanics, Computers, and the Mind

David H. Glass and Mark McCartney

School of Computing and Mathematics, University of Ulster, Newtownabbey, Co. Antrim, BT37 0QB, Northern Ireland, dh.glass@ulster.ac.uk, m.mccartney@ulster.ac.uk

Summary. The claim that there is some fundamental relationship between quantum mechanics and the mind is controversial, but it has amongst its defenders a number of notable scientists and philosophers. Some have claimed that a proper understanding of quantum mechanics requires that conscious minds play a fundamental role. Alternatively, some have claimed that classical physics is inadequate for providing an account of the mind, and thus understanding the mind requires that quantum mechanics play a fundamental role. Assessing these claims is far from straightforward partly because there is widespread disagreement about how quantum mechanics should be interpreted, let alone how it should be applied to the mind. In this chapter, we review particular proposals relating quantum mechanics and the mind. First, we investigate proposals claiming that the mind is somehow related to the collapse of quantum mechanical wave functions. Second, we consider variations of the many-worlds interpretation and how they might be relevant to the discussion. Finally, we explore some possible implications for artificial intelligence (AI).

6.1 Introduction

It is only in relatively recent times that the nature of consciousness has begun to be investigated as a scientific problem. Previously assumptions had been made that ruled out serious scientific study in this area. Consciousness seemed to involve a subjectivity that was not appropriate for scientific investigation and so it could be dismissed as meaningless or else left for the speculation of philosophers. However, now that consciousness is being considered, the size of the challenge has become obvious. Consider, for example, the problem of qualia: as conscious beings we have qualitative, subjective experiences such as the experience of seeing red. How could such a subjective experience be accounted for in terms of objective, quantitative physical processes such as neuron firings?

Perhaps the greatest scientific achievement of the twentieth century was the development of quantum mechanics. This theory has proved to be remarkably successful in terms of the predictions it makes, but despite having been around for 80 years there is still widespread disagreement about how it should be understood or what exactly it says about the world. As with consciousness, the problem of finding an adequate interpretation of quantum mechanics was often dismissed as a philosophical problem. However, work carried out by John Bell in the 1960s brought the problem back to the attention of physicists.

Is it possible that there is a link between consciousness and quantum mechanics? Many notable scientists and philosophers, such as Albert, Lockwood, Penrose, Squires, Stapp, and Wigner, have claimed that there might be such a link. In this chapter, we assess this claim and discuss its relevance to artificial intelligence. In Section 6.2, we consider the measurement problem and briefly discuss the Copenhagen interpretation of Bohr and the related orthodox interpretation of von Neumann. Sections 6.3 and 6.4 focus on particular proposals for relating quantum mechanics and the mind, with the former dealing with accounts involving a collapse of the wave function and the latter dealing with variations of the many-worlds interpretation. Section 6.5 gives a brief overview of other interpretations of quantum mechanics that do not necessarily have any implications for the mind. Finally, in a concluding section, we summarize the main positions and look at their implications for artificial intelligence as well as briefly discuss whether quantum mechanics has any implications for free will.

6.2 The Measurement Problem in Quantum Mechanics

Many of the philosophical problems arising in quantum mechanics can be discussed in the context of a very simple problem: the spin angular momentum of an electron. Since the spin of an electron is given by $\hbar/2$, a measurement of any of the three Cartesian components of the spin will give the result $+\hbar/2$ or $-\hbar/2$. Each of the three components has an operator associated with it, and these are denoted by S_x, S_y, and S_z. Furthermore, the electron has a state-vector associated with it. Both the operator and the state-vector are important in Dirac's formulation of quantum mechanics, which will now be used. Consider first of all the z-component of the spin, S_z. If the state-vector is such that a measurement of the z-component is guaranteed to produce the result $+\hbar/2$, then the electron is in an eigenstate of S_z that is denoted by $|\alpha\rangle$. This means that when the operator acts on this state-vector, it gives the eigenvalue $+\hbar/2$ times the state-vector as expressed by the equation

$$S_z|\alpha\rangle = \frac{\hbar}{2}|\alpha\rangle. \tag{6.1}$$

A similar expression holds for the case where the outcome is guaranteed to be $-\hbar/2$, and in this case the eigenstate of S_z is denoted $|\beta\rangle$. Similar pairs of eigenstates exist for the S_x and S_y operators. Denoting the eigenstates of S_x by $|\gamma\rangle$ and $|\delta\rangle$, a measurement of the x-component of its spin will give the result $+\hbar/2$ whenever the electron is in the state $|\gamma\rangle$ and $-\hbar/2$ whenever the state is $|\delta\rangle$. Now consider a measurement of the z-component of spin when the electron is in the state $|\gamma\rangle$ (i.e., an eigenstate of S_x). It is helpful to note that $|\gamma\rangle$ can be expressed in terms of the eigenstates of S_z, $|\alpha\rangle$, and $|\beta\rangle$ as

$$|\gamma\rangle = \frac{1}{\sqrt{2}}(|\alpha\rangle + |\beta\rangle). \tag{6.2}$$

From equation (6.2), it is clear that the electron is not in one of the two eigenstates of S_z and so there is no guarantee what the result of the measurement will be (i.e., whether it will be $+\hbar/2$ or $-\hbar/2$). Nevertheless, equation (6.2) does indicate that the electron is in some kind of combination of these two states. In more technical language, the electron is in a superposition of the two states. Quantum mechanics tells us that the probability of measuring the z-component of spin to be $+\hbar/2$ is $1/2$ and that the probability of measuring it to be $-\hbar/2$ is also $1/2$. This value is obtained by squaring the coefficient of the relevant state in equation (6.2), so the probability of getting the result $+\hbar/2$ is found by squaring $1/\sqrt{2}$, the coefficient of $|\alpha\rangle$, which is the eigenstate having the associated eigenvalue of $+\hbar/2$. It is important to note that the basic ideas introduced in this simple example and the rules for calculating probabilities, which originate from the work of Born, result in remarkable agreement with experiment when they are applied to a wide range of phenomena.

To emphasize the point, consider the total state representing the measuring device and electron prior to measurement when the electron is in the state $|\gamma\rangle$,

$$\begin{aligned}|0\rangle_M|\gamma\rangle &= |0\rangle_M\left\{\frac{1}{\sqrt{2}}(|\alpha\rangle + |\beta\rangle)\right\}\\ &= \frac{1}{\sqrt{2}}|0\rangle_M|\alpha\rangle + \frac{1}{\sqrt{2}}|0\rangle_M|\beta\rangle,\end{aligned} \tag{6.3}$$

where $|0\rangle_M$ represents the state of the measuring device before a measurement takes place. Assuming the measuring device works properly and that the state in equation (6.3) evolves deterministically, then the state after measurement should be

$$|0\rangle_M|\gamma\rangle \rightarrow \frac{1}{\sqrt{2}}|+\rangle_M|\alpha\rangle + \frac{1}{\sqrt{2}}|-\rangle_M|\beta\rangle, \tag{6.4}$$

where $|+\rangle_M$ represents the measuring device indicating a value for the spin of $+\hbar/2$ (which it should do when the particle is in the state $|\alpha\rangle$) and $|-\rangle_M$ represents the measuring device indicating a value for the spin of $-\hbar/2$. This leads to the seemingly bizarre conclusion that the measuring device is in a state in which it indicates two different values, whereas we know, merely by looking at it, that the measuring device actually ends up either in the state $|+\rangle_M$ or the state $|-\rangle_M$. It seems that the equations of quantum mechanics, which apply in the absence of measurement and lead to equation (6.4), cannot be used to describe the measurement process since they lead to this strange conclusion. Instead the wave function seems to undergo a collapse so that equation (6.4) should be replaced by

$$|0\rangle_M|\gamma\rangle \rightarrow |+\rangle_M|\alpha\rangle$$
$$\text{OR}$$
$$|-\rangle_M|\beta\rangle, \tag{6.5}$$

each occurring with probability $1/2$. The difference between equations (6.4) and (6.5) is the essence of the measurement problem. The equations suggest that, after a measurement, the state of the measuring device plus electron should be given by equation (6.4), whereas it is actually given by equation (6.5).

No consensus has been reached as to how to make sense of these (and other) strange features of quantum mechanics, even though many different interpretations have been proposed. Of these, the Copenhagen interpretation, which was developed by Niels Bohr, was by far the most dominant for most of the subject's history. More than that, some defenders claim that it is not merely *an* interpretation but the *only* interpretation; to quote Rudolf Peierls, "There is only one way in which you can understand quantum mechanics" [DB86, p. 71]—and it is via the Copenhagen interpretation. The central tenets of Copenhagenism are that:

(a) The world must be divided into a quantum system and a classical apparatus.

(b) Wave and particle aspects of quantum mechanics are complementary (and irreconcilable) aspects of the behavior of the system.

(c) Quantum mechanics is a fundamentally epistemological theory in that Heisenberg's uncertainty relations place a limit on our knowledge of the system, and when an observation is made, our knowledge of the system and hence the system itself is changed.

It is, however, very difficult to give a precise account of the Copenhagen interpretation, and some of its features seem rather unsatisfactory. For example, why is there a division between the quantum and classical systems? Is this just a useful technique to keep things simple, or does it reflect a difference in nature? Furthermore, Bohr sometimes gives the impression that quantum mechanics is not telling us what the world of atoms and molecules is really like but just giving us a useful formalism for making predictions. Seemingly influenced by positivism, this suggests that the theory only applies to observations and does not tell us about what is going on between observations. A more precise, and perhaps less problematic, formulation was proposed by von Neumann. It is sometimes referred to as the orthodox interpretation, although it could be seen as a development of the Copenhagen interpretation. Basically it states that there are two types of processes:

1. When a measurement is not taking place, the system evolves deterministically (in the nonrelativistic case, it can be described by the Schrödinger equation) and so superpositions occur and the system may not be in a definite state.

2. When a measurement occurs, the system collapses so that the quantity being measured takes on a definite state.

As it stands, this also seems unsatisfactory since there is no indication as to what constitutes a measurement or when measurements occur. Various attempts to resolve the problem try to account for the notion of measurement. One of these will be considered in the next section.

The issues of measurement and collapse are often discussed using the Schrödinger's cat paradox, which is the classic *Gedanken* experiment in quantum mechanics. In the imagined experiment, a cat is placed in a box with a phial of poison, a Geiger counter, and some radioactive material. A radioactive material is chosen such that within, say, 30 minutes, there is a 50% chance that a decay will have occurred. If the Geiger counter is triggered the phial is broken and the cat killed. Thus, after 30 minutes there is a 50% chance that when the box is opened, the cat will be dead. However, according to the Schrödinger equation, the moment before we open the box, the wave function for the system will be in the state

$$\frac{1}{\sqrt{2}}|decayed\rangle_{nuclei}|dead\rangle_{cat} + \frac{1}{\sqrt{2}}|undecayed\rangle_{nuclei}|alive\rangle_{cat}. \qquad (6.6)$$

This sets the problem of collapse in bold relief. When does collapse occur? Does it occur when we open the box? In such a case, the cat is in a curious position of being both alive and dead beforehand, and it appears that a human conscious observation is crucial to collapse. Or has collapse already occurred because the cat is itself conscious or because the microscopic world of the quantum has been linked to a macroscopic physical world of equipment (such as the Geiger counter)? Or perhaps collapse does not occur at all. In the following sections, we shall concentrate on those interpretations that involve some sort of relationship between quantum mechanics and conscious minds.

6.2.1 Common Misconceptions

Before going any further, it is worth clarifying some misconceptions that people often have about quantum mechanics.

1. *In a superposition, a particle really is in a definite state—we just don't know which one it's in.*

Tempting as this view is, it cannot be quite right. First of all, there is substantial experimental evidence of interference phenomena, which seems to be incompatible with this view. Second, if we assume that variables such as spin do have definite values, we are led, via Bell's theorem, to nonlocality. Furthermore, even if we accept nonlocality, certain mathematical results show that not all variables can have definite values at all times.

2. *Uncertainty in quantum mechanics arises because there is a physical disturbance that changes the state of the system when a measurement takes place.*
Heisenberg initially used this kind of argument, but it seems to have been given up after the formulation of Einstein's EPR paradox, which was intended to show that the restrictions of the uncertainty principle could be circumvented. The orthodox viewpoint is that uncertainty is intrinsic to quantum systems and so is present even if there is no direct physical interaction.

3. *Quantum mechanics shows that determinism is false.*
This is almost always assumed in popular discussions about quantum mechanics, but it is not necessarily correct. Note that in the two processes (noncollapse and collapse) noted earlier, the first is completely deterministic. Does the second process (the collapse process) not count against determinism? Not necessarily, because according to some interpretations, such as the many-worlds interpretation (see Section 6.4) and Bohm's theory (see Section 6.5), there is no collapse. These interpretations are completely deterministic.

6.3 Collapse Theories

So far we have considered the superposition of states of a measuring device that arises from the dynamical equations of quantum mechanics, but we have not included any representation of a conscious observer in the description. Suppose that a conscious observer looks at the measuring device to determine what reading it gives for the spin. If the dynamical equations of quantum mechanics can be applied to this observer, then the state in expression (6.4) should evolve into

$$\frac{1}{\sqrt{2}}|+\rangle_O|+\rangle_M|\alpha\rangle + \frac{1}{\sqrt{2}}|-\rangle_O|-\rangle_M|\beta\rangle, \tag{6.7}$$

where $|+\rangle_O$ corresponds to the conscious observer believing that the measuring device indicates "+" and similarly for the $|-\rangle_O$ state. It may have seemed extremely odd that the measuring device could have been in two conflicting states at the same time (in some sense), but now things are even worse. Now it seems that the conscious observer is in two conflicting states. It is important to note that being in this state (expression (6.7)) is not the same as saying that the observer is confused or unsure about which state the measuring device is in but rather that (in some sense) the observer is in both states. Surely this cannot be correct. It must be the case that, by the time a conscious observer has come on the scene, the wave function has collapsed into a definite state. But when does this collapse occur?

6.3.1 The Consciousness Interpretation

A link between consciousness and quantum mechanics is usually associated with Wigner [Wig61] and his view that conscious agents cause wave function collapse. The idea is quite straightforward and provides an intelligible solution to the measurement problem. Basically, everything physical can be described by the dynamical equations of quantum mechanics, but conscious minds cannot. This means that electrons can be in superpositions of spin states, macroscopic devices can be in superpositions of their states (e.g., a super-position of pointing to "+" and pointing to "–"), and even brain states can be in superpositions. Minds, however, cannot. Once an observer looks at the measuring device, the wave function collapses, so that, for example, one of the definite states in expression (6.5) obtains rather than the superposition in expression (6.4). This interpretation does have some pretty odd consequences. For example, Schrödinger's cat really is in a superposition of dead and alive states until someone looks in the box (unless the cat is conscious!). Furthermore, before conscious beings ever appeared on Earth, the world must have been a very strange place indeed, as superposed states would have been the order of the day. If this view is correct, the nature of the world depends very strongly on minds. For these kinds of reasons, many people reject this interpretation of quantum mechanics.

How does this interpretation sit with theories of the mind? Clearly this is a dualist position since minds are not part of the physical world. Furthermore, it is an interactionist position since minds exert an influence on the world by collapsing wave functions. As with all versions of dualism, questions naturally arise as to how a nonphysical mind can affect the physical world. A final point to note is that although this viewpoint sits most comfortably with an interactive dualist account of the mind, it does differ in a notable way from Cartesian dualism. According to Cartesianism, the conscious being is in control of changes made, whereas according to this interpretation the mind brings about changes but does so passively—it collapses the wave function so that Schrödinger's cat will be either dead or alive but has no way of determining which outcome will be realized.

This view finds a modern and more subtle exponent in the work of Stapp, who, rather than focusing on the role of a conscious observer in macroscopic scenarios such as Schrödinger's cat, considers the link between consciousness and the human brain, with consciousness giving rise to wave function collapse at the neural level. The link has also been made in the other direction by

Penrose and Hameroff, who argue that rather than consciousness giving rise
to collapse, wave function collapse gives rise to consciousness. We discuss both
of these views below.

6.3.2 Henry Stapp

Henry Stapp sees quantum mechanics as being crucial to a proper understanding of the mind. At a chemical level, he sees firing at a synaptic junction
as an essentially quantum event since it can occur via the capture of a
small number of calcium ions [HHNM94]. At a philosophical level, he views
classical mechanics as a complete theory leaving no room for consciousness and
thus pushing any possible explanation inevitably into the realm of quantum
mechanics. Finally, at an interdisciplinary level, he feels that a quantum
mechanical interpretation of mind fits well with work of psychologists such
as William James [Sta03, pp. 9–12], who viewed consciousness as the selector
of brain states, and Harold Pashler [Sta06, p. 35], who classifies brain processes
in a way that Stapp believes could correspond to the quantum processes of
unitary evolution of the Schrödinger equation and collapse.

In work from the early 1990s and republished later in book form [Sta03, ch.
2] Stapp identified a conscious event with a wave function collapse in the brain
and implied that before collapse occurs, the brain may be in a macroscopic
quantum superposition, stating that a conscious event is "an event that *selects
one of the alternative possible high-level metastable configurations of brain
activity from among the host of such patterns mechanically generated by the
Schrödinger equation*" [Sta03, p. 45, emphasis in original].

In later work, however, Stapp has nuanced and clarified this by taking
as his starting point the ideas put forward by von Neumann [Neu55]. For
any physical experiment, von Neumann considered that the "Heisenberg cut"
dividing the world into the observer and the observed could be placed in a
number of places without affecting the measurement. Thus, if we have

(I) a (microscopic) system to be observed,
(II) a (macroscopic) piece of measuring apparatus, and
(III) a (macroscopic) human observer,

the cut, according to von Neumann, could be placed between (I) and (II) or
between (II) and (III). Von Neumann then goes on to divide (III) further into

(IIIa) the body and brain of the human observer and
(IIIb) the "abstract ego" or mind of the observer

and suggests that the cut could occur between (IIIa) and (IIIb).

Stapp comments on this, stating that von Neumann thus "showed that
[the Heisenberg] cut could be pushed all the way up, so that the entire
physically describable universe, including the bodies and brains of the agents,
are described quantum mechanically" [Sta07]. This leads Stapp to conclude

that quantum mechanics provides a natural and scientific basis for what he calls quantum interactive dualism. Dualism has traditionally been criticized because it is unclear how the mental can interact with the physical, but Stapp asserts in contradiction to this that quantum mechanics not only allows the presence of the mental but provides a mechanism for its operation within the physical world via collapsing wave functions. Stapp is reticent to state what the mind or "abstract ego" is, although he has speculated that it may be identified with the soul-spirit, or perhaps, more difficult to understand in the context of his work to date, a mechanical explanation for collapse may be found [Sta04].

Further, although Stapp's comment on von Neumann's movement of the cut allowing the brain to be described quantum mechanically is congruent with his previous work on the quantum nature of brain activity, he has recently gone on to clarify this by ruling out the existence of macroscopic quantum states in the brain due to "the fact that the living brain is large, warm, and wet, and interacts strongly with its environment" [Sta07]. Stapp believes that the brain, however, can be maintained in a particular configuration by the action of the quantum Zeno effect [MS77]. This effect is the quantum equivalent of the adage that "a watched kettle never boils" in that if a quantum system is observed to be in a particular state at some time t and is then observed repeatedly and frequently at subsequent times $t + \Delta t$, $t + 2\Delta t$, $t + 3\Delta t \ldots$, where Δt is small, then quantum mechanics predicts that the system will stay in the same state—or equivalently the probability of the system having evolved into another of the states permitted by the Schrödinger equation will be negligible over the short time period between observations. Stapp believes that this Zeno "holding effect is probably the only robust kind of effect of mind on brain that the theory predicts" [Sta07] and that this is in line with William James's idea that an act of will is to "attend to a difficult object and hold it fast before the mind" [Jam92, p. 417].

Thus, in summary, Stapp believes that quantum mechanics invites the introduction of a mind/matter dualism into science, with collapse of the wave function being caused by the mind and giving rise to well-defined conscious brain states.

6.3.3 Penrose-Hameroff

As part of his 1995 Tanner Lectures at the University of Cambridge, Roger Penrose [PSCH97] stated that he has three "prejudices" at the foundation of his scientific worldview. The first is that the entire physical world is describable in terms of mathematics. The second is that he is a physicalist; i.e., "there are not mental objects out there which are not based in physicality" [PSCH97, p. 97]. The third is that there is a Platonic world of mathematical forms that are accessible to our minds. None of these "prejudices" are thought of as particularly controversial in the scientific world. The first, however, is not infrequently seen by the scientific community as a strange but fruitful truth (with Eugene Wigner's essay title regarding "The Unreasonable Effectiveness of Mathematics in the Natural Sciences" [Wig67] often being quoted to make the point), and the third is often viewed as no more than one of two metaphysical alternatives describing mathematics as either Platonic discovery or human construction. Even though none of these "prejudices" are controversial, they each impact on Penrose's view of the mind: the physical world may be describable in terms of mathematics, but he feels that at least one part of that world, the yet to be discovered quantum theory of gravity, will contain aspects that are noncomputable, and although he is a physicalist, he believes that this noncomputable aspect plays a crucial role in allowing us to access the Platonic world of mathematical truth.

Penrose views consciousness as the result of the collapse of wave functions in the brain but, crucially, denies that this can be simulated computationally. Moreover, Penrose believes that the physics required to explain collapse has not yet been discovered—a problem that he expects to be resolved only within the context of a quantum theory of gravity. Further still, he believes that the correct theory of quantum gravity will be noncomputable. This noncomputable aspect of physical reality placed as part of the brain mechanism implies that the brain, and hence consciousness, cannot be simulated on a computer [Pen89, Pen94]. Penrose also tentatively links this noncomputable aspect of the brain with our ability to make "contact with some sort of Platonic world" [PSCH97, p. 125].

The view that the correct theory of quantum gravity will have noncomputable aspects is based on the existence of at least one already existing model that attempts to unify quantum theory and gravitation [GH86]. However, it must be emphasized that there is no widely accepted theory of quantum gravity in existence, and thus the link between quantum gravity and noncomputability is speculative.

Penrose's ideas on the relationship between consciousness and quantum theory find a root in the study of the role of microtubules in neurons. Microtubules are, amongst other things, involved in determining the strength of the signal between neurons at the synapses (i.e., the junctions where signals are transferred from one neuron to another) and are tubes (diameter of $\sim$25 nm) built from a lattice of the protein tubulin. Significantly, each protein can be in one of two conformations. Hameroff and Watt [HW82] have suggested that because of this the microtubule may be thought of as a cellular automaton, with each tubulin protein corresponding to a cell, which can be in one of two states. Each microtubule may thus be thought of as performing computations, thus making the behavior of the neuron much more complex than the traditional idea of it being merely a switch that fires above a certain threshold. This basic idea of complex mechanisms at the subcellular level was first speculated upon by Sherrington [She57] in the context of how to explain the diverse behavior of single-celled organisms, which although clearly not possessing a nervous system exhibited apparently purposeful behavior such as avoidance of obstacles and approach toward food. Crucially, the long tubular nature of the microtubules and the possible presence of ordered water outside them may help isolate the interior and permit large-scale quantum behavior to occur within them [HP96, Ham06]. This would mean the states of the cellular automaton could be in a quantum superposition. This, although contended may be possible, but Penrose and Hameroff go on to suggest that this quantum superposition extends over many neurons and lasts on the order of a second. The brain is thus seen as being in a macroscopic quantum superposition. This is more controversial since the criticism by Stapp that such states cannot persist in the "large, warm, and wet" brain [Sta07] is widely held to be valid. Penrose and Hameroff argue that basic conscious acts are to be identified with wave function collapse. Penrose notes that this in itself will not lead to a noncomputable aspect of consciousness unless wave function collapse itself is ultimately found to be explicable using noncomputable aspects of an as yet undiscovered theory of quantum gravity.

Penrose admits that "there is a good deal of speculation in many of these ideas" [PSCH97, p. 134]. However, Hameroff has emphasized the testable nature of a number of aspects of the Penrose-Hameroff approach [Ham06]. The approach has been criticized with regard to the roles of both noncomputability and quantum gravity (see, for example [Kle95] and [PSCH97]) with, for example, Stephen Hawking, Penrose's long-term collaborator on general relativity, quipping that "his argument seemed to be that consciousness is a mystery and quantum gravity is another mystery so they must be related" [PSCH97, p. 171]. It may be that the correct theory of quantum gravity turns out to be computable, or that the collapse issue is resolved without recourse to quantum gravity. The Penrose-Hameroff focus on the role of the microtubule has also been challenged by Tegmark [Teg00], who claims that superpositions in the microtubule cannot last long enough to be significant, although this has been countered by Hagan et al. [HHT02].

6.4 No-Collapse Theories

The different viewpoints described under collapse theories in Section 6.3 all agree with each other in that states like that described in expression (6.7) do not occur in nature. Interference phenomena appear to provide a good reason to believe that quantum superpositions such as that represented in expression (6.3) occur in nature. Some collapse theorists (e.g., Stapp) will even allow the possibility that even superpositions such as that in expression (6.4) can occur so that a macroscopic measuring device might not be in a definite state. But all will agree that by the time human observers become involved, as in expression (6.7), the collapse will have occurred so that the observer is in a definite state rather than a quantum superposition.

There is, however, a school of thought going back to Everett [Eve57] that resists this conclusion. According to this view, there is no collapse of the wave function and so quantum superpositions involving human observers, as in expression (6.7), do occur. The main advantage of this view is that it does not appear to require anything beyond the mathematics of quantum theory. Consider processes 1 and 2 discussed in Section 6.2. Only process 1 is described by the theory, according to which the Schrödinger equation describes the evolution of the wave function. According to the orthodox interpretation, there is no physical theory to account for process 2 (i.e., the collapse)—it is added to the theory to try to make sense of it. But this seems problematic. Quantum theory provides a remarkably accurate account of atomic and molecular phenomena and so one would expect it to be applicable to macroscopic objects since they consist of atoms and molecules. Another way of putting this is to say that quantum theory should be a universal theory, applying to all of nature and not merely to some limited domain. Now we can see why the orthodox interpretation is problematic: it seems to deny that quantum theory is universal, and it does so by introducing a collapse that is not accounted for in terms of any physical theory.

Despite this theoretical advantage, adopting the Everett no-collapse view seems to face insurmountable problems, the most obvious of which is that the existence of quantum states like that given in expression (6.7) appears to directly contradict our experience. We know that when a measurement is carried out on the spin of an electron, the human observer will observe it either to be in the up state or the down state and not in the indefinite state of expression (6.7). Another problem, which has been pointed out by Albert and Loewer ([AL88]; see also [Alb92]), is that a person who is in the state in expression (6.7) will be deceived about their own state of mind. Suppose we ask someone who has carried out a measurement of spin whether they have a definite belief about the value of spin of the electron. Clearly, if this question is asked when the state of the system is $|+\rangle_O|+\rangle_M|\alpha\rangle$, and assuming that the person will answer honestly, she will answer "yes". Similarly, whenever the state of the system is $|-\rangle_O|-\rangle_M|\beta\rangle$, she will also answer "yes". It follows from this, according to Albert and Loewer, that whenever the state is that in expression (6.7), she will also answer "yes" (since it is just a linear combination of the two states we have been considering). But clearly she is deceived, for she cannot have a definite belief about the value of the spin if the system is in the state given by expression (6.7). Albert and Loewer argue that an acceptable account of mental states should respect a *principle of charity* so that whenever someone reports on their own mental state they can be regarded as reporting something true. This seems plausible since even though my beliefs might be mistaken, it seems reasonable to say that I am not generally mistaken about what beliefs I have.

If the argument above is correct, it creates a serious problem for the idea that quantum superpositions involving observers, such as expression (6.7), can occur. Albert and Loewer do not conclude from this that collapses must occur after all, as we shall see in Section 6.4.2, but rather that mental states cannot be identified with physical states if quantum mechanics is universal in its application to the physical world (i.e., they move towards a form of dualism). Below we shall consider several ways of trying to make sense of the Everett account as outlined above.

6.4.1 The Many-Worlds Interpretation

Although the Everett view is often described as the many-worlds interpretation, it seems to have been DeWitt [DeW70] who introduced this terminology. According to a literal way of understanding this interpretation, there are no collapses, but whenever a state such as that in expression (6.7) occurs, there are now two worlds: one in which the system can be represented by $|+\rangle_O|+\rangle_M|\alpha\rangle$ and one in which it can be represented by $|-\rangle_O|-\rangle_M|\beta\rangle$. Thus, if we apply this to our earlier discussion of Schrödinger's cat, there is one world in which the cat is dead and another world in which it is alive. This means, of course, that there are multiple universes, some of which are very different from each other and some of which are very similar. It also means that there are multiple versions of each person. There is another world where we decided not to write this chapter, another one where we did write it but you decided not to read it, and so on.

All of this strikes many people (including the authors) as implausible, and indeed there are problems with it. One problem is that it is difficult to see how the probabilities that are central to quantum mechanics can arise in this account. Since *all* outcomes occur, it doesn't seem to make much sense to talk about the probability of a particular outcome. According to Deutsch [Deu85], there are a continuous infinity of worlds at all times, and these worlds divide in such a way as to mirror the quantum probabilities. This is not a straightforward solution, however. If it is understood in a literal way (i.e., that these are physically distinct worlds that literally divide so that, for example, half of the worlds end up with the electron in a spin-up state and half with it in a spin-down state), then many of the problems associated with collapse return: when does the division between worlds occur, and what causes the division? Understood in this way, it is difficult to see any advantage to the many-worlds interpretation, and the number of worlds involved is even more extravagant than we might at first have thought since there is not only a single world corresponding to each branch of the wave function but an infinity of them! Alternatively, if the terminology is to be understood in a metaphorical way so that there is no literal division of worlds, then it is difficult to see how the "continuous infinity of worlds" could account for quantum probabilities.

Our main focus here is on whether this interpretation might have any implications for our understanding of the mind. At first glance, it appears that it does not. Even though there are many versions of each person, this is only because there are many versions of the corresponding worlds. How a given mind is related to its particular world (or branch of the wave function) is left untouched by the many-worlds account. All of the typical debates about how the mind is related to the physical world appear to be unaffected by this interpretation. But things are not quite so simple. Considering again expression (6.7), which represents the state of the system plus measuring device plus observer after the measurement has been completed and assuming that no collapse occurs, we note that it can be expressed in terms of a different set of basis vectors. For example, expressing it in terms of $|\gamma\rangle$ and $|\delta\rangle$, the eigenstates of spin in the x-direction, we obtain

$$\frac{1}{2}\Big(|+\rangle_O|+\rangle_M + |-\rangle_O|-\rangle_M\Big)|\gamma\rangle$$
$$+ \frac{1}{2}\Big(|-\rangle_O|-\rangle_M - |+\rangle_O|+\rangle_M\Big)|\delta\rangle. \tag{6.8}$$

Mathematically, expressions (6.7) and (6.8) are equivalent, so why should the division between worlds correspond to expression (6.7) rather than (6.8)? If the worlds correspond to the branches of the wave function in expression (6.7), then these worlds will have definite values of the spin of the particle in the z-direction (and indefinite values in the x-direction), while if the worlds correspond to the branches of the wave function in expression (6.8), then these worlds will have definite values of the spin of the particle in the x-direction (and indefinite values in the z-direction). Since the two representations are equivalent according to the theory, the question as to which worlds exist seems to have no definite answer. This is referred to as the "preferred basis" problem. Of course, the division of worlds corresponding to the terms in expression (6.7) might seem more plausible since it will mean that in each of the resulting worlds the observer will find herself in a definite state rather than a quantum superposition. But if this is actually the case, then there is a very fundamental link between the many-worlds interpretation and consciousness, for the very worlds that exist according to the interpretation will depend on what conscious beings there are. To avoid this dualist conclusion seems to require (a) that there be some physical reason for a preferred basis, and (b) that this preferred basis should be the same basis that ensures conscious beings are in definite states. We are not aware of any convincing reasons for thinking that either of these claims is true.

6.4.2 The Many-Minds Interpretation

The main idea in the Everett viewpoint is that collapses of the wave function do not occur. As noted earlier, this is often linked with the idea of "many-worlds", but it is not really clear how this is to be understood. If it is understood in a very literal way in terms of distinct physical worlds that are constantly dividing, it seems very implausible and problematic. Alternatively, if it is merely a denial that collapses occur, it seems to contradict our experience since we are conscious of being in definite states after making observations. The many-minds interpretation is an alternative way of thinking about the Everett viewpoint and, as the name suggests, involves postulating

multiple minds that divide rather than worlds. To quote Lockwood, a propo-
nent of this interpretation, "A many-minds theory, as I understand it, is
a theory which takes completely at face value the account which unitary
quantum mechanics gives of the physical world and its evolution over time. ...
It has no truck with the idea that the laws of physics prescribe an *objectively*
preferred basis. For a many-minds theorist, the *appearance* of there being a
preferred basis, like the *appearance* of state vector reduction, is to be regarded
as an illusion. And both illusions can be explained by appealing to a theory
about the way in which *conscious mentality* relates to the physical world as
unitary quantum mechanics describes it" [Loc96, p. 170, emphasis in original].

Thus, as far as the physical world is concerned, there is no splitting
taking place, but there is no collapse either. Quantum superpositions occur
throughout the physical world, including macroscopic objects as well as
microscopic objects, and so buildings, trees, and even the bodies and brains of
humans are involved in the strange indefinite quantum states discussed earlier.
Nevertheless, there is only one world, albeit a very big and strange one. How
is all of this to be reconciled with our experience of the world, which is much
more mundane? Here we summarize the many-minds interpretation proposed
by Albert and Loewer [AL88]. Consider the state of the particle plus measuring
device plus observer before a measurement of spin in the z-direction is carried
out, assuming the particle is initially in the state described in equation (6.2).
This can be written as

$$|\underline{0}\rangle_O |0\rangle_M \left\{ \frac{1}{\sqrt{2}}(|\alpha\rangle + |\beta\rangle) \right\}, \qquad (6.9)$$

where $|0\rangle_M$ represents the state of the measuring device before measurement
and $|\underline{0}\rangle_O$ represents the state of the observer's brain before the measurement,
with the underline indicating that the mind of the observer is in a state
corresponding to this brain state. After the measurement is completed (and
the observer is conscious of an outcome), the state in expression (6.9) will
have evolved into either

$$\frac{1}{\sqrt{2}} \{|\underline{\pm}\rangle_O |+\rangle_M |\alpha\rangle + |-\rangle_O |-\rangle_M |\beta\rangle)\}$$
$$\text{OR}$$
$$\frac{1}{\sqrt{2}} \{|+\rangle_O |+\rangle_M |\alpha\rangle + |\underline{-}\rangle_O |-\rangle_M |\beta\rangle)\}. \qquad (6.10)$$

Note that these two states are identical *physically*, but in the first case
the observer is conscious of the outcome being spin-up (even though the
physical state of the particle plus measuring device plus the observer's brain
state is in a quantum superposition), while in the second case the observer
is conscious of the outcome being spin-down (as indicated by the underline).
Note that the mental state is not the same as the physical brain state, but
rather it latches onto one of the brain states in a particular branch of the wave

function. Thus, the picture here is a very dualistic one since different mental states can be associated with exactly the same physical state of the brain. In order to incorporate the probabilistic element of quantum mechanics, Albert and Loewer specify a probabilistic element in the evolution of the mind so that, for example, in the transition from the state in expression (6.9) to one of the states in expression (6.10), there is a probability of 1/2 of going to the first state and 1/2 of going to the second state. These probabilities are specified to correspond with the square of the amplitude of the wave function so that the normal quantum probabilities are recovered. Thus, the evolution of the physical world, including human brains, is entirely deterministic in accordance with the Schrödinger equation, but the evolution of minds involves this random component.

The final step to this version of the many-minds interpretation is to specify that with each brain there is associated not a single-mind but a *continuous infinity* of minds. The reason for this will become clear in the next section. Roughly speaking, the idea is that in a transition such as that from expression (6.9) to expression (6.10), these minds will be equally divided between the first and second states in expression (6.10). Like the many-worlds interpretation, the many-minds view is extremely counterintuitive. First of all, the physical world both microscopic and macroscopic is in quantum superposition. Second, each person has a continuous infinity of minds in each branch of the wave function. Third, each of these minds will be radically mistaken about the actual state of the world since individual minds will experience a world in a definite state that does not correspond with the real state of the world. Despite these problems, it does appear to have some advantages over the more literal many-worlds viewpoint. One of these, is that there is only one physical world in this perspective and so there is no literal splitting of worlds taking place. Furthermore, it does not seem to require the preferred basis of the many-worlds interpretation since, as far as the physical world is concerned, the basis in which its state is expressed does not matter. However, it does matter as far as subjective conscious states are concerned and leaves a question as to why they are associated with physical states in a particular basis.

In terms of its relevance for ways of understanding the mind, it is worth noting that the many-minds interpretation as presented by Albert and Loewer is dualistic in nature. This is slightly lessened by the fact that the distribution of the totality of mental states of each person is fixed by the physical state of the world and so could be said to supervene on it, but this is not so for individual minds. Lockwood's version of the many-minds interpretation avoids this dualism since in his account the mental state of individual minds also supervenes on the corresponding brain state (in that branch of the wave function) [Loc89, Loc96]. This, however, makes it less clear how his version accounts for the probabilistic nature of quantum mechanics. It also raises a question about how a single physical state of the world could give rise to an infinity of conscious minds.

6.4.3 A Single-Mind Approach

In the discussion of the many-minds interpretation above, it is apparent that a simpler account is available. Instead of supposing that there are an infinity of minds associated with the physical state in expression (6.9), why not postulate just one, which then becomes associated with one of the branches of the wave function as in expression (6.10)? In fact, Albert and Loewer [AL88] discuss this possibility but reject it in favor of their many-minds account. A serious problem with this single-mind version is known as the *mindless hulk* problem. Suppose that person A's mind becomes associated with a different branch of the wave function from person B's mind. Recall that the physical world is the same for A and B since the world does not divide, but their experiences of that world will differ. Suppose that A is conscious of having a conversation with B. Since B's mind is on a different branch of the wave function, this will mean that A will be talking not to a conscious person but to a mindless hulk. However, since there is no physical difference arising from the fact that B is not conscious on A's branch of the wave function, A will not be able to tell that there is "no-one at home".

The concern of the philosophical problem of other minds is how we can know that other people are not zombies but are conscious and have beliefs, experiences, emotions, etc., that are similar to our own. According to this interpretation, we cannot know that other people have minds because most of them on our (or should I say my) branch of the wave function do not have them. Thus, on my branch of the wave function this chapter is being read by zombies (and indeed coauthored by one; see Sections 6.3.2 and 6.3.3 for confirmation of this point), and on your branch it was written by zombies!

This mindless hulk problem motivated Albert and Loewer to propose their many-minds account discussed in Section 6.4.2. An alternative way of avoiding this problem is discussed by Squires [Squ90]. Consider person A measuring the spin in the z-direction of a particle initially in the state given in equation (6.2), and suppose that he becomes conscious of the outcome being spin-up. Now suppose person B also measures the spin in the z-direction of the same particle. What result will she obtain? Since we are still working within the Everett framework, no collapse has occurred, so there is no guarantee that B's mind will track the same branch of the wave function as A's mind. Thus, it is possible that B will become conscious of the outcome being spin-down. This is just the mindless hulk problem again. Squires discusses the possibility of a universal consciousness, which somehow contains individual minds, that determines which branch of the wave function A's mind will track and ensures that B's mind will track the same branch, and so A and B become aware of the same outcome. Thus, in contrast to the many-minds interpretation, which associates an infinity of minds with each person, this account goes to the other extreme and claims that each person's mind is really a part of a single universal mind. An intermediate position would also be possible, whereby each person has their own individual mind but there is in addition a supreme mind that plays the role of determining what the outcomes of observations of the individual minds will be.

It is clear that each of the no-collapse viewpoints described in this section involves highly counterintuitive ideas about the nature of reality and, in particular, the nature of conscious minds. Most people (including the authors) find all the positions in this section difficult to take seriously, although it must be admitted that Everett-type interpretations of quantum mechanics have become much more popular in recent years [Teg01]. But which of these interpretations is best or perhaps least problematic? If someone is committed to an Everett-type interpretation, we would suggest that something along the lines of the single-mind account is least problematic in terms of the ontology it proposes since it avoids distinct physical worlds and also multiple minds for each person. However, it is extremely dualistic in its view of the mind and requires a universal consciousness or supreme mind to avoid the mindless hulk problem, and so if one's chief concern is to avoid dualism, then Lockwood's viewpoint seems like the best on offer, but this is at the expense of accepting the existence of an infinity of minds for each person.

6.5 Remarks on other Interpretations of Quantum Mechanics

The interpretations of quantum mechanics outlined above are not the only ones in existence. However, they encompass the majority of approaches to the problem that have been taken and thus serve to illustrate the perplexing role that many philosophers and physicists believe consciousness to have within the physical world. For completeness, however, two other widely discussed interpretations should be noted.

6.5.1 De Broglie-Bohm Interpretation

Following early work by de Broglie, Bohm produced an interpretation of quantum mechanics that is both deterministic and overtly nonlocal (see, for example, [BH93] and [Hol93]). In Bohmian quantum mechanics, particles have objective trajectories that can be calculated in the normal way as would be done in classical mechanics. The difference is that these trajectories are calculated from the sum of the usual classical potentials (e.g., due to the presence of electromagnetic fields) and an additional quantum potential that is derived from the wave function. It is this quantum potential that explicitly lays bare the nonlocal nature of quantum mechanics in that it can be nonvanishing at arbitrarily large distances and that it in some sense encodes the entire experimental setup. With reference to the interpretations laid out above, the de Broglie-Bohm approach is a no-collapse theory, and observers are superfluous. It is surprising (to at least one of the current authors) that the de Broglie-Bohm interpretation has not been more widely adopted by physicists, given that it retains particle trajectories and determinism, avoids the measurement problem, and, last but by no means least, was favorably regarded by no less than John Bell [Bel87]. The rejection of the de Broglie-Bohm approach by the vast majority of physicists is, however, partly because it is felt in some quarters that the rewriting of the Schrödinger equation to obtain the trajectories and the quantum potential is somewhat contrived and that the Bohmian approach has not been successfully generalized to encompass relativity. Further, because collapse does not occur, and the quantum potential is derived from the uncollapsed wave function, this means that even though we observe a system in a definite state, its subsequent behavior can still in principle be influenced by those parts of the wave function that describe the states in which it was not found.

6.5.2 Nonlinear Quantum Mechanics

One final approach is to gain the transition from expression (6.4) to expression (6.5) by adding extra nonlinear terms to the Schrödinger equation. In such models, collapse occurs via the evolution of the modified Schrödinger equation. The best-known version of such an approach is that given by Ghirardi, Rimini, and Weber [GRW86] in which individual particles are randomly localized (i.e., their wave function is collapsed). The large timescale chosen between these localizations (10^{16} seconds) ensures that for individual atoms the probability of collapse is very low and so the Schrödinger equation accurately describes the behavior of a microscopic system, whereas for macroscopic systems (of mass greater than, say, 10^{-9} kg) collapse is very likely to occur and thus classical observations of the world are obtained.

6.6 Implications for AI and the Mind

Having surveyed a number of viewpoints relating quantum mechanics to the mind, we now try to show how such accounts might impinge on more traditional debates about the mind, particularly debates about artificial intelligence. According to strong AI, the mind is a computer program and so all mental phenomena can be accounted for in terms of computation. Weak AI is the thesis that the mind can be *simulated* by a computer but that not all mental phenomena can be accounted for in terms of computation. According to this latter point of view, any simulation will be lacking in some respect. For example, according to Searle [Sea92], although a computer program might in principle be able to simulate the thinking of humans, it will not have any understanding since it is merely executing instructions that manipulate uninterpreted symbols. Since several of the positions described in previous sections are explicitly dualistic in nature, it might be thought that they would involve denying both versions of AI, but this is not necessarily the case.

Consider first of all the consciousness interpretation of Wigner, which has also been defended by Stapp. The most plausible way to think of this is in terms of dualism (i.e., that it is a nonphysical mind collapsing a physical state). This seems to amount to a rejection of strong AI since there is more to a mind than computation, but does it also involve a rejection of weak AI? It seems that it does not for if the only interaction between the mind and the brain is in terms of collapsing wave functions and assuming this is done in such a way that the probabilistic rules of quantum mechanics are not violated, then collapse could be simulated by including a random number generator.[1] Furthermore, if it is assumed that the physical brain, subject as it is to the laws of quantum mechanics, can be simulated by a computer program, then weak AI could be possible.

A similar line of reasoning applies to the dualistic versions of the many-minds interpretation such as that of Albert and Loewer. According to this viewpoint, a conscious mind does not collapse wave functions but tracks a particular branch of the wave function as it evolves. All of the behavior associated with a conscious being is accounted for purely in terms of brain states, with no interaction from the nonphysical mind. Thus, once again, if the brain states can be simulated by a computer program, then weak AI is possible.

By way of contrast to these dualistic accounts, Penrose, who is a physicalist, ends up rejecting both strong and weak AI. Even though the mind is to be accounted for in terms of physics, Penrose's key claim is that this must be a noncomputable physics. It is not a mind causing collapses to occur but rather collapses of appropriate brain states that give rise to consciousness. Since the process that causes collapse to occur is noncomputable, the mind must be more than a computer program, and so strong AI must be false, but equally the same noncomputable process is what affects the behavior of the individual and so simulation of a mind is not even possible, and so weak AI must also be false.

It should not surprise us that claims that quantum mechanics is essential for an adequate account of the mind are likely to result in a rejection of strong AI. After all, the basic idea is that a nonquantum-mechanical account of the mind is leaving out something essential and so a fortiori a classical

---

[1] Perhaps things are not quite so straightforward. Traditional debates about AI ignore the environment, so that the computer program only interacts with the environment through communication with a human. But how such a computer program would respond to input coming from other sources also seems relevant. In particular, if input were received from a measurement of spin in a case where there is a superposition between spin-up and spin-down states, then no collapse would occur since, by definition, the computer is not conscious. Thus, if interaction with the environment were to be permitted, weak AI would not be possible in the case where the mind is simulated in a real environment, but it would be possible in the case where both the mind and the environment are simulated.

computer program will not be able to fully account for the mind.[2] What is perhaps more interesting is that dualistic accounts of the relationship between quantum mechanics and the mind are compatible with weak AI, whereas at least one leading nondualistic account rules out weak AI.

Perhaps a classical computer could not account for all mental behavior, but what about a quantum computer? Could the brain be a quantum computer? Other chapters in this volume will discuss quantum computing, but here we make just two observations. First, although the idea that the brain might support coherent macroscopic quantum states required for quantum processing has been discussed (see [Frö68] and [PSCH97]), it has not gained many followers due to the fact that the brain does not seem to be the right kind of environment for such states. Second, even if quantum processing is possible in the brain, it is far from clear how this would help to explain the relationship between the brain and the mind. In particular, although quantum computers can in principle solve certain types of problems more efficiently than classical computers, anyone who objects to the mind being a computer program does not do so on the basis that the classical computers are too slow.

To conclude the chapter, we briefly comment on two more general issues about the relationship between quantum mechanics and the mind, one a problem and one a possibility. A serious problem in trying to make sense of the mind is the fundamental difference between brain states and mental states. The former are clearly physical and can be given an objective, quantitative description in terms of the matter of which they are constituted, while the latter have a subjective, qualitative character and cannot be described in terms of physical concepts. As a consequence of this difference, there seems to be an *explanatory gap* when trying to account for mental states in terms of brain states (see [Cha96] for further discussion on this point). Sometimes the claim is made that such an account is impossible in terms of the concepts of classical physics, whereas it is made possible by quantum mechanics. But it is far from obvious that this is true. The concepts of forces, fields, particles, and waves may not be able to account for the subjectivity of mental phenomena, but do wave functions, collapses, superpositions, and entanglements fare any better?

A further way in which quantum mechanics might be relevant to the mind is in terms of free will. Our intuitive notion of free will is such that it finds no place within the determinism of classical physics. The claim is often made that the indeterminism of quantum mechanics opens the door again.[3] The consensus is generally against this viewpoint on the grounds that even if indeterminism is true at the microscopic level, it is irrelevant for the relevant brain processes and, furthermore, indeterminism is not sufficient for free will

---

[2] This is not to say that all attempts to relate quantum mechanics and the mind must result in a rejection of strong AI (see [Cha96] for a case in point).

[3] As noted earlier, quantum mechanics does not necessarily establish that determinism is false since, for example, Bohm's theory is completely deterministic.

anyway, and thus free will is often considered to be an illusion. John Searle [Sea01, p. 512], however, who has in general been sceptical of any link between quantum mechanics and the mind, offers the following "strict argument for requiring the introduction of quantum indeterminism" into the discussion [Sea01, p. 512]:

Premise 1: All indeterminism in nature is quantum indeterminism.
Premise 2: Consciousness is a feature of nature that manifests indeterminism.
Conclusion: Consciousness manifests quantum indeterminism.

While Searle is not necessarily committed to premise 2 and hence the conclusion of the argument, he does consider the possibility that it may be true. The problem is that if quantum indeterminism is merely due to randomness, it cannot, it would seem, account for free will. One possibility, open to a dualist, is that the mind could exploit this indeterminism in nature to select (or increase the probability of selecting) a desired state of affairs [BE92]; e.g., by selecting particular outcomes when collapsing wave functions rather than collapsing them randomly. This suggestion has not found much favor and is not open to Searle, as he eschews any form of dualism. Instead, Searle notes that properties possessed by individual elements of a system need not be properties of a system as a whole; e.g., a table does not have the electrical properties of its atoms, and so "randomness at the micro level does not thereby imply randomness at the system level". It is far from clear how this randomness at the micro level could give rise to an indeterminism suitable for free will at the system level, but perhaps such a possibility cannot be ruled out.

Having considered various ways of relating quantum mechanics to the mind, we do not view any specific proposal as being particularly convincing. Nevertheless, it would be incorrect to conclude from this that quantum mechanics is irrelevant to the mind. In light of the fact that quantum mechanics is our most fundamental and accurate theory of the physical world, the various topics considered in this chapter provide enough reason to show that the possibility of a connection between consciousness and quantum mechanics cannot be easily disregarded.

References

[AL88]   D.Z. Albert and B. Loewer. Interpreting the many-worlds interpretation. *Synthese*, 77:195–213, 1988.
[Alb92]   D.Z. Albert. *Quantum Mechanics and Experience*. Harvard University Press, Cambridge, MA, 1992.
[BE92]   F. Beck and J. Eccles. Quantum aspects of brain activity and the role of consciousness. *Proceedings of the National Academy of Sciences of the USA*, 89:11357–11361, 1992.
[Bel87]   J.S. Bell. *Speakable and Unspeakable in Quantum Mechanics*. Cambridge University Press, Cambridge, 1987.

[BH93]   D. Bohm and B.J. Hiley. *The Undivided Universe: An Ontological Interpretation of Quantum Theory*. Routledge, London, 1993.

[Cha96]   D.J. Chalmers. *The Conscious Mind*. Oxford University Press, Oxford, 1996.

[DB86]   P.C.W. Davies and J.R. Brown. *The Ghost in the Atom*. Cambridge University Press, Cambridge, 1986.

[Deu85]   D. Deutsch. Quantum theory as a universal physical theory. *International Journal of Theoretical Physics*, 24:1–41, 1985.

[DeW70]   B.S. DeWitt. Qunatum mechanics and reality. *Physics Today*, 23:30–35, 1970.

[Eve57]   H. Everett. Relative state formulation of quantum mechanics. *Reviews of Modern Physics*, 29:454–462, 1957.

[Frö68]   H. Fröhlich. Long-range coherence in biological systems. *International Journal of Quantum Chemistry*, 2:641–649, 1968.

[GH86]   R. Geroch and J. Hartle. Computability and physical theories. *Foundations of Physics*, 16:533, 1986.

[GRW86]   G.C. Ghirardi, A. Rimini, and T. Weber. Unified dynamics for microscopic and macroscopic systems. *Physical Review D*, 34:470–491, 1986.

[Ham06]   S.R. Hameroff. Conscious neurobiology and quantum mechanics. In J.A. Tuszynski, editor, *The Emerging Physics of Consciousness*, pages 193–254. Springer, Berlin, 2006.

[HHNM94]   R. Heidelberger, C. Heinmann, E. Neherm, and G. Matthews. Calcium dependence of the rate of exocytosis in a synaptic terminal. *Nature*, 371:513–515, 1994.

[HHT02]   S. Hagan, S.R. Hameroff, and J.A. Tuszynski. Quantum computation in brain microtubules: decoherence and biological feasibility. *Physical Review E*, 65(061901), 2002.

[Hol93]   P.R. Holland. *The Quantum Theory of Motion: An Account of the de Broglie-Bohm Causal Interpretation of Quantum Mechanics*. Cambridge University Press, Cambridge, 1993.

[HP96]   S.R. Hameroff and R. Penrose. Conscious events as orchestrated space-time selections. *Journal of Consciousness Studies*, 3:36–53, 1996.

[HW82]   S.R. Hameroff and R.C. Watt. Information processing in mircotubules. *Journal of Theoretical Biology*, 98:549–561, 1982.

[Jam92]   W. James. Psychology: the briefer course. In *William James: Writings 1878–1899*. New York Library of America, New York, 1892.

[Kle95]   S.A. Klein. Is quantum mechanics relevant to understanding consciousness? *Psyche*, 2(3), 1995. A Review of Shadows of the Mind by Roger Penrose, available at http://psyche.cs.monash.edu.au/v2/psyche-2-03-klein.html.

[Loc89]   M. Lockwood. *Mind, Brain and the Quantum*. Blackwell, Oxford, 1989.

[Loc96]   M. Lockwood. Many minds interpretations in quantum mechanics. *British Journal for the Philosophy of Science*, 47:159–188, 1996.

[MS77]   B. Misra and E.C.G. Sudarshan. The Zeno's paradox in quantum theory. *Journal of Mathematical Physics*, 18:756–763, 1977.

[Neu55]   J. von Neumann. *Mathematical Foundations of Quantum Mechanics*. Princeton University Press, Princeton, NJ, 1955. Translated by R.T. Beyer, first published in German in 1932.

[Pen89]   R. Penrose. *The Emperor's New Mind: Concerning Computers, Minds, and the Laws of Physics*. Oxford University Press, Oxford, 1989.

[Pen94]   R. Penrose. *Shadows of the Mind: An Approach to the Missing Science of Consciousness*. Oxford University Press, Oxford, 1994.

[PSCH97]   R. Penrose, A. Shimony, N. Cartwright, and S. Hawking. *The Large, the Small and the Human Mind*. Cambridge University Press, Cambridge, 1997.

[Sea92]   J.R. Searle. *The Rediscovery of the Mind*. MIT Press, Cambridge MA, 1992.

[Sea01]   J.R. Searle. Free will as a problem in neurobiology. *Philosophy*, 76:491–514, 2001.

[She57]   C.S. Sherrington. *Man on His Nature*. Cambridge University Press, Cambridge, 2nd edition, 1957.

[Squ90]   E.J. Squires. *Conscious Mind in the Physical World*. Adam Hilger, Bristol, 1990.

[Sta03]   H.P. Stapp. *Mind, Matter and Quantum Mechanics*. Springer, Berlin, 2nd edition, 2003.

[Sta04]   H.P. Stapp. Quantum physics and the psycho-physical nature of the universe. Presented at Survival of Bodily Death, An Esalen Invitational Conference, May, 2–7, 2004. Available at `http://www.esalenctr.org/display/confpage.cfm?confid=19&pageid=146&pgtype=1` (last accessed November 2006).

[Sta06]   H.P. Stapp. The mindful universe, 2006. Available at `http://www-physics.lbl.gov/~stapp/MU.doc` (last accessed November 2006).

[Sta07]   H.P. Stapp. Quantum mechanical theories of consciousness. In M. Velmans and S. Schneider, editors, *Blackwell Companion to Consciousness*. Blackwell, Oxford, 2007.

[Teg00]   M. Tegmark. Importance of quantum decoherence in brain processes. *Physical Review E*, 61:4194–4206, 2000.

[Teg01]   M. Tegmark. 100 years of quantum. *Scientific American*, 284:68–75, 2001.

[Wig61]   E.P. Wigner. Remarks on the mind-body question. In I.J. Good, editor, *The Scientist Speculates*, pages 284–302. Basic Books, New York, 1961.

[Wig67]   E.P. Wigner. *Symmetries and Reflections*. Indiana University Press, Bloomington, 1967.

Part III

Brain-Computer Interfaces
and Computational Neuroscience

7

Restoration of Movement and Thought from Neuroelectric and Metabolic Brain Activity: Brain-Computer Interfaces (BCIs)

Niels Birbaumer[1,2] and Klaus Haagen[3]

[1] Institute of Medical Psychology and Behavioral Neurobiology, University of Tübingen, Tübingen, Germany, niels.birbaumer@uni-tuebingen.de

[2] National Institutes of Health (NIH), NINDS, Human Cortical Physiology, Bethesda, MD 20892-1430, USA

[3] Department of Economy, University of Trento, Trento, Italy, khaagen@economia.unitn.it

Summary. This chapter provides an overview of noninvasive and invasive brain-computer interfaces (BCIs). From a higher-level view, the chapter contains two major sections. Initially, the chapter describes fundamental mechanisms underlying BCI control. The chapter then describes several applications of BCIs in clinical environments.

7.1 Introduction

This overview of noninvasive and invasive BCIs describes the scientific and clinical progress in direct brain-derived communication and motor restoration in paralysis. Essentially, BCI uses electric, magnetic, and metabolic brain activity for the activation of external devices and computers. Its principal applications are in verbal communication in locked-in paralyzed patients and in restoration of movement in victims of stroke and spinal cord injury. While direct brain communication in paralysis is possible and useful, motor restoration still poses algorithmic problems, signal-to-noise ratio problems, and clinical limitations. Newly developed metabolic BCIs using functional magnetic resonance imaging (fMRI) and near-infrared spectroscopy (NIRS) allow manipulation of very localized and subcortical brain changes, mainly for the modification of emotional/motivational variables. In general, BCI research is a rich, large, and complex field. This chapter aims to provide an introduction to the field.[4] Our aim is to describe some of the major goals and concepts in the field in some detail. The remainder of this chapter therefore

---

[4] Part of this chapter has been published in the Journal of Physiology (2007) and Brain Research Bulletin (2007).

has the following organization. Section 7.2 describes the essential mechanisms underlying BCI control. The section starts with a brief introduction and then reports on the curarisation and operant control of physiology, the metabolic BCI BOLD control as a model system, neuroelectric and neuromagnetic BCIs, and learning and neural plasticity in BCI control. Section 7.3 describes several clinical applications of BCIs including epilepsy and attention regulation, amyotrophic lateral sclerosis (ALS), and communication with BCI, ethical and quality of life issues in BCI research, paralysis from spinal cord lesions, restoration of movement in chronic stroke, and fMRI-BCI and psychopathy and anxiety.

7.2 Neurophysiological and Behavioral Mechanisms Underlying BCI Control

7.2.1 Introduction

A brain-computer interface (BCI) or brain-machine interface (BMI) transforms brain signals into signals that can be used for activating or blocking an external device or computer without any peripheral motor activity. Invasive BCIs record brain activity from neural or neurovascular tissue using surgical or other invasive medical interventions. Non-invasive BCIs do not involve a tissue-penetrating medical procedure but record brain signals from electrodes, sensors, or electromagnetic fields.

Brain-computer interfaces can be categorized according to the brain activity they use. During the short history of BCI research originating from operant training of single-neuron spike trains [Fet69] and EEG (electroencephalogram) alpha waves [Kam71], the following neuronal activities were used (for a comprehensive review, see [Bir06a]):

- EEG oscillations ranging from 4 to 40 Hz, primarily mu-or SMR (sensorimotor rhythm), and its harmonics (8 to 30 Hz from sensorimotor cortex).
- Electrocorticogram (ECoG) from implanted macro electrodes.
- Event-related brain potentials (ERPs), primarily the P 300 and slow cortical potentials (SCP) (for an overview, see [ERLB84]), fast latency sub-cortical potentials, and visual evoked potentials.
- Action potential spike trains from implanted microelectrodes (for a review, see [NBM04]).
- Synaptic field potentials from implanted electrodes.
- Metabolic brain activity, the BOLD response recorded through functional magnetic resonance imaging (fMRI), and blood oxygenation with near-infrared spectroscopy (NIRS).

Hans Berger, who discovered the human EEG, speculated in his first comprehensive review of his experiments with the "Elektrenkephalogramm" about the possibility of reading thoughts from the EEG traces by using sophisticated mathematical analysis [Ber29]. Grey Walter, the brilliant EEG pioneer who described the contingent negative variation (CNV), often called the "expectancy wave", built the first automatic frequency analyzer and the computer of "average transients" with the intention of discriminating covert thoughts and language in the human EEG [Wal64]. Fetz published the first paper on invasive operant conditioning of cortical spike trains in animals [Fet69]. Only the recent development of BCIs, however, has brought us a bit closer to the dreams of these pioneers of EEG research.

For noninvasive BCI research, the historic roots and most of the literature originated from neurofeedback and operant conditioning of neuroelectric brain activity. Most of the clinical BCI studies in human patients use biofeedback of EEG oscillations or ERP (see [ERLB84]), but the term "biofeedback" at present is rarely used because of exaggerated and scientifically unsound claims of its clinical efficacy by its clinical representatives. In neurofeedback or biofeedback, the patient receives visual or auditory online feedback of his or her brain activity and tries to modify voluntarily a particular type of brain wave. The information of the feedback also provides the reward for successful instigated changes of the patient's own brain activity. Self-regulation of brain waves as described in the biofeedback literature was reported to have therapeutic effects on many psychiatric and neurological conditions, but only a few indications passed rigorous clinical-experimental testing as described below.

7.2.2 Curarization and Operant Control of Physiology

The root of BCI research is intimately tied to this tradition of biofeedback and instrumental-operant learning of autonomic functions. During the late 1960s and early 1970s, Neal E. Miller and his collaborators opposed the traditional wisdom of the autonomic nervous system (ANS) as autonomous and independent of voluntary control of the somatic central nervous system (CNS). Miller [Mil69], in a landmark paper in *Science*, challenged the view that voluntary control is acquired through operant (instrumental) condi-tioning, while modification of involuntary ANS functions is learned through classical (Pavlovian) conditioning, a distinction first emphasized by Skinner [Ski53, HS61]. Miller presented experimental evidence in curarized and artifi-cially ventilated rats showing that even after long-term curarization of several weeks and the animals learned to increase and decrease heart rate, renal blood flow, and dilation and constriction of peripheral arteries in an operant conditioning paradigm that rewarded the animals for increases and decreases of these specific physiological functions. These studies stirred an enormous interest in the scientific and clinical community, particularly in psychosomatic medicine and behavior modification. The results suggested that instrumental ("voluntary") control of autonomic functions is possible without any mediation of the somatic-muscular system. Operant training of any internal body functions seemed possible, opening the door for psychological and learning treatment of many medical diseases, such as high blood pressure, cardiac arrhythmias, vascular pathologies, renal failure, gastrointestinal disorders, and many others. In the clinic, biofeedback of these functions replaced the operant conditioning in rats, and the feedback from the specific physiological variable constituted the reward (for an overview of these years' enthusiasm, see the Aldine series on Biofeedback and Self-Control [Kam71]).

During the next two decades, Miller and his students at Rockefeller University tried to replicate their own findings. However, the steady decline of the size of the conditioning effect with each replication created a severe credibility problem for operant learning of autonomic functions and bio-feedback. Finally, by the mid-1980s, it was impossible to replicate the effects in curarized rats. Barry Dworkin, Neal Miller's last and most prolific student, continued to try and build the most sophisticated "intensive care unit" for curarized rats, but again, operant training of autonomic function or nerves in the curarized rat was impossible.

In contrast, classical conditioning succeeded even in single facial nerve fibers [DM86, Dwo93]. Dworkin attributed the failure of operant techniques to the missing homeostatic effect of the reward: the reward acquires its positive effect through homeostasis-restoring effects (i.e., ingestion of food restores glucostatic and fluid balance). In the curarized rat (and the completely paralyzed respirated and fed patient), where all body functions are kept artificially constant, the homeostatic function of the reward is no longer present because imbalances of the equilibrium do not occur. The chronically curarized rat and the completely paralyzed, artificially ventilated and fed locked-in patient share many similarities, and difficulties in communicating with these patients may be understood based on these similarities (see below). The difficulties in replicating the operant learning of autonomic variables were accompanied by an "awakening" in the clinical arena of biofeedback applications: the most impressive clinical results were achieved with electromyographic feedback in chronic neuromuscular pain [FB93], neuro-muscular rehabilitation of various neurological conditions [BK79], particularly external sphincter control in enuresis end encopresis [HW83], and posture control in kyphosis and scoliosis [DMD⁺85, BFC⁺94], but clinically un-impressive or negligible results in essential hypertension [Eng81, MOK95], heart rate [CKS⁺81], and gastric hyperfunction [HW83]. It became painfully clear that only very limited positive effects of biofeedback on visceral pathol-ogy with clinically and statistically relevant changes occur. There was one notable exception, however—neurofeedback of brain activity [ERLB84].

7.2.3 The Metabolic BCI: BOLD Control as a Model System

Functional magnetic resonance imaging measures increases and decreases of the paramagnetic load of blood flow to activated pools of neurons, particularly apical dendrites [LPA⁺01]. Paramagnetic charge is determined by blood oxygenation level dependent (BOLD) flow, which reflects local metabolic deficiencies of the vascular bed supplying the neurons. Logothetis et al. have shown that the correlation of local blood flow change and the BOLD signal is particularly high for the neuronal inflow to the apical dendrites reflecting primarily intracortical activity. Slow cortical potentials (SCP) seem to be the closest electrophysiological relative of the BOLD signal, and simultaneous recording of BCI-regulated SCP and BOLD demonstrated a strong relationship between self-regulated increases and decreases of SCP at central electrodes and BOLD variations in the anterior basal ganglia and premotor cortex as predicted by neurophysiological considerations of SCP sources [BECR90, HVW+05].

All BCI systems need some form of learned voluntary control or cognitive voluntary attentional modulation such as the P 300 BCI (see below) and fMRI with its exquisite anatomical resolution allowing study of the neuronal processes necessary for BCI control. Figure 7.1 shows the first fMRI-BCI system developed in the authors' laboratory [WVE+03] using extremely fast echo-planar gradient sequences in a 1.5 to 3T MR scanner (results in press).

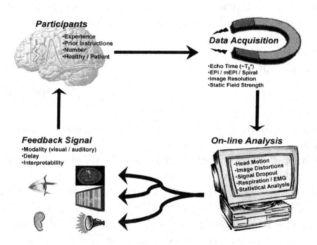

Fig. 7.1. The first fMRI-BCI system developed in the authors' laboratory.

Subjects observe the visual feedback reflecting the movement-corrected BOLD changes of a circumscribed cortical or subcortical brain area. Caria et al. [CVS+07] gives an example of the anterior insular region implicated in the regulation of negative emotions and affective pain. The latency of the BOLD change to the neural discharge is 3s, but the feedback to the subject or patient to the physiological response is instantaneous and constant and therefore functions as an effective reward for voluntary BOLD changes. Subjects are instructed to use emotional motor, or cognitive imagery to influence the feedback signal in the required direction. Areas with unknown function or subjects without cognitive abilities to imagine are treated identically but subjects receive only the instruction to affect the feedback signal in the required direction and subjects are rewarded for successful attempts to modify the metabolic flow in the particular brain region.

Weiskopf et al. (in press) provide an overview of recent results of fMRI-BCI, and DeCharms et al. [DMG+05] reported its effects on pain perception. Apart from several cortical areas, amygdalae, anterior cingulate, anterior insula, and parahippocampal gyrus were shown to respond differentially with increased and decreased BOLD response to self-regulation within two to ten sessions of one hour each. Even more important, area-specific effects on behavior were demonstrated: voluntary increases of insular activation intensified negative emotional valence ratings of emotional slides, anterior cingulate affects arousal, and parahippocampal gyrus BOLD reduced memory performance (probably through overactivation of the region).

In an ongoing series of experiments, Birbaumer et al. [BVL+05] demonstrated that criminal psychopaths show a dramatic deficit in metabolic activity of the fear circuit: lateral orbital prefrontal cortex, amygdalae, anterior cingulate, anterior insula, and superior parietal cortex are not activated during aversive classical conditioning. Learning to reactivate these areas in fear-evoking situations should reduce the central deficit of psychopathic traits, a complete lack of anticipatory fear.

These studies on fMRI-BCI and behavior illustrate some important properties of BCI control:

- Voluntary control of circumscribed brain areas is possible within several hours of training in healthy subjects.
- The learned regulation is specific and does not unspecifically coactivate other brain sites.
- The behavioral effects of self-induced local brain changes are functionally specific for the respective brain region.
- The central motor systems need not be coactivated during brain self-regulation, indicating that motor mediation of the brain is not a necessary prerequisite for its regulation, and learned brain control should be possible in completely paralyzed people and animals unable to use motor projections for peripheral physiological regulation [DM86].
- Cognitive activity such as imagery may assist the acquisition of brain control but is not a necessary condition to manipulate brain regions locally.

7.2.4 Neuroelectric and Neuromagnetic BCIs

The reconstruction of movement from patterns of single-cell firing patterns of the motor cortex [Nic03] or parietal neuronal pools [SMA05] in animals and two human patients [HSF+06] using extremely densely packed microelectrode arrays of up to several hundred microelectrodes [Don02] was remarkably successful. Monkeys learned to move cursors into moving goals on a computer screen in a predetermined sequence by successively activating motor, premotor, and parietal motor neuron pools. In one particularly successful preparation [Nic03], 32 cells were sufficient to move an artificial arm and perform skillful reaching movements after extensive training with their hand first and then with spiking patterns only. The plasticity of the cortical circuits allows learned control of movement directly from the cellular activity even outside the primary or secondary homuncular representations of the motor cortex [TTS02].

A multielectrode array recording spike and field potentials simultaneously was implanted in the motor hand area of two quadriplegic patients by Donoghue's group [HSF+06]. Within a few training sessions, the patients learned to use neuronal activity from field potentials to move a computer cursor in several directions, comparable to the tasks used for multidimensional cursor movements in the noninvasive SMR-BCI reported by Wolpaw and McFarland [WM04]. In contrast to the noninvasive approach, none of the invasive procedures allowed restoration of skillful movement in paralyzed animals or people in everyday-life situations. The animals studied in BMI research [Nic03] were all intact animals that learned to move an artificial device or cursor for a food reward without moving their intact arm in highly artificial laboratory situations. Any generalization from the invasive animal BCI approach to paralyzed people is premature.

For the noninvasive case and clinical use, three types of EEG-based BCIs and one neuromagnetic BCI using magnetoencephalography (MEG, see the paragraph on stroke rehabilitation below) were developed. Figure 7.2 depicts the three thoroughly tested BCI systems: an SCP-based spelling BCI for paralyzed patients [BGH+99], which was originally tested for the behavioral treatment of intractable epilepsy [KSU+01] (Figure 7.2a), a BCI with sensorimotor rhythm (SMR) as the critical EEG oscillation to be controlled [WBM+02, WM04] (Figure 7.2b), and the P 300 event-related brain potential (ERP)-BCI developed by Donchin [FD88] (Figure 7.2c). SCP control and SMR (often called mu-rhythm) control is learned through visual and auditory feedback and reward and needs 5 to 20 training sessions in patients before significant production of SCP or mu-rhythm is achieved, while the P 300 BCI needs no training: as depicted in Figure 7.2c, rows and columns of a matrix consisting of the letters of the alphabet are lightened in rapid succession. The subject is instructed to concentrate on the letter he or she wants to spell. Whenever the desired letter (P in Figure 7.2c) is among the lightened string and a P 300 ERP appears in the EEG selecting the desired letter [SD06]. Sellers and Donchin developed an auditory P 300 BCI also with a few letters spelled in rapid succession. However, auditory feedback is less easy to control than visual BCIs, and performance drops considerably.

The SCP-BCI: Beginning in 1979, our laboratory published an extensive series of experiments that demonstrated operant control of slow cortical potentials (SCP) of the EEG. These demonstrations differed from previous work on brain biofeedback, as they documented the following in well-controlled experimental paradigms:

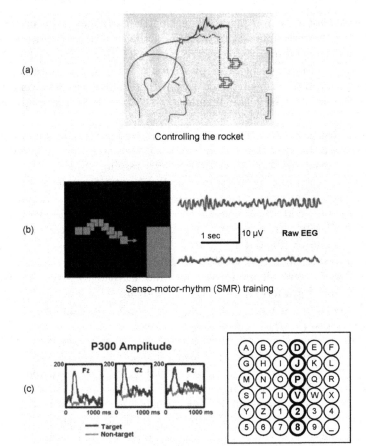

(a)

Controlling the rocket

(b)

1 sec   10 µV   Raw EEG

Senso-motor-rhythm (SMR) training

(c)

P300 Amplitude

Target
Non-target

P300 Brain-Computer-Interface (BCI)

Fig. 7.2. Most frequently used BCI systems: (a) the slow cortical potential BCI or thought translation device described by Birbaumer et al. [BGH+99]; (b) the SMR (sensorimotor-rhythm) BCI described by Pfurtscheller et al. [PNB05]; (c) the P 300 BCI described by Farwell and Donchin [FD88], as shown in a carefully controlled study by Hinterberger et al. [HBMB04].

(a) Strong and anatomically specific effects of self-induced cortical changes on behavior and cognition, and

(b) Solid neurophysiological evidence about the anatomical sources and physiological function of slow cortical potentials (SCPs) (e.g., see [BECR90, BRL+92, BFLE95], and see [Bir99] for a review).

Of particular interest in the context of central nervous system motor mediation of voluntary control of brain activity was the fact that SCPs originating from posterior parietal sources were resistant to operant learning, while central and frontal SCPs could be brought under voluntary operant control after one to five training sessions [LRB93]. Several clinical studies confirmed the critical importance of the anterior brain systems for physiological regulation of CNS functions: Lutzenberger et al. [LBE+80] showed that patients with extended prefrontal lobe lesions were unable to learn SCP control despite intact intellectual functioning. Patients with prefrontal dysfunctions, such as attention deficit disorder (ADD, [BERL86]) and schizophrenia [SRH+92], exhibited extreme difficulties in acquiring SCP control, and attentional improvement after SCP or SMR neurofeedback training required long training periods [SLG+06]. Again, peripheral motor function played no role in SCP conditioning [BK79], but intact prefrontal systems seemed to be a prerequisite for successful brain control. Figure 7.1 shows the results of a study where healthy subjects learned SCP control and fMRI (BOLD response) was recorded simultaneously during training.

Subjects received visual feedback of positive and negative SCPs of 6 seconds duration and were rewarded for the production of target amplitudes [HWV+04, HVW+05, HBF05]. As can be seen in Figure 7.2, successful voluntary brain control depends on activity in premotor areas and the anterior parts of the basal ganglia. Birbaumer et al. [BECR90] had proposed earlier that physiological regulation of SCP and attention depends critically on anterior basal ganglia activity regulating local cortical activation thresholds and SCP in selective attention and motor preparation. Braitenberg [BS91] created the term "thought pump" ("Gedankenpumpe" in German) for this basal ganglia-thalamus-cortical loop. Taken together, the extensive literature on the SCP also suggests that operant-voluntary control of local cortical excitation thresholds underlying goal-directed thinking and preparation depends on an intact motor and/or premotor cortical and subcortical system.

The SMR-mu-BCI: The Wolpaw group in Albany and the Pfurtscheller lab in Graz, Austria, demonstrated in an extensive series of experiments that healthy subjects and paralyzed patients achieve voluntary control of right- and left-hemispheric SMR at the rolandic cortex by imagining movements. Sterman [Ste81, SF72] was the first to propose self-control of epileptic seizures [ERLB84] by an augmentation of sensorimotor rhythm (SMR). Sensorimotor rhythm (SMR) in human subjects is recorded exclusively over sensorimotor areas with frequencies of 10 to 20 Hz and variable amplitudes. Pfurtscheller and colleagues [PNB05] localized the source of human SMR in the sensorimotor regions following the homuncular organization of the motor and somatosensory cortical strip. Imagery of hand movement abolishes SMR over the hand region, and imagery or actual movement of the legs blocks SMR in the interhemispheric sulcus. With MEG, even single fingers can be localized using SMR desynchronization.

Pfurtscheller called this phenomenon event-related desynchronization and synchronization [PNB05]. On the basis of careful animal experiments, Sterman demonstrated incompatibility of seizures in motor and premotor areas in the presence of sensorimotor rhythm (SMR) [SC62a, SC62b]. Cats exhibited maximum SMR during motor inhibition and various sleep stages. The presence

of spindles during different sleep stages, particularly during rapid eye movement (REM) sleep, indicated recruitment of inhibitory thalamo-cortical circuits and blocked experimentally induced seizures. Sleep spindles and SMR
share identical physiological mechanisms. However, it is not clear whether the
neurophysiological bases of the two phenomena are really comparable, and
therefore we recommend that the term SMR as used by Sterman et al. be
retained because of its well-defined theoretical and experimental background.

It is not accidental that SMR-operant control is achieved through activation and deactivation of the central motor loops. Again, successful voluntary
regulation of a physiological variable is tied to the regulation of the motor
system. The results of SMR control in animals and patients seem to demonstrate that manipulation (mediation) of the peripheral motor efferents is not a
necessary requirement of SMR control, however, at least on the basis of EMG
recordings of the arm muscles that showed no measurable variation during
motor imagery with central nervous system event-related desynchronization
[PNB05]. The successful brain regulation of SMR in completely paralyzed
patients reported below confirms that changes of the peripheral motor system
do not mediate central nervous system (CNS) activity responsible for SMR
origination. The notion of the critical role of central motor activity in
voluntary action and thought remains.

The P 300 BCI: The P 300 ERP is the best-studied brain-evoked potential evoked by new surprising stimuli and by stimuli asking for an update
of current memory traces [Don81, Ver88]. Depending on the complexity
of the stimulus, its latency varies from 300 ms to 1 second. It can be
recorded best over anterior parietal areas, but its anatomical sources are often
hippocampal, depending upon the memory trace violations of the stimulus
material. The positive polarity of the P 300 indicates an inhibitory function,
probably blocking competing information processing in the presence of new
and challenging material. The P 300 is widely used in the clinic to evaluate
deficits in attentional processing and has recently been used in lie detection
research. Donchin exploited in his BCI system the reliability and validity of
the P 300: even after long time periods, the P 300 amplitude to the desired
letter does not habituate, and very few subjects lack a P 300 (Nijboer et al.,
current work, submitted).

In contrast to all other existing BCIs, learning and feedback is not
necessary, and the short latency of the P 300 (300 ms instead of seconds in
the SCP and mu BCIs) allows much faster selection of letters than with any
other BCI system. For high speed spelling and selection, however, it requires
an intact visual system and intact attention not always present in completely
paralyzed patients.

7.2.5 Learning and Neural Plasticity Involved in BCI Control

As described above, acquisition of operant learning control over autonomic
functions and brain activity without an intact somatic central or peripheral

system was demonstrated initially in the curarized rat but turned out to be impossible to replicate. Of seven patients with ALS who started training after they had entered the completely locked-in state without any muscular control (no eye movement, no sphincter control), none acquired sufficient brain control to communicate, and only one patient communicated for a limited time period of 3 hours with a ph-imagery technique developed in our lab [WJB06]. We hypothesized [Bir06b] that loss of the contingency between a voluntary response and the feedback or reward of a response prevents learning even if the cognitive system (attention, memory, verbal imagery, and thinking) is intact. If the voluntary response is only cognitive, such as non-overt imagery, the feedback or reward does not reliably follow the response in an environmental context causing extinction. Psychophysical studies [HCK02] demonstrate that if the behavioral response is elicited independently of a conscious decision, the conscious awareness of the contingency and the decision vanishes. We termed this process "extinction of thinking", which may reduce synaptic plasticity as described at the molecular level, leading to a more generalized deficit in learning [BS05]. A single case of a completely locked-in patient able to communicate with a BCI after entering that state would disprove our speculation. In the BCI literature, no case at a completely locked-in state case has been reported.

A possible solution to the extinction of thinking problem may consist in the creation of artificial contingencies with transcranial magnetic stimulation pulses delivered to frontal or motor brain areas and rewarding the elicited brain or peripheral nerve responses. Another possibility are metabolic BCIs using fMRI or NIRS (near infrared spectroscopy) BCIs as described above and by Sitaram et al. (in press). Metabolic changes and vascular variations are sensed by receptors and allow contingent perceptive responses other than neuroelectric brain activity without any visceral perception, which renders it difficult to produce a voluntary control response contingent on a perceived internal stimulus [Ada98].

7.3 Clinical Applications of BCIs

7.3.1 Epilepsy and Attention Regulation

Slow cortical potential (SCP) control allowed anatomically specific voluntary regulation of different brain areas with area-specific effects on behavior and cognition (for an overview, see [REBL89]). Sterman [Ste81, SF72] was the first to propose self-control of epileptic seizures [ERLB84] by an augmentation of sensorimotor rhythm (SMR). In human subjects, SMR is recorded exclusively over sensorimotor areas with frequencies of 10 to 20 Hz and variable amplitudes. Pfurtscheller and colleagues [PNB05] localized the source of human SMR in the sensorimotor regions following the homuncular organization of the motor and somatosensory cortical strip. Imagery of hand movement abolishes

SMR over the hand region, and imagery or actual movement of the legs blocks SMR in the interhemispheric sulcus. Pfurtscheller called this phenomenon event-related desynchronization and synchronization [PNB05]. On the basis of careful animal experiments, Sterman demonstrated incompatibility of seizures in motor and premotor areas in the presence of SMR [SC62a, SC62b]. Cats exhibited maximum SMR during motor inhibition and various sleep stages. The presence of spindles during different sleep stages, particularly during REM sleep, indicated recruitment of inhibitory thalamo-cortical circuits and blocked experimentally induced seizures. Sleep spindles and SMR share identical physiological mechanisms. Epileptic cats and humans were trained to increase SMR, and after extensive training ranging from 20 to more than 100 sessions, Sterman [Ste77] was able to demonstrate seizure reduction and complete remission in some patients with drug-resistant epilepsy. It is important to note that SMR is often called mu-rhythm, following a suggestion by Gastaut [Gas52, GTG52], who noted its abolition in some types of seizures.

However, we mentioned already in Section 7.2.4 that it is not clear whether the neurophysiological bases of the two phenomena are really comparable and thus, recommended that the term SMR as used by Sterman et al. be retained because of its well-defined theoretical and experimental background.

Section 7.2.4 also mentioned that it is not accidental that SMR-operant control is achieved through activation and deactivation of the central motor loops. The section indicated that one of the reason for this is that successful voluntary regulation of a physiological variable is tied to the regulation of the motor system. It was also mentioned that the results available for SMR control in animals and patients seem to indicate that manipulation (mediation) of the peripheral motor efferents is not a necessary prerequisite of SMR-control (at least based on EMG-recordings of the arm muscles showing no measurable variation during motor imagery with central nervous system event-related desynchronization [PNB05]). The successful brain regulation of SMR in completely paralyzed patients mentioned later are going to confirm that changes of the peripheral motor system do not mediate central nervous system (CNS) activity responsible for SMR origin. This also reinforces that the critical role of CNS activity in voluntary action and thought remains, as was mentioned earlier.

Earlier in this chapter (see text on SCP-BCI in Section 7.2.4) we mentioned that in the context of CNS motor mediation of voluntary control of brain activity, the fact that SCPs originating from posterior parietal sources were resistant to operant learning, while central and frontal SCPs could be brought under voluntary, operant control after one to five training sessions is of particular interest.

We also mentioned that several clinical studies confirmed the critical importance of the anterior brain systems for physiological regulation of CNS fuctions (e.g., in Section 7.2.4 the relevant literature discussed included [LBE+80, BERL86, SRH+92, BK79, HWV+04, HVW+05, BECR90], and [BS91]). Combined, the extensive literature on the SCP also suggests that operantvoluntary control of local cortical excitation thresholds underlying goal directed thinking and preparation depends on an intact motor or/and premotor cortical and subcortical system.

Encouraged by the reliable and lasting effects of brain self-regulation on various behavioral variables and by Sterman's case demonstrations, Birbaumer and colleagues conducted several controlled clinical studies on the effect of SCP regulation on intractable epilepsy [REBL89, REB+93, KSU+01]. Based on their neurophysiological model of SCP regulation, patients with focal epileptic seizures were trained to down-regulate cortical excitation by rewarding them for cortical positive potentials and perception of SCP changes. After extremely long training periods, some of these patients gained close to 100% control of their SCPs and seizure suppression, tempting Birbaumer and colleagues to apply cortical regulation as a BCI for paralyzed patients. Given that epileptic patients suffering from a dysregulation of cortical excitation and inhibition and consequent brain lesions learn to control their brain responses both within the laboratory and on the "outside", it is not unreasonable to ask whether a paralyzed patient could learn to activate an external device or computer in order to move a prosthetic arm or to convey messages to a voice system.

The same procedure was applied in several controlled studies [FBL+03, SLG+06] to treat children with attention deficit disorder (ADD). It was shown that both learned increase of central-frontal negativity of SCP and increase of SMR improve ADD as efficiently as medication (Ritalin). No difference between SCP training, beta training, or SMR was found, which indicates unspecific treatment factors of BCI effects or that the different types of brain activity converge at a final common therapeutic endpath. That endpath could well be an improvement in the general capacity to regulate attention via brain regulation.

7.3.2 ALS and Verbal Communication with BCI

Over the past 15 years, 28 patients with ALS and 5 patients with other severe brain disorders have been trained with BCIs, most of them in their homes [BGH+99, KKK+01, Bir06b]. Stages of impairment ranged from completely locked-in (no eye movements or other forms of motor activity present) to paralysis of legs or arms at the beginning stage of the disease. Most patients were trained with the SCP BCI system described earlier, and more recently the P 300 and the SMR system were used. All of the patients achieved significant control of their brain activity, and most of them were able to select letters and write words with one of the three BCI systems, except those seven patients who started BCI training in the completely locked-in state [KNM+05]. None of these patients was able to communicate with a BCI, and one patient communicated with a ph-based device for two sessions but lost control after these sessions without regaining it [WJB06]. We described the possible reasons for the learning deficit of completely locked-in patients and curarized animals in previous paragraphs.

From the studies summarized in the cited work, it is not clear which of the three BCIs is the most promising. In a recently completed study (Nijboer et al., current work, submitted) eight severely paralyzed patients with ALS were trained with SCP, P 300 and SMR BCIs in a balanced crossover within-subject design. Each training block of each BCI type lasted 20 sessions. The results were clear-cut: the SCP BCI did not succeed in this short training period, and the voluntary brain control was significant but not good enough (70% minimum success rate) for selecting letters with SCP. The fastest acquisition and fastest spelling rates were achieved with the P 300 BCI; SMR was also successful but not as fast as the P 300 system. In the locked-in state, eye control is lost, and it is unclear from this study whether an auditory P 300 BCI with only a few letters presented simultaneously is still the superior alternative. Open to empirical investigation remains the question of whether a patient with sufficient brain control in the locked-in state is able to carry over the voluntary control into the completely locked-in state (see [Bir06b]).

7.3.3 Ethical and Quality of Life Issues in BCI Research and Application

Most ALS patients opt against artificial respiration and feeding and die of respiratory problems. In many countries, doctors are allowed to assist the transition with sedating medication to ease respiration-related symptoms. If doctor-assisted suicide or euthanasia is legal, as it is in the Netherlands or Belgium, very few patients vote for continuation of life. The vast majority of family members and doctors (usually neurologists) believe that the quality of life in total paralysis is extremely low and continuation of life constitutes a burden for the patient, and that it is unethical to use emergency measures such as tracheostomy to continue life. The pressure on the patient to discontinue life is enormous.

The facts on end of life issues and quality of life do not support hastened death decisions in ALS, however, and the scientific literature and our own studies challenge the pervasive myth of helplessness, depression and poor quality of life in respirated and fed paralyzed persons, particularly those with ALS [Qui05, ARDB+05]. Most instruments measuring depression and quality of life, such as the widely used Beck or Hamilton depression scales, are invalid for paralyzed people living in protected environments because most of the questions do not apply to the life of a paralyzed person ("I usually enjoy a good meal", "I like to see a beautiful sunset"). Special instruments had to be developed for this population [KWL+05]. In studies by Breitbart, Rosenfeld, and Penin [BRP00] and by our group [KWL+05], only 9% of the patients showed long episodes of depression, most of them in the time period following the diagnosis and a period of weeks after tracheostomy. Figure 7.3 shows the results for depression (a) and for quality of life (b) rated by patients and family members and caretakers.

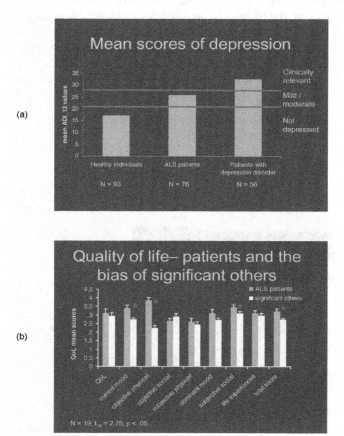

Fig. 7.3. Depression (a) and quality of life (b; adapted from [KWL+05]) in ALS. ALS patients are within the normal range for depression (a, horizontal lines). Quality of life is rated higher by patients (b, dark histogram) than significant others (white histogram).

As can be seen, ALS patients are not clinically depressed. In fact, they are in a much better mood than psychiatrically depressed patients who have no life-threatening bodily disease. Likewise, patients rate their quality of life as much better than their caretakers and family members do, even when these patients are completely paralyzed and respirated. None of the patients of our sample (some of them in the locked-in state) requested hastened death.

It is possible to argue that questionnaires and interviews more reflect social desirability and social pressure than the "real" behavioral-emotional state of the patient. The social pressure in ALS, however, directs the patient toward death and interruption of life support. The data therefore may "underestimate" the positive attitude in these groups. This hypothesis is strongly supported by a series of experiments with ALS patients at all stages of their disease using the International Affective Picture System (IAPS) [LBC99]. Lule et al. [LKJ+05], using a selection of IAPS pictures with social content, found more positive emotions with positive pictures and less negative ratings with negative pictures in ALS patients than in matched healthy controls. Even more surprising are the brain responses to the IAPS slides (Figure 7.4).

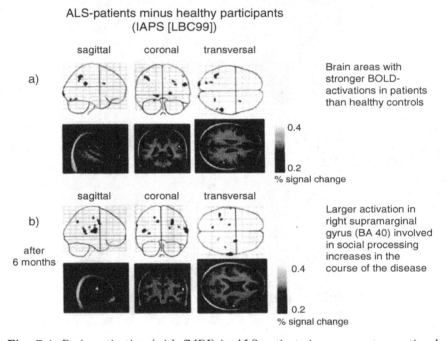

Fig. 7.4. Brain activation (with fMRI) in ALS patients in response to emotional slides in the course of disease progression (from Lule et al., see the text).

FMRI measurement in nine patients with ALS and controls demonstrated increased activation in the supramarginal gyrus and other areas responsible for empathic emotional responses to others comparable to the "mirror neuron network" identified first by Rizolatti and colleagues [GKR04]. Furthermore, brain areas related to the processing of negative emotional information, such as the anterior insulae and amygdala, show less activation in ALS. These differences become stronger with progression of the disease six months later.

One is tempted to speculate that with progression of this fatal disease, emotional response on the behavioral and central nervous system level toward positively valenced social cues improves, resulting in a more positive emotional state than in healthy controls! The positive response and positive interaction of the social environment and caretakers to a fatally ill, paralyzed person may in part be responsible for the pro-social emotional behavior and for the modified brain representation of the ALS patients depicted in Figure 7.4 as predicted by social learning theory [Ban69].

Taken together, the results on emotional response and quality of life in paralyzed ALS patients suggest a more cautious and ethically more responsive approach toward hastened death decisions and last-will orders of patients and their families. The data reported here also speak pervasively for the usefulness and necessity of noninvasive BCI in ALS and other neurological conditions leading to complete paralysis.

7.3.4 Paralysis from Spinal Cord Lesions

Pfurtscheller et al. [PNB05] were the first to apply the SMR BCI to a patient with a high spinal cord lesion. The patient learned to self stimulate electrical stimulation to hand and arm muscles by activating electrical muscle stimulation with brain-controlled electrical muscle stimulation using SMR increase or decrease. The patient was able to grab a glass and lift it to his mouth with successive activations of electrostimulation.

Donoghue [HSF$^+$06] implanted an array of 100 microelectrodes in the primary motor cortex of two high spinal cord patients. The patients were able to move a computer cursor on a screen in circular fashion with neuronal spike activation of single cells, but no restoration of movement was possible.

Several studies (see [Nic03] for a summary) trained healthy monkeys and rats to perform skillful movements with spike patters from single motor or parietal neurons. It is not clear why the human preparations (see also [KKM$^+$04] for a single electrode preparation) failed.

7.3.5 Restoration of Movement in Chronic Stroke

Figure 7.5a and Figure 7.5b show a BCI based on magnetoencephalography (MEG) for chronic stroke patients developed by Cohen, Birbaumer, and their groups (results in print).

MEG oscillations and evoked magnetic fields offer a better spatial resolution and the same exquisite time resolution as EEG, SCP, and P 300. The whole cortex magnetic activity is recorded in patients with subcortical stroke without remaining hand function from 270 sensors. Three sensors over the lesioned hemisphere most sensitive to imagery of movement of the paralyzed hand are selected for the BCI training. In most cases, 10 to 15 Hz SMR or one of its high-frequency harmonics is used for training. An artificial hand is fixed to the paralyzed hand (see Figure 7.5), and the patient learns with visual feedback to open the hand by increasing SMR over the lesioned hemisphere and close the hand by decreasing it. By choosing brain activity from the lesioned hemisphere only, overuse of the healthy hemisphere with a negative effect on brain reorganization [MDMC04] and nonuse of the lesioned

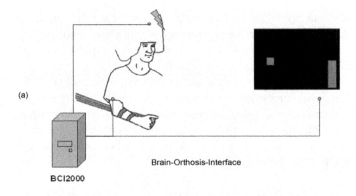

(a)

BCI2000

Brain-Orthosis-Interface

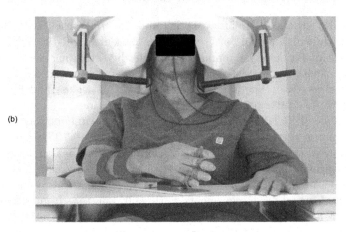

(b)

Fig. 7.5. The MEG BCI for chronic stroke: (a) a patient's paralyzed hand is fixed to a flexible orthosis, and with motor imagery decrease of SMR (goal bar at feedback screen up) and increase of SMR (goal bar at feedback screen down) the hand opens (more SMR, cursor moves downward) or closes (less SMR, cursor up); (b) patient in a 270 channel MEG system with orthosis.

hemisphere is avoided. Preliminary data on five patients demonstrate clearly that voluntary control of the artificial hand is possible from the lesioned hemisphere within 20 sessions. Patterns of cortical reorganization and motor improvement without the prosthetic device are being explored at present.

7.3.6 Psychopathy, Anxiety and the fMRI BCI

The fMRI BCI described in the first and second paragraphs was applied in preliminary pilot studies to increase emotions of anxiety and fear in healthy subjects and criminal psychopaths [CVS+07]. Caria et al. [CVS+07] describe the effects of training to increase BOLD in the anterior insula involved in the fear circuit in 12 healthy subjects. After only three sessions, significant increase of BOLD in this area compared with a sham control and imagery control condition was achieved, resulting in a more negative emotional valence rating of fear-evoking pictures of the IAPS series [LBC99] during insula-BOLD increase only. The effect is not only area-specific but also valence-specific: only aversive slides change their valence; other types of emotional slides are not affected. In contrast to the results of [Bir06b] finding a complete lack of activation of the fear circuit (amygdala, anterior insula, and cingulate, orbitofrontal cortex) in criminal psychopaths during aversive Pavlovian conditioning, the first three psychopaths were able to learn to increase activation of the anterior insula. Behavioral effects of the training are presently being investigated.

7.4 Summary

This chapter reported on a field that has gained a lot of attention in the scientific community in recent years—the field of BCIs. From a higher level, the chapter contains two larger sections. Section 7.2 provided an introduction to BCIs, the motivation and goals of the field, and several techniques and procedures we find in the field today. Section 7.3 provided an insight into several BCI applications in clinical environments. Although the chapter revealed that there are still many open problems and many unanswered questions in the field, the chapter has also shown that BCI research has the potential to contribute to our understanding in several important areas on a fundamental level.

Acknowledgments

This work is supported by the German Research Society (DFG) and the National Institutes of Health (NIH).

References

[Ada98]   G. Adam. *Visceral Perception*. Plenum Press, New York, 1998.

[ARDB+05] S. Albert, J. Rabkin, M. Del Bene, M. Tider, and H. Mitsumoto. Wish to die in end-stage ALS. *Neurology*, 65:68–74, 2005.

[Ban69]   A. Bandura. Social learning of moral judgements. *Journal of Personality and Social Psychology*, 11(3):275–279, 1969.

[BECR90]   N. Birbaumer, T. Elbert, A. Canavan, and B. Rockstroh. Slow potentials of the cerebral cortex and behavior. *Physiological Reviews*, 70:1–41, 1990.

[Ber29]   H. Berger. Über das Elektrenkephalogramm des Menschen. *Archiv für Psychiatrie und Nervenkrankheiten*, 87:527–570, 1929.

[BERL86]   N. Birbaumer, T. Elbert, B. Rockstroh, and W. Lutzenberger. Biofeed-back of slow cortical potentials in attentional disorders. In W.C. McCallum, R. Zappoli, and F. Denoth, editors, *Cerebral Psychophysiology: Studies in Event-Related Potentials*, pages 440–442. Elsevier, Amsterdam, 1986.

[BFC⁺94]   N. Birbaumer, H. Flor, B. Cevey, B. Dworkin, and N.E. Miller. Behavioral treatment of scoliosis and kyphosis. *Journal of Psychosomatic Research*, 6:623–628, 1994.

[BFLE95]   N. Birbaumer, H. Flor, W. Lutzenberger, and T. Elbert. Chaos and order in the human brain. In G. Karmos and M. Molnar, editors, *Perspectives of Event-Related Potentials Research*, volume 44, pages 450–459. Elsevier, Amsterdam, 1995. Supplements to Clinical Neurophysiology, 44.

[BGH⁺99]   N. Birbaumer, N. Ghanayim, T. Hinterberger, I. Iversen, B. Kotchoubey, A. Kübler, J. Perelmouter, E. Taub, and H. Flor. A spelling device for the paralysed. *Nature*, 398:297–298, 1999.

[Bir99]   N. Birbaumer. Slow cortical potentials: plasticity, operant control, and behavioral effects. *The Neuroscientist*, 5(2):74–78, 1999.

[Bir06a]   N. Birbaumer. Brain-computer-interface research: coming of age. *Clinical Neurophysiology*, 117:479–483, 2006.

[Bir06b]   N. Birbaumer. Breaking the silence: brain-computer interfaces (BCI) for communication and motor control. *Psychophysiology*, 43:517–532, 2006.

[BK79]   N. Birbaumer and H. Kimmel, editors. *Biofeedback and Self-Regulation*. Erlbaum, Hillsdale, NJ, 1979.

[BRL⁺92]   N. Birbaumer, L. Roberts, W. Lutzenberger, B. Rockstroh, and T. Elbert. Area-specific self-regulation of slow cortical potentials on the sagittal midline and its effects on behavior. *Electroencephalography and Clinical Neurophysiology*, 84:353–361, 1992.

[BRP00]   W. Breitbart, B. Rosenfeld, and H. Penin. Depression, hopelessness, and desire for hastened death in terminally ill patients with cancer. *The Journal of the American Medical Association*, 284:2907–2911, 2000.

[BS91]   V. Braitenberg and A. Schüz. *Anatomy of the Cortex*. Springer, Berlin, 1991.

[BS05]   N. Birbaumer and R.F. Schmidt. *Biologische Psychologie*. Springer-Verlag, Berlin, 6th edition, 2005.

[BVL⁺05]   N. Birbaumer, R. Veit, M. Lotze, M. Erb, C. Hermann, W. Grodd, and H. Flor. Deficient fear conditioning in psychopathy: a functional magnetic resonance imaging study. *Archives of General Psychiatry*, 62:799–805, 2005.

[CKS⁺81]   B. Cuthbert, J. Kristeller, R. Simons, R. Hodes, and P.J. Lang. Strategies of arousal control: biofeedback, meditation, and motivation. *Journal of Experimental Psychology*, 110(4):518–546, 1981.

[CVS⁺07]   A. Caria, R. Veit, R. Sitaram, M. Lotze, N. Weiskopf, W. Grodd, and N. Birbaumer. Regulation of anterior insular cortex activity using real-time fMRI. *NeuroImage*, 35(3):1238–1246, 15 April 2007.

[DM86]   B.R. Dworkin and N.E. Miller. Failure to replicate visceral learning in the acute curarized rat preparation. *Behavioral Neuroscience*, 100:299–314, 1986.

[DMD+85]   B. Dworkin, N.E. Miller, S. Dworkin, N. Birbaumer, M. Brines, S. Jonas, E. Schwentker, and J. Graham. Behavioral method for the treatment of idiopathic scoliosis. *Proceedings of the National Academy of Sciences, USA*, 82:2493–2497, 1985.

[DMG+05]   R.C. DeCharms, F. Maeda, G.H. Glover, D. Ludlow, J.M. Pauly, D. Soneji, J.D. Gabrieli, and S.C. Mackey. Control over brain activation and pain learned by using real-time functional MRI. *Proceedings of the National Academy of Sciences, USA*, 102(51):18626–18631, 2005.

[Don81]   E. Donchin. Surprise!...surprise? *Psychophysiology*, 18:493–513, 1981.

[Don02]   J.P. Donoghue. Connecting cortex to machines: recent advances in brain interfaces. *Nature Neuroscience*, 5:1085–1088, 2002.

[Dwo93]   B.R. Dworkin. *Learning and Physiological Regulation*. University of Chicago Press, Chicago, 1993.

[Eng81]   B.T. Engel. Clinical biofeedback: a behavioral analysis. *Neuroscience and Biobehavioral Reviews*, 5(3):397–400, 1981.

[ERLB84]   T. Elbert, B. Rockstroh, W. Lutzenberger, and N. Birbaumer, editors. *Self-Regulation of the Brain and Behavior*. Springer, New York, 1984.

[FB93]   H. Flor and N. Birbaumer. Comparison of the efficacy of EMG biofeedback, cognitive behavior therapy, and conservative medical interventions in the treatment of chronic musculoskeletal pain. *Journal of Consulting & Clinical Psychology*, 61(4):653–658, 1993.

[FBL+03]   T. Fuchs, N. Birbaumer, W. Lutzenberger, J.H. Gruzelier, and J. Kaiser. Neurofeedback training for attention-deficit/hyperactivity disorder in children: a comparison with methylphenidate. *Applied Psychophysiology and Biofeedback*, 28(1):1–12, 2003.

[FD88]   L.A. Farwell and E. Donchin. Talking off the top of your head: toward a mental prosthesis utilizing event-related brain potentials. *Electroencephalography and Clinical Neurophysiology*, 70:510–523, 1988.

[Fet69]   E.E. Fetz. Operant conditioning of cortical unit activity. *Science*, 163:955–958, 1969.

[Gas52]   H. Gastaut. Electrocorticographic study of the reactivity of rolandic rhythm. *Review Neurologique (Paris)*, 87(2):176–182, 1952.

[GKR04]   V. Gallese, C. Keysers, and G. Rizzolatti. A unifying view of the basis of social cognition. *Trends in Cognitive Sciences*, 8(9):396–403, 2004.

[GTG52]   H. Gastaut, H. Terzian, and Y. Gastaut. Study of a little electroencephalographic activity: rolandic arched rhythm. *Marseille Medical*, 89(6):296–310, 1952.

[HBF05]   T. Hinterberger, N. Birbaumer, and H. Flor. Assessment of cognitive function and communication ability in a completely locked-in patient. *Neurology*, 64:1307–1308, 2005.

[HBMB04]   T. Hinterberger, G. Baier, J. Mellinger, and N. Birbaumer. Auditory feedback of human EEG for direct brain-computer communication. In S. Barrass and P. Vickers, editors, *Proceedings of the 10th Meeting of the International Conference on Auditory Display ICAD04*, Sydney, Australia, 6–9 July 2004. International Community for Auditory Display. Available online.

[HCK02]   P. Haggard, S. Clark, and J. Kalogeras. Voluntary action and conscious awareness. *Nature Neuroscience*, 5:382–385, 2002.

[HS61]   J. Holland and B.F. Skinner. *The Analysis of Behavior*. McGraw-Hill, New York, 1961.

[HSF+06]   L.R. Hochberg, M.D. Serruya, G.M. Friehs, J.A. Mukand, M. Saleh, A.H. Caplan, A. Branner, D. Chen, R.D. Penn, and J.P. Donoghue. Neural ensemble control of prosthetic devices by a human with tetraplegia. *Nature*, 442:164–171, 2006.

[HVW+05]   T. Hinterberger, R. Veit, B. Wilhelm, N. Weiskopf, J.J. Vatine, and N. Birbaumer. Neuronal mechanisms underlying control of a brain-computer-interface. *European Journal of Neuroscience*, 21:3169–3181, 2005.

[HW83]   R. Hölzl and W. Whitehead, editors. *Psychophysiology of the Gastrointestinal Tract*. Plenum Press, New York, 1983.

[HWV+04]   T. Hinterberger, N. Weiskopf, R. Veit, B. Wilhelm, E. Betta, and N. Birbaumer. An EEG-driven brain-computer-interface combined with functional magnetic resonance imaging (fMRI). *IEEE Transactions on Biomedical Engineering*, 51(6):971–974, 2004.

[Kam71]   J. Kamiya, editor. *Biofeedback and Self-Control: An Aldine Reader on the Regulation of Bodily Processes and Consciousness*. Aldine, Chicago, 1971.

[KKK+01]   A. Kübler, B. Kotchoubey, J. Kaiser, J. Wolpaw, and N. Birbaumer. Brain-computer communication: unlocking the locked-in. *Psychological Bulletin*, 127(3):358–375, 2001.

[KKM+04]   P.R. Kennedy, M.T. Kirby, M.M. Moore, B. King, and A. Mallory. Computer control using human intracortical local field potentials. *IEEE Transactions on Neural Systems and Rehabilitation Engineering*, 12(3):339–344, 2004.

[KNM+05]   A. Kübler, F. Nijboer, J. Mellinger, T.M. Vaughan, H. Pawelzik, G. Schalk, D.J. McFarland, N. Birbaumer, and J.R. Wolpaw. Patients with ALS can use sensorimotor rhythms to operate a brain-computer interface. *Neurology*, 64:1775–1777, 2005.

[KSU+01]   B. Kotchoubey, U. Strehl, C. Uhlmann, S. Holzapfel, M. König, W. Fröscher, V. Blankenhorn, and N. Birbaumer. Modification of slow cortical potentials in patients with refractory epilepsy: a controlled outcome study. *Epilepsia*, 42(3):406–416, 2001.

[KWL+05]   A. Kübler, S. Winter, A.C. Ludolph, M. Hautzinger, and N. Birbaumer. Severity of depressive symptoms and quality of life in patients with amyotrophic lateral sclerosis. *Neurorehabilitation and Neural Repair*, 19(3):182–193, 2005.

[LBC99]   P. Lang, M. Bradley, and B. Cuthbert. International affective picture system, 1999. The Center for Research in Psychophysiology. University of Florida, Gainesville.

[LBE+80]   W. Lutzenberger, N. Birbaumer, T. Elbert, B. Rockstroh, W. Bippus, and R. Breidt. Self-regulation of slow cortical potentials in normal subjects and in patients with frontal lobe lesions. In H.H. Kornhuber and L. Deecke, editors, *Motivation, Motor and Sensory Processes of the Brain: Electrical Potentials, Behavior and Clinical Use*, pages 427–430. Elsevier, Amsterdam, 1980.

[LKJ+05]   D. Lulé, A. Kurt, R. Jürgens, J. Kassubek, V. Diekmann, E. Kraft, N. Neumann, A.C. Ludolph, N. Birbaumer, and S. Anders. Emotional responding in amyotrophic lateral sclerosis. *Journal of Neurology*, 252:1517–1524, 2005.

[LPA+01]   N. Logothetis, J. Pauls, M. Augath, T. Trinath, and A. Oeltermann.
            Neurophysiological investigation of the basis of the fMRI signal. *Nature*,
            412:150–157, 2001.
[LRB93]   W. Lutzenberger, L.E. Roberts, and N. Birbaumer. Memory per-
            formance and area-specific self-regulation of slow cortical potentials:
            dual-task interference. *International Journal of Psychophysiology*, 15:
            217–226, 1993.
[MDMC04]   N. Murase, J. Duque, R. Mazzocchio, and L. Cohen. Influence of inter-
            hemispheric interactions on motor function in chronic stroke. *Annals of
            Neurology*, 55:400–409, 2004.
[Mil69]   N. Miller. Learning of visceral and glandular responses. *Science*,
            163:434–445, 1969.
[MOK95]   A. McGrady, P. Olson, and J. Kroon. Biobehavioral treatment of essen-
            tial hypertension. In M. Schwartz, editor, *Biofeedback*. Guilford, New
            York, 2nd edition, 1995.
[NBM04]   M.A.L. Nicolelis, N. Birbaumer, and K.L. Müller. Brain-computer inter-
            faces. *IEEE Transactions on Biomedical Engineering*, 51(6):877–880,
            2004. Guest Editorial.
[Nic03]   M.A. Nicolelis. Brain-machine interfaces to restore motor function and
            probe neural circuits. *Nature Reviews Neuroscience*, 4(5):417–422, 2003.
[PNB05]   G. Pfurtscheller, C. Neuper, and N. Birbaumer. Human brain-computer
            interface (BCI). In A. Riehle and E. Vaadia, editors, *Motor Cortex in
            Voluntary Movements: A Distributed System for Distributed Functions*,
            pages 367–401. Boca Raton, FL, CRC Press, 2005.
[Qui05]   T.E. Quill. ALS, depression, and desire for hastened death: (how) are
            they related? *Neurology*, 65:1, 2005.
[REB+93]   B. Rockstroh, T. Elbert, N. Birbaumer, P. Wolf, A. Düchting-Röth, and
            M. Reker. Cortical self-regulation in patients with epilepsies. *Epilepsy
            Research*, 14:63–72, 1993.
[REBL89]   B. Rockstroh, T. Elbert, N. Birbaumer, and W. Lutzenberger. *Slow
            Brain Potentials and Behavior*. Urban & Schwarzenberg, Baltimore,
            2nd edition, 1989.
[SC62a]   M.B. Sterman and C.D. Clemente. Forebrain inhibitory mechanisms:
            cortical synchronization induced by basal forebrain stimulation. *Exper-
            imental Neurology*, 6:91–102, 1962.
[SC62b]   M.B. Sterman and C.D. Clemente. Forebrain inhibitory mechanisms:
            sleep patterns induced by basal forebrain stimulation in the behaving
            cat. *Experimental Neurology*, 6:103–117, 1962.
[SD06]   E.W. Sellers and E.A. Donchin. A P300 based brain-computer interface:
            initial tests by ALS patients. *Clinical Neurophysiology*, 117(3):538–548,
            2006.
[SF72]   M.B. Sterman and L. Friar. Suppression of seizures in an epileptic
            following sensorimotor EEG feedback training. *Electroencephalography
            and Clinical Neurophysiology*, 33(1):89–95, 1972.
[Ski53]   B.F. Skinner. *Science and Human Behavior*. Macmillan, New York,
            1953.
[SLG+06]   U. Strehl, U. Leins, G. Goth, C. Klinger, and N. Birbaumer. Self-
            regulation of slow cortical potentials: a new treatment for children
            with attention-deficit/hyperactivity disorder. *Pediatrics*, 118:1530–
            1540, 2006.

[SMA05]   H. Scherberger, J.R. Murray, and R.A. Andersen. Cortical local field potentials encodes movement intentions in the posterior parietal cortex. *Neuron*, 46:347–354, 2005.

[SRH⁺92]   F. Schneider, B. Rockstroh, H. Heimann, W. Lutzenberger, R. Mattes, T. Elbert, N. Birbaumer, and M. Bartels. Self-regulation of slow cortical potentials in psychiatric patients: schizophrenia. *Biofeedback & Self-Regulation*, 17(4):277–292, 1992.

[Ste77]   M.B. Sterman. Sensorimotor EEG operant conditioning: experimental and clinical effects. *The Pavlovian Journal of Biological Science*, 12(2):63–92, 1977.

[Ste81]   M.B. Sterman. EEG biofeedback: physiological behavior modification. *Neuroscience and Biobehavioral Reviews*, 5:405–412, 1981.

[TTS02]   D.M. Taylor, S.I. Tillery, and A.B. Schwartz. Direct cortical control of 3D neuroprosthetic devices. *Science*, 296:1829–1832, 2002.

[Ver88]   R. Verleger. Event-related brain potentials and memory. *Behavioral and Brain Sciences*, 11:343–427, 1988.

[Wal64]   W.G. Walter. The contingent negative variation: An electrical sign of significance of association in the human brain. *Science*, 146:434, 1964.

[WBM⁺02]   J.R. Wolpaw, N. Birbaumer, D. McFarland, G. Pfurtscheller, and T. Vaughan. Brain-computer interfaces for communication and control. *Clinical Neurophysiology*, 113:767–791, 2002.

[WJB06]   B. Wilhelm, M. Jordan, and N. Birbaumer. Communication in locked-in syndrome: effects of imagery on salivary pH. *Neurology*, 67:534–535, 2006.

[WM04]   J.R. Wolpaw and D.J. McFarland. Control of a two-dimensional movement signal by a noninvasive brain-computer interface in humans. *Proceedings of the National Academy of Sciences USA*, 101(51):17849–17854, 2004.

[WVE⁺03]   N. Weiskopf, R. Veit, M. Erb, K. Mathiak, W. Grodd, R. Goebel, and N. Birbaumer. Physiological self-regulation of regional brain activity using real-time functional magnetic resonance imaging (fMRI): methodology and exemplary data. *NeuroImage*, 19:577–586, 2003.

8

Computational Neuroscience and Cognitive Brain Functions

Gustavo Deco[1] and Edmund T. Rolls[2]

[1] Institució Catalana de Recerca i Estudis Avançats (ICREA), Departament de Tecnologia, Universitat Pompeu Fabra, Passeig de Circumval·lació, 8, 08003 Barcelona, Spain, gustavo.deco@upf.edu

[2] University of Oxford, Department of Experimental Psychology, South Parks Road, Oxford OX1 3UD, England, edmund.rolls@psy.ox.ac.uk

Summary. Understanding how biological brains, most notably the human brain, work is one of the great challenges in science today. This chapter is related to this challenge and presents work we have undertaken in the fields of cognitive neuroscience and cognitive brain functions. Among other things, the chapter investigates attention as an emergent network phenomenon that can result from purely additive synaptic effects, nonlinear effects in the neurons, and cooperation-competition dynamics in the network, which together yield a variety of modulatory effects.

8.1 Introduction

To understand how the brain works, including how it functions in vision, it is necessary to combine different approaches, including neural computation. Neurophysiology at the single-neuron level is needed because this is the level at which information is exchanged between the computing elements of the brain. Evidence from the effects of brain damage, including that available from neuropsychology, is needed to help understand what different parts of the system do, and indeed why each part is necessary. Neuroimaging is useful to indicate where in the human brain different processes take place and to show which functions can be dissociated from each other. Knowledge of the biophysical and synaptic properties of neurons is essential to understand how the computing elements of the brain work and therefore what the building blocks of biologically realistic computational models should be. Knowledge of the anatomical and functional architecture of the cortex is needed to show what types of neuronal networks actually perform the computation. And, finally, the approach of neural computation must be known, as this is required to link together all the empirical evidence to produce an understanding of how the system actually works. A test of whether one's understanding is correct is to simulate the processing on a computer and to show whether the simulation can perform the tasks and whether the simulation has properties similar to the real brain. The approach of neural computation leads to a precise definition of how the computation is performed and to precise and quantitative tests of the theories produced.

In humans and mammals with higher cognitive capabilities, the neocortex is a very prominent brain structure. As such, it seems to be crucially involved in cognitive processes. The neocortex can be subdivided into a set of functionally different areas, and it communicates with most of the other brain systems. It is a structure with high internal functional complexity and diversity that is involved in most aspects of cerebral processing. How are all these different partial representations, held in cortical areas, being integrated to form a coherent stream of perception, cognition, and action? Instead of a central coordinating brain structure, a massive recurrent connectivity between cortical brain areas is found. This line of evidence has led to the hypothesis that integration of incomplete partial representations held in different cortical areas might be integrated by mutual cross talk, mediated by the inter-areal neural fibers. Based on this view and further neurophysiological evidence, it has been hypothesized that each cortical area is capable of representing a set of alternative hypotheses encoded in the activities of alternative cell assemblies. Representations of different conflicting hypotheses inside each area compete with each other for activity and to be represented. However, each area represents only a part of the environment and/or internal state. In order to arrive at a coherent global representation, different cortical areas bias each other's internal representations by communicating, through interareal connections, their current states to other areas, thereby favoring certain sets of local hypotheses over others. For example, the representation of conflicting hypotheses in one area might be resolved by a bias given toward one of the two hypotheses from another area, as obtained from this other area's local view. By recurrently biasing the competitive internal dynamics of each area, the global neocortical system dynamically arrives at a global representation in which each area's state is maximally consistent with those of the other areas. This view has been referred to as the biased competition hypothesis [RD02, DR05b, Dun96].

In parallel to this competition-centered view, a cooperation-centered picture of brain operation has been formulated, where global representations find their neural correlate in assemblies of co-activated neurons. Co-activation is achieved by stronger than average mutual connections between the members of each assembly. Reverberatory communication between the members of the assembly then leads to persistent activation of the member neurons and gives rise to a representation extended in time. The concept of neural assemblies was later formalized in the framework of statistical physics, where assemblies of co-activated neurons form attractors of the recurrent neural dynamics. Even more recently, attractor dynamics have been investigated in biologically plausible networks of spiking neurons and mean-field descriptions [DR05a].

In summary, the theoretical and computational framework of biased competition and cooperation offers a unifying principle for neurocognitive modeling of higher neocortical functions.

In this chapter, we review briefly the principle of biased competition/cooperation (Section 8.2) and the main aspects of the theoretical framework (Section 8.3). We also exemplify this philosophy by reviewing a specific example in the context of visual attention (Section 8.4).

8.2 The Biased Competition and Cooperation Framework

How cognitive vision works is a paradigm example of this approach because it is a sufficiently complex problem that it requires a computational approach and indeed has not been solved in artificial vision systems operating in natural scenes. At the same time, vision raises fundamental issues in cognitive neuroscience, such as how attention works. The computational neuroscience approach is being used to produce a unified theory of attention and working memory and how these processes are influenced by rewards to influence decision making. Cognitive behavior requires complex context-dependent processing of information that emerges from the links between attentional perceptual processes, working memory, and reward-based evaluation of the actions performed. Computational studies have already provided models remarking on the role of feedforward bottom-up effects in visual attention (see [IK01] for an excellent review). We stress here the role of biased competition and cooperation mechanisms for attention involving bottom-up and top-down interactions. The biased competition mechanism has already been used in several models for explaining attentional effects in neural responses observed in the inferotemporal cortex [UN96] and in V2 and V4 [RCD99]. The hypothesis for this mechanism can be traced back to the "adaptive resonance" model [Gro87] and the "interactive activation" model [MR81] in the neural network and connectionist literatures.

We review here a biased competition and cooperation theoretical framework that is able to show how an attentional state held in a short-term memory in the prefrontal cortex can by top-down processing influence ventral and dorsal stream cortical areas using biased competition to account for many aspects of visual attention [RD02, DR05a, DR04]. Attention then appears as an emergent effect related to the dynamical evolution of the whole network. This formulation incorporates spiking and synaptic dynamics that enable simulation and explanation within a unifying framework of visual attention in a variety of tasks and at different cognitive neuroscience experimental measurement levels, namely single cells [DL02, DR04, DR05a], fMRI [CD02, CD04], psychophysics [DPZ02], and neuropsychology [DR02]. In the context of working memory, further developments [DR03, DRH04, SADS04] managed to model in a unifying form attentional and memory effects in the prefrontal cortex, integrating single-cell and fMRI data and different paradigms in the framework of biased competition. The models also directly address how bottom-up and top-down processes interact in visual cognition and show how some apparently serial processes reflect the operation of interacting parallel distributed systems. It is also possible to show how within the prefrontal cortex an attentional bias can influence the mapping of sensory inputs to motor outputs and thus play an important role in decision making. Furthermore, the absence of expected rewards can switch the attentional bias signal and thus rapidly and flexibly alter cognitive performance [DR05b].

In this chapter, as an example of the biased competition/cooperation theoretical framework, we review the systematic analysis of the synaptic and neural spiking dynamics underlying visual attention [DR05a].

8.3 Theoretical Framework

The theoretical analysis of experimental neural responses associated with visual attention aims to reveal the nature of the dynamical mechanisms underlying visual perception. A proper level of description at the microscopic level is captured by the spiking and synaptic dynamics of one-compartment, point-like models of neurons, such as *integrate-and-fire-models* [Tuc88, BW01]. The realistic dynamics allows the use of realistic biophysical constants (such as conductances, delays, etc.) in a thorough study of the realistic timescales and firing rates involved in the evolution of the neural activity underlying cognitive processes for comparison with experimental data. This is essential because we are describing a complex dynamical system that is sensitive to the underlying different spiking and synaptic time courses and to the nonlinearities involved in these processes. For this reason, it is convenient to include a thorough description of the different time courses of the synaptic activity by including fast and slow excitatory receptors (AMPA and NMDA) and GABA-inhibitory receptors. The nonstationary temporal evolution of the spiking dynamics is addressed by describing each neuron by an integrate-and-fire model. The subthreshold membrane potential $V(t)$ of each neuron evolves according to the equation [Tuc88]

$$C_{\mathrm{m}}\frac{dV(t)}{dt} = -g_{\mathrm{m}}(V(t) - V_L) - I_{\mathrm{syn}}(t),\qquad(8.1)$$

where $I_{\mathrm{syn}}(t)$ is the total synaptic current flow into the cell, V_L is the resting potential, C_{m} is the membrane capacitance, and g_{m} is the membrane conductance. When the membrane potential $V(t)$ reaches the threshold θ, a spike is generated, and the membrane potential is reset to V_{reset}. The neuron is unable to spike during the first τ_{ref}, which is the absolute refractory period.

The total synaptic current is given by the sum of glutamatergic excitatory components (NMDA and AMPA) and inhibitory components (GABA)(I_G). We consider that external excitatory contributions are produced through

AMPA receptors (I_{Ae}), while the excitatory recurrent synaptic currents are produced through AMPA and NMDA receptors (I_{Ar} and I_{Nr}). The total synaptic current is therefore given by

$$I_{syn}(t) = I_{Ae}(t) + I_{Ar}(t) + I_{Nr}(t) + I_G(t), \qquad (8.2)$$

where the current generated by each receptor type follows the general form

$$I(t) = g(V(t) - V_E) \sum_{j=1}^{N} w_j s_j(t) \qquad (8.3)$$

and $V_E = 0$ mV for the excitatory (AMPA and NMDA) synapses and -70 mV for the inhibitory (GABA) synapses. The synaptic strengths w_j are specified by the architecture. The time course of the current flow through each synapse is dynamically updated to describe its decay by altering the fractions of open channels s according to equations with the general form

$$\frac{ds_j(t)}{dt} = -\frac{s_j(t)}{\tau} + \sum_k \delta(t - t_j^k), \qquad (8.4)$$

where the sums over k represent a sum over spikes emitted by presynaptic neuron j at time t_j^k, and τ is set to the time constant for the relevant receptor. In the case of the NMDA receptor, the rise time as well as the decay time is dynamically modeled, as it is slower.

The simulation of a network of integrate-and-fire neurons determines the time evolution of the activity of each neuron as a function of the other neurons. However, we also assume that some of the inputs to the neurons are random. This implies that the sample paths of the system are realizations of a random process, meaning that the spiking activities fluctuate from time point to time point and from trial to trial. Consequently, these simulations are computationally expensive and their results probabilistic, which makes them rather unsuitable for systematic parameter explorations. To solve this problem, we simplify the dynamics via the *mean-field* approach, at least for the stationary conditions (i.e., for periods after the dynamical transients), and analyze there the bifurcation diagrams of the dynamics. The essence of the mean-field approximation is to simplify the integrate-and-fire equations by replacing after the diffusion approximation [Tuc88, AB97, BW01] the sums of the synaptic components by the average DC component and a fluctuation term. The stationary dynamics of each population can be described by the *population transfer function*, which provides the average population rate as a function of the average input current. The set of stationary, self-reproducing rates ν_i for the different populations i in the network can be found by solving a set of coupled self-consistency equations. The equations governing the activities in the mean-field approximation can hence be studied by standard methods of dynamical systems. In particular, we can use these equations to investigate how the stable fixed points of the mean-field system change as a function of two critical parameters of the model. Under the assumption that the stable fixed points of the mean-field system qualitatively correspond to the attractors of the network model, this analysis gives us a characterization of the network behavior for a wide range of parameter values. The mean-field analysis performed in this work uses the formulation derived in [BW01], which is consistent with the network of neurons used. Their formulation departs from the equations describing the dynamics of one neuron to reach a stochastic analysis of the mean first-passage time of the membrane potentials, which results in a description of the population spiking rates as functions of the model parameters in the limit of very large N.

8.4 An Example: Biased Competition Underlying Visual Attention

Several experimental results of single-cell recording studies in monkeys are consistent with the biased competition hypothesis in showing that attention serves to modulate the suppressive interaction between two or more stimuli within the receptive field [MD85, CMDD93, RD99]. In particular, we concentrate here on the experimental protocol of [RCD99] because they performed single-cell recordings of V2 and V4 neurons in a behavioral paradigm that explicitly separated sensory processing mechanisms from attentional effects in order to test the biased competition hypothesis more directly. They first examined the presence of competitive interactions in the absence of attentional effects within the receptive field by having the monkey attend to a location far outside the receptive field of the neuron that they were recording. They used oriented bars as visual stimuli. They compared the firing activity response of the neuron when a single reference stimulus was within the receptive field with the response when a second, "probe" stimulus was added to the field. When the probe was added to the field, the activity of the neuron was shifted toward the activity level that would have been evoked if the probe had appeared alone. When the reference was an effective stimulus (high response) and the probe was an ineffective stimulus (low response), the firing activity was suppressed after adding the probe. On the other hand, the response of the cell increased when an effective probe stimulus was added to an ineffective reference stimulus. Thus the response of a V4 neuron to two stimuli in its field is not the sum of its responses to both but rather is a weighted average of the responses to each stimulus alone. Attentional modulatory effects have been independently tested by repeating the same experiment but now having the monkey attend to the reference stimulus within the receptive field of the recorded neuron. The effect of the attention on the response of the V2 or V4 neuron was to almost compensate for the suppressive or excitatory effect of the probe. That is, if the probe caused a suppression of the firing response to the reference when the attention was outside the receptive field, then attending to the reference restored the neuron's activity to the level corresponding to

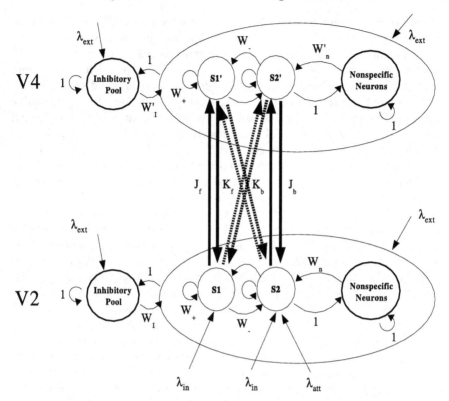

Fig. 8.1. Minimal model corresponding to the "biased competition" experiments of Reynolds et al. [RCD99]. The model considers two cortical areas, V2 and V4.

the response of the neuron to the reference stimulus alone. Symmetrically, if the probe stimulus increased the neuron's level of activity, attending to the reference stimulus compensated the response by shifting the activity to the level that had been recorded when the reference was presented alone.

We analyze the synaptic and spiking mechanisms underlying biased competition for the experimental design described in the previous section by introducing a minimal model of the dynamics between the two cortical brain areas involved (see Figure 8.1).

These two cortical areas correspond to V2 and V4 for the Reynolds et al. design [RCD99, RD03]. Both cortical areas have the same internal architecture and implement a dynamical competition between different neurons. Each cortical area contains N_E (excitatory) pyramidal cells and N_I inhibitory interneurons. In our simulations, we use $N_E = 800$ and $N_I = 200$, consistent with the neurophysiologically observed proportion of 80% pyramidal cells versus 20% interneurons. In each cortical area, the neurons are fully connected (with synaptic strengths as specified below). Neurons in each cortical area of the network shown in Figure 8.1 are clustered into populations or pools.

There are two different types of pools: excitatory and inhibitory. There are two subtypes of excitatory pool, namely specific and nonselective. Specific pools are encoding, for example, the identity of the visual features. Layer V2 contains two specific pools encoding bar orientation, spatial frequency, and location. We denote these pools $S1$ and $S2$, respectively, and consider that each of them has a small nonoverlapping receptive field (i.e., they are sensitive to two different locations) and is sensitive to two different orientations/spatial frequencies, denoted by $O1$ and $O2$, respectively. Layer V4 also contains two specific pools, which we denote $S1'$ and $S2'$. Each of these pools has a larger receptive field that covers the two receptive fields considered in layer V2. We consider that the pool $S1'$ has a preferred stimulus that is the one preferred by the pool $S1$ (i.e., $O1$), and the pool $S2'$ has a preferred stimulus that is the one preferred by the pool $S2$ (i.e., $O2$). On the other hand, the stimulus $O1$ ($O2$) is a nonpreferred stimulus of pool $S2'$ ($S1'$). This is implemented by considering that the synaptic feedforward connections J_f and feedback connections J_b between $S1 - S1'$ and $S2 - S2'$ are much stronger than the weak synaptic feedforward connections K_f and feedback connections K_b between $S1 - S2'$ and $S2 - S1'$. We set $K_f = cJ_f$ and $K_b = cJ_b$, with $c = 0.1$. Each specific pool of excitatory cells contains fN_E neurons (in our simulations $f = 0.1$). In both layers, the remaining excitatory neurons do not have specific sensory inputs and are in a nonselective pool. All the inhibitory neurons are clustered into a common inhibitory pool for each module, so that there is global competition throughout each module. We assume that the synaptic coupling strengths between any two neurons in the network act as if they were established by Hebbian learning (i.e., the coupling will be strong if the pair of neurons have correlated activity and weak if they are activated in an uncorrelated way). As a consequence of this, neurons within a specific excitatory pool are mutually coupled with a strong weight $w_+ = 1.5$, and neurons in the inhibitory pool are mutually connected with an intermediate weight $w = 1$. These parameters have been studied and fixed via mean-field techniques [DR05a].

They are also connected with all excitatory neurons in the same layer with the same intermediate weight, which for excitatory-to-inhibitory connections is $w = 1$ (in both layers) and for inhibitory-to-excitatory connections is denoted by a weight w_I in layer V2 and w_I' in layer V4. Because in our model the specific V4 pools have overlapping receptive fields, while the specific V2 pools do not have overlapping receptive fields, we consider that the level of competition in V4 is higher than in V2. This is because the inhibition in both layers is local, and therefore the stronger the neighborhood relationship, then the stronger is the inhibition. Consequently, in topographically organized layers, the more overlapping of the receptive fields, then the stronger is the competition. We therefore use in our simulations $w_I = 1$ and $w_I' = 1.25$. The connection strength between two neurons in two different specific excitatory pools in the same layer is weak and given by $w_- = 1 - f(w_+ - 1)/(1 - f)$, so that the overall recurrent excitatory synaptic drive in the spontaneous state remains constant as w_+ is varied [BW01]. Neurons in a specific excitatory pool are connected to neurons in the nonselective pool in the same layer with a feedforward synaptic weight $w = 1$ and a feedback synaptic connection of weight $w_n = (-fJ_b - fK_b)/(1 - 2f) + w_-$ in layer V4 and $w'_n = (-fJ_f - fK_f)/(1-2f)+w_-$ in layer V2, and these connections normalize each layer so that the overall recurrent excitatory synaptic drive in the spontaneous state remains constant as the external intercortical connections J_f, J_b, K_f, and K_b are varied.

Each neuron receives $N_{ext} = 800$ excitatory AMPA synaptic connections from outside the network. The external inputs are given by a Poisson train of spikes with a rate of 3 Hz, consistent with the spontaneous activity observed in the cerebral cortex. The presentation of a stimulus is simulated by selectively increasing the external rates afferent to the corresponding specific population in layer V2, $\nu_{ext} = \nu_{ext} + \lambda_{in}$. Attentional biasing is also simulated by selectively increasing the external rates afferent to the corresponding specific population, $\nu_{ext} = \nu_{ext} + \lambda_{att}$, in layer V2 for spatial attention. In our simulations, we use $\lambda_{in} = 250$ Hz and $\lambda_{att} = 10$ Hz.

We consider first a detailed parameter analysis of the possible stationary states of the simplified model. We explore the behavior of the network as a function of the feedforward and feedback synaptic connections between the two cortical brain areas described in the model (i.e., as a function of J_f and J_b). With this analysis, we aim to characterize the different modes of operation of the network and their robustness, which arise from the complex dynamical interplay between the two cortical modules, with intercortical cooperation and intracortical competition mutually biasing each other.

In the standard experimental design, both stimuli are presented simultaneously. We consider this by externally exciting the two specific pools $S1$ and $S2$ simultaneously. This is done by selectively increasing the external rates afferent to both specific pools $S1$ and $S2$ in layer V2 (i.e., $\nu_{ext}^{S1} = \nu_{ext}^{S1} + \lambda_{in}$ and $\nu_{ext}^{S2} = \nu_{ext}^{S2} + \lambda_{in}$) (the superscript denotes the name of the pool). Let us denote with ν_{Si}^{noatt} the stationary values of the averaged population activity in pool Si under this condition of simultaneous presentation of both visual stimuli in the absence of attention. In order to examine the effects of attention across neurons, the experimental work computed a change measurement M in which the difference between the attended and unattended responses is scaled by the size of the unattended responses. If spatial attention is allocated to the preferred stimulus, the neural activity is enhanced. On the other hand, if spatial attention is allocated to the nonpreferred stimulus, the neural activation is partially suppressed. To consider both effects, we computed the same attentional change measurement M on all four specific pools in both cortical modules. Let us denote with ν_{Si}^{att} the stationary values of the averaged population activity in pool Si under the condition of simultaneous presentation of both visual stimuli, with spatial attention allocated to stimulus $S1$. The enhancement effect of attention on the activity of a pool S is measured by $M^S = \frac{\nu_S^{att}-\nu_S^{noatt}}{\nu_S^{noatt}}$. The experimental values reported in the literature for attentional enhancement modulation in V2 are approximately 8% and in V4 approximately 30%. On the other hand, the experimental value reported for attentional suppressive modulation in V2 is approximately 8% and in V4 approximately 25%. To consider all attentional effects in one measure M^{BC}, we define a modulation index that incorporates all these experimental quantitative values into one, which is given by

$$
\begin{aligned}
M^{BC} = 1 - \frac{1}{4}\Bigg[& \left|\frac{M^{S1} - 0.1}{0.1}\right| + \left|\frac{M^{S1'} - 0.3}{0.3}\right| + \\
& \left|\frac{M^{S2} - 0.08}{0.08}\right| + \left|\frac{M^{S2'} - 0.25}{0.25}\right| \Bigg].
\end{aligned}
\tag{8.5}
$$

The modulation index M^{BC} takes into account quantitatively all up-regu-lating and down-regulating attentional effects as observed in the experiments and is therefore a sensitive measure of the underlying competitive and cooperative dynamics that cause it. Values of M^{BC} close to 1 mean a suitable fit with the quantitative attentional modulation values observed in the experiments under all stimulation conditions and in the V2 and V4 layers.

Figure 8.2 shows the intercortical parameter exploration, plotting the attentional modulation measure M^{BC} for the stationary states as a function of the feedforward and feedback V2–V4 synaptic connections J_f and J_b. This figure shows a narrow parameter region where a delicate dynamical equilibrium between intracortical competition (in each layer) and mutual intercortical cooperation yields biased competition according to the quantitative experimental observation. This narrow region where M^{BC} is close to 1 is around the point "A" with $J_f = 1.5$ and $J_b = 0.6$. Therefore, the region of intercortical parameter space where the system shows biased competition according to the experimental modulation and response values is very narrow. This implies a delicate dynamical interplay between intercortical cooperation and intracortical competition. Furthermore, these results show that the feedback intercortical interactions (at least in the visual cortex) must be weaker (by a factor of approximately 3) than the feedforward connections, which is a frequent assumption in the neurophysiological literature but not based on quantitative analysis of the dynamics. The region at the top around the point "D" (high J_f and high J_b) corresponds to a region that we call "No Biased Competition: High Response Activity" because there is low attentional modulation (both up-regulating and down-regulating) and relatively high neural responses in both specific pools of areas V2 and V4. The region around point "B", which has higher feedback values as required for biased competition, corresponds to a dynamical attractor that we call "Overmodulation" because the attentional modulation effects are unrealistically high in spite of the fact that the level of response activity in the absence of attention is in the experimental range. There are large regions of the parameter space, which we characterize as "Weak Biased Competition",

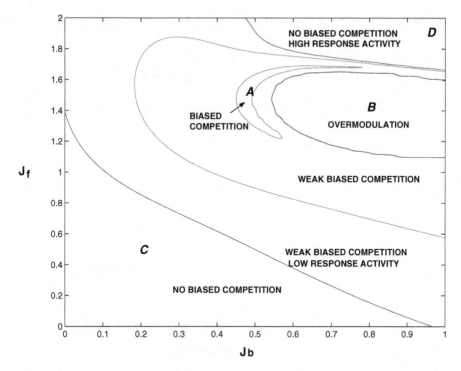

Fig. 8.2. Intercortical parameter exploration plotting the attentional modulation measure M^{BC} for the stationary states as a function of the feedforward and feedback V2–V4 synaptic connections J_f and J_b. The figure shows where the different stationary dynamical regions occur.

corresponding to a dynamical attractor that shows attentional modulation qualitatively according to biased competition but quantitatively too weak and with the normal level of neural response when attention is absent. This region is followed by another region, "Weak Biased Competition: Low Activity Response", which also shows a low level of neural response in the absence of attention. The last region, corresponding to low feedforward values and called "No Biased Competition", shows a low level of response in the absence of attention and no attentional modulation at all.

Figure 8.3 shows the nonstationary behavior of the neurodynamical activity in the full spiking and synaptic simulation of the network for the particular point "A" of the region showing biased competition. The simulation corresponds to the experimental design of Reynolds et al. [RCD99, RD99]. After a period of spontaneous activity of 100 ms without stimulation, the stimuli are presented for 250 ms. After that, the stimuli disappear again and a period of 250 ms is shown. Figure 8.3 plots the development of the firing rate activity for specific V4 neurons tuned to the preferred stimulus, showing that the attended stimulus controls the response of the neuron. The rates

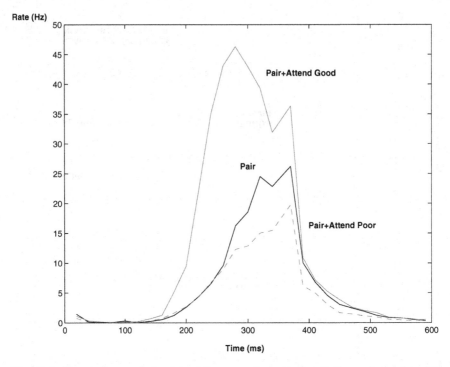

Fig. 8.3. Nonstationary behavior of the neurodynamical activity performed by the full spiking and synaptic simulation of the network for the particular point "A" of the region showing biased competition. The simulation corresponds to the experimental design of Reynolds et al. [RCD99].

were calculated by averaging the responses over 20 trials of all the neurons (80) in the pool of specific V4 neurons responding to the preferred stimulus. The line in the middle shows the response when the two stimuli are shown, a preferred (good or effective) stimulus and a nonpreferred (poor) stimulus, with attention directed away from the receptive field ("Pair" condition). The line at the top shows the response when the two stimuli are presented together, with attention directed to the good stimulus ("Pair+Attend Good" condition). An attentional enhancement is observed. The line at the bottom shows the response when the two stimuli are presented together, with attention directed to the poor stimulus ("Pair+Attend Poor" condition). An attentional suppression is observed.

8.5 Summary

We believe that theoretical and computational neuroscience provides a solid mathematical framework for investigating the basic computational principles and mechanisms underlying perceptual and cognitive brain function, such as visual attention, working memory, and the control of behavior by reward mechanisms. Neurodynamical models integrate in a unifying form evidence from functional, neurophysiological, and psychological findings. This kind of analysis is fundamental for a deep understanding in neuroscience.

In particular, we have reviewed here how attention is an emergent network phenomenon that can result from purely additive synaptic effects, nonlinear effects in the neurons, and cooperation-competition dynamics in the network, which together yield a variety of modulatory effects. The analyses presented here extend previous concepts of the role of biased competition in attention [Dun96, DD95, UN96] by providing the first analysis we know at the integrate-and-fire neuronal level, which allows the neuronal nonlinearities in the system to be explicitly modeled in order to investigate realistically the processes that underlie the apparent gain modulation effect of top-down attentional control. In the integrate-and-fire model, the competition is implemented realistically by the effects of the excitatory neurons on the inhibitory neurons and their return inhibitory synaptic connections. This is also the first integrate-and-fire analysis of top-down attentional influences in vision that explicitly models the interaction of several different brain areas (including V2, V4, IT, V3, and MT in the different simulations).

Biased competition effects are not intuitive because they result from a complex dynamical interplay that can only be analyzed with the theoretical tools and with the biologically plausible and realistic modeling elements that we assumed (i.e., realistic synaptic and spiking dynamics). Hence, this is a good example of the relevance of computational neuroscience in the analysis of experimental data.

References

[AB97]   D. Amit and N. Brunel. Model of global spontaneous activity and local structured activity during delay periods in the cerebral cortex. *Cerebral Cortex*, 7:237–252, 1997.

[BW01]   N. Brunel and X. Wang. Effects of neuromodulation in a cortical networks model of object working memory dominated by recurrent inhibition. *Journal of Computational Neuroscience*, 11:63–85, 2001.

[CD02]   S. Corchs and G. Deco. Large-scale neural model for visual attention: Integration of experimental single cell and fMRI data. *Cerebral Cortex*, 12:339–348, 2002.

[CD04]   S. Corchs and G. Deco. Feature-based attention in human visual cortex: simulation of fMRI data. *Neuroimage*, 21:36–45, 2004.

[CMDD93] L. Chelazzi, E. Miller, J. Duncan, and R. Desimone. A neural basis for visual search in inferior temporal cortex. *Nature*, 363:345–347, 1993.

[DD95]   R. Desimone and J. Duncan. Neural mechanisms of selective visual attention. *Annual Review of Neuroscience*, 8:193–222, 1995.

[DL02]   G. Deco and T.S. Lee. A unified model of spatial and object attention based on inter-cortical biased competition. *Neurocomputing*, 44–46: 775–781, 2002.

[DPZ02]   G. Deco, O. Pollatos, and J. Zihl. The time course of selective visual attention: theory and experiments. *Vision Research*, 42:2925–2945, 2002.

[DR02]   G. Deco and E.T. Rolls. Object-based visual neglect: a computational hypothesis. *European Journal of Neuroscience*, 16:1994–2000, 2002.

[DR03]   G. Deco and E.T. Rolls. Attention and working memory: a dynamical model of neuronal activity in the prefrontal cortex. *European Journal of Neuroscience*, 18:2374–2390, 2003.

[DR04]   G. Deco and E.T. Rolls. A neurodynamical cortical model of visual attention and invariant object recognition. *Vision Research*, 44:621–644, 2004.

[DR05a]   G. Deco and E.T. Rolls. Neurodynamics of biased competition and cooperation for attention: a model with spiking neurons. *Journal of Neurophysiology*, 94:295–313, 2005.

[DR05b]   G. Deco and E.T. Rolls. Synaptic and spiking dynamics underlying reward reversal in the orbitofrontal cortex. *Cerebral Cortex*, 15:15–30, 2005.

[DRH04]   G. Deco, E.T. Rolls, and B. Horwitz. 'What' and 'where' in visual working memory: a computational neurodynamical perspective for integrating fMRI and single-neuron data. *Journal of Cognitive Neuroscience*, 16:683–701, 2004.

[Dun96]   J. Duncan. Cooperating brain systems in selective perception and action. In T. Inui and J.L. McClelland, editors, *In Attention and Performance XVI*, pages 549–578. MIT Press, Cambridge, MA, 1996.

[Gro87]   S. Grossberg. Competitive learning: from interactive activation to adaptive resonance. *Cognitive Science*, 11:23–63, 1987.

[IK01]   L. Itti and C. Koch. Computational modelling of visual attention. *Nature Reviews Neuroscience*, 2:194–203, 2001.

[MD85]   J. Moran and R. Desimone. Selective attention gates visual processing in the extrastriate cortex. *Science*, 229:782–784, 1985.

[MR81]   J.L. McClelland and D.E. Rumelhart. An interactive activation model of context effects in letter perception. part i: an account of basic findings. *Psychological Review*, 88:375–407, 1981.

[RCD99]   J. Reynolds, L. Chelazzi, and R. Desimone. Competitive mechanisms subserve attention in macaque areas V2 and V4. *Journal of Neuroscience*, 19:1736–1753, 1999.

[RD99]   J. Reynolds and R. Desimone. The role of neural mechanisms of attention in solving the binding problem. *Neuron*, 24:19–29, 1999.

[RD02]   E.T. Rolls and G. Deco. *Computational Neuroscience of Vision*. Oxford University Press, Oxford, 2002.

[RD03]   J. Reynolds and R. Desimone. Interacting roles of attention and visual saliency in V4. *Neuron*, 37:853–863, 2003.

[SADS04]   M. Szabo, R. Almeida, G. Deco, and M. Stetter. Cooperation and biased competition model can explain attentional filtering in the prefrontal cortex. *European Journal of Neuroscience*, 19:1969–1977, 2004.

[Tuc88]   H. Tuckwell. *Introduction to Theoretical Neurobiology*. Cambridge University Press, Cambridge, 1988.

[UN96]   M. Usher and E. Niebur. Modelling the temporal dynamics of IT neurons in visual search: a mechanism for top-down selective attention. *Journal of Cognitive Neuroscience*, 8:311–327, 1996.

Part IV

Bioinformatics and DNA Computing

GeneSim™: Intelligent IT Platform for the Biomedical World

Martin Stetter[1], Andreas Nägele[1,2], and Mathäus Dejori[1]

[1] Siemens Corporate Technology, Information & Communications, Munich,
Germany, `mathaeus.dejori@siemens.com`, `stetter@siemens.com`
[2] Technical University of Munich, Garching, Germany
`andreas.naegele.ext@siemens.com`

Summary. Today's biomedical research and practice operate in a world where data
and knowledge sources are ubiquitous, complex, and diverse. At the same time, we
face the challenge to provide new, innovative, and targeted postblockbuster drugs
and to combat the health care cost explosion by increasing its quality at reduced
expense. Bioinformatics and computational systems biology exploit intelligent and
learning computing technologies to integrate heterogeneous data, to extract the biomedical information hidden in the data, to discover knowledge about normal and
abnormal life processes, and to transform this knowledge into value added for pharmaceutical products and health care delivery. GeneSim™, a learning technology
platform dedicated to supporting genomic and molecular medicine, is introduced
as an example of how intelligent computing can help boost the biomedical world.
Based on a context-sensitive knowledge base, GeneSim provides solutions for learning and predictive modeling of genotype-phenotype relationships, molecular pathways, aspects of cellular function, and their relationships with macroscopic disease
states. Topological pathway analysis enables researchers to hunt molecular targets
of drugs and contrast agents for molecular imaging. In silico drug application and
RNAi (ribonucleic acid interference) experiments can be carried out to identify disease mechanisms and to assess the putative therapeutic efficiency and side effects of
drugs, eventually reaching a "kill early" decision for investigational drugs. Pharma-
cogenomics is supported to stratify patients according to the genetic and molecular
state of their disease, allowing for an individualized therapy with reduced side effects.

9.1 Challenges of the Biomedical World

The demographic change toward an aging population of developed nations
is one of the megatrends of the 21st century. As the health care costs for
persons above 65 years in the United States and other developed countries
are estimated to be 3–5 times greater than for those younger than 65 [JO02],
a considerable growth in health care spending will challenge public programs
and health insurance. Adverse drug events (ADEs), which are caused by errors

in diagnosis and/or therapy and range all the way from allergic reactions to death, are seen as a major cause of avoidable health care expenditures [Ins99]. In the United States, over 2 million ADEs could be prevented and about \$4.5 billion could be saved per year [HBB+05] by applying the right drug at the right dose for the right patient. For example, the most common medication error as a cause of ADEs is wrong dosing [AHR01]. It has been shown that a pharmacogenomic approach, in which patients are stratified into extensive and poor drug metabolizers by genotyping of the drug metabolizer enzyme CYP2D6, has the potential to reduce ADEs. More generally, prevention and early detection of disease, differentiated diagnostics, and individualized therapy are seen as major cornerstones of increased health care quality at reduced cost. Molecular medicine, which makes use of a mechanistic understanding of diseases and the quantification of the relationships between molecular causes and phenotypic outcomes, is a crucial determinant of improved health care delivery.

The growing demand for improved quality of health care also imposes pressure on the pharma- and red biotechnology industries (red biotechnology involves medical processes such as getting organisms to produce new drugs). A large number and variety of specific and selective biomarkers as surrogate endpoints will be required, which provide the means for differentiated and accurate molecular diagnostics and yield stratifications of patients into therapeutically relevant groups. Drugs will have to be tailored to these patient subgroups, which are characterized by different molecular profiles and disease mechanisms.

In the postgenomic era, since the completion of the sequencing of the human genome [But01, HGP03], biomedical research has focused on a functional understanding of the life processes encoded in the DNA sequence. As a consequence, a rapidly growing body of biomedical data, information, and knowledge has accumulated, which has the potential to trigger quantum leaps in molecular medicine, pharmacology, and biotechnology. With the above-mentioned growth and diversification of the biomedical data landscape, various IT platforms and repositories have been built up, and it is easy to understand that they are gaining importance in all fields of biomedical research and practice.

By 2006, a considerable fraction of the estimated 30,000 human genes had been functionally annotated in a structured way such as in the Gene Ontology (GO) [GO06]. Other public repositories have been designed to store information about genetic variations including, single-nucleotide polymorphisms (SNPs) [ESN06] and haplotypes [IHP06], information about gene expression and the mechanism-dependent activation of genes [GEO06, Arr06], protein function [SPD06], and metabolic pathways [KEG06], just to mention a few. Millions of scientific publications related to clinical research, genomics, and proteomics have been archived [EPM06] in a searchable way and are being structured by the polyhierarchical thesaurus MeSH [MSH06]. Over 40 biomedical repositories have been combined by the National Center for

Biotechnology Information [NCB06] and can be accessed by the meta search engine Entrez [ELS06]. The rapid pace of postgenomic R&D and the resulting growth of data and knowledge, however, increasingly transform the landscape of public repositories themselves into a jungle that is difficult to explore even for experts. But this is not the end! Whereas most of the mentioned efforts and initiatives still try to uncover the functional principles of a single "average" human genome, the "thousand dollar genome" (i.e., the affordable full sequencing of each patient's complete genome for reasons of improved prevention, diagnosis, and therapy) is already being discussed [SMVC04]. When turned into reality, individual whole genome sequencing will cause a data avalanche of a so far unseen order of magnitude, only an extremely small fraction of which will be of clinical value in any given disease context.

The molecular biological and molecular medical knowledge accumulating in the postgenomic era can form the basis required to tackle the challenges of molecular medicine, pharmacology and biotechnology. To achieve this goal, however, it is absolutely crucial to be able to select which information is relevant and should be retrieved for a given problem, disease, and context: there is an urgent need for IT solutions that discover, retrieve, and make available the right pieces of knowledge at the right time around the right topic, ranked by their relevance for a given problem.

9.2 GeneSim^{TM} Platform

Intelligent knowledge management used in a learning framework can provide efficient and effective workflows to navigate in the biomedical world. Here we introduce GeneSim^{TM}, a learning and integrating IT platform designed to support molecular medicine, biomarkers, and drug discovery [DSS03].

Most of the existing repositories and platforms collect and manage information about biomedical entities. The term entity is used to refer to genes, RNA, proteins, metabolites, or other biomolecules in the molecular domain and to biomarkers, diseases, or other phenotypic features in the macroscopic domain. Links between different entities are often provided as well but are considered as additional, second-order information.

Life processes, in contrast, are dominated by interactions. The web of mutual biochemical interactions between DNA, RNA, and proteins forms the basis for the complexity of the genetic network that controls all life processes [Bro99, SDD03]. Many complex diseases, such as cancer, are seen today to arise from accumulating perturbations of cellular molecular interaction networks rather than from the malfunction of individual key molecules [HW00]. In pharmacological research and molecular medicine, it is important to know the links between molecular-biological configurations and macroscopic outcomes. For example, a genetic predisposition for disease or for an adverse drug event is given by a link between the genotype—typically one or a number of SNPs—of a patient and the outcome of diagnosis or therapy. Whether or not some blood concentration of a protein or a number of proteins serves as a good biomarker or *surrogate endpoint* for some disease depends on whether or not there exists a reliable strong link between the two. Whether or not a new investigational drug shows strong or weak side effects depends on which pathways in the web of the genetic network of treated cells it affects.

GeneSim adopts the high importance of interactions and links as an IT architecture: the central concept of GeneSim is a relationship. In other words, the platform manages knowledge in terms of relationships, which link together entities. Figure 9.1 illustrates the general structure of GeneSim.

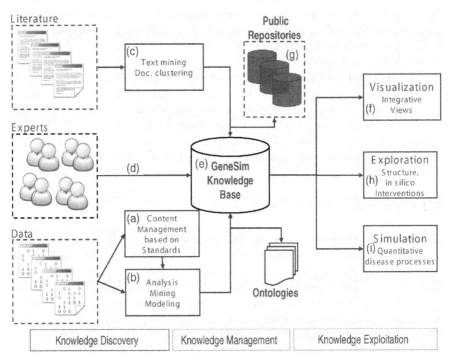

Fig. 9.1. Outline of the structure of GeneSim. The central part is the GeneSim knowledge base, which stores information about relationships between molecular and/or phenotypic entities by using a specialized ontology (e). Information about the entities themselves is provided by links to public information (g) and literature repositories (c). Information about relationships arises from knowledge discovery in biomedical data (a, b) or directly from human experts (d). Various services, including visualization (f), exploration (h), and simulation (i), can operate on the knowledge base.

The central part of the platform is a knowledge base that stores known relationships between entities together with information associated with these relationships. Information about the relations is integrated from various sources: it can be automatically learned from data in a knowledge discovery setting, can be explicitly input or curated by human experts, and can be enriched by information from the literature by means of text mining (Figure 9.1, left part). The web of relationships is stored in a structured and quantitative way and can be operated on by computational tools. It forms the basis of a number of services that allow the user to interactively navigate in the knowledge base (visualization), to explore the structure and function of the network of relationships (exploration), and to simulate biochemical scenarios (simulation). Access to GeneSim as well as the communication between components is based on web services for maximum flexibility.

9.2.1 Data Analysis, Mining, and Modeling

The platform provides a number of statistical analysis and machine-learning modules for knowledge discovery from biomedical categorical or numerical data. Irrespective of the raw data type, most molecular biological, pharmaceutical, and clinical measurements are usually subject to feature extraction. Features are then often digitized into categorical values. For example, genotypic information is usually directly given as a set of alleles of a gene carried by the subject under consideration, resulting in categories of genotype. Gene expression levels in microarray measurements are usually detected by fluorescence microscopy. Absolute or relative expression levels are extracted by platform-dependent algorithms, and the resulting numerical values are often categorized, for example into overexpressed, normally expressed, and underexpressed. Clinical lab data are often provided in numeric format (e.g., blood concentrations of a protein or cell counts in tissues). Also, clinical data (blood pressure, tumor size, etc.) are often categorized into diagnostically and therapeutically relevant intervals.

Gene expression measurements, especially from high-throughput microarray experiments, to date represent the most ubiquitous data source in molecular biology. GeneSim includes a web service based content management system for gene expression data, BioChipDB, which enables the user to upload, store, retrieve, and download data from high-throughput microarray experiments as well as serial analysis (SAGE) data (Figure 9.1a). The system is largely based on the established standard MIAME [BHQ+01]. Submission is supported for the commercial formats Affymetrix and GenPix as well as for academic formats GEO and SMD [BST+05, BAD+05]. Communication and export occurs via MAGE-ML. BioChipDB provides content-sensitive links to external repositories, including Affymetrix, Entrez, and GO, where applicable, and provides a direct interface to the Affymetrix measurement platforms. Besides local data storage in BioChipDB, data from external databases can be accessed as well. In particular, linkage of gene expression data with other data modalities is flexibly possible in this way.

The platform provides a number of state of the art statistical techniques for initial screening and visualization of molecular biological data (Figure 9.1b). Statistical tests, including the t-test, and ANOVA, and other methods such as enrichment analysis, PCA, and false discovery rate, allow extraction of biomolecules that act differently under different conditions. Conditions are typically phenotypic features or different interventions, such as healthy vs. disease, early vs. late disease, stress vs. normal, etc. The extent of differential activity can be statistically quantified by the p-value or related measures. Moreover, one- or two-dimensional clustering techniques can be used to group together biomolecules, phenotypes (e.g., patients), or both by means of the similarity of their measurement profiles. The results of any analysis are kept in a general analysis results repository together with a link to the data and the history of the analysis performed. Finally, strong coincidences between biomolecules, or between biomolecules and a phenotype, can be fed into the GeneSim knowledge base GeneSimKB as relationships.

The central tool of the data-driven knowledge discovery engine is the GeneSim model learner (Figure 9.1b). It provides machine-learning tools that extract a web of mutual statistical relationships directly from datasets. The tool incorporates extensions for learning Bayesian networks [DS03, DS04, DSS04] as well as Markov networks. All techniques learn from data to which entities are likely to be linked by a relationship and in which way one entity affects another. They are powerful enough to describe any order of collaborative, competitive, or mixed influences of a set of entities on a target entity. For example, the joint effect of a number of genetic variations as a common risk factor for a disease can be extracted like this, even if any single genetic variation has little or no predictive power. Likewise, molecular origins of a certain disease can be identified even if the activities (e.g., gene expression levels) of more than one biomolecule are contributing to it. The common strength of the platform's machine-learning approaches is that they can extract links between any kind of data, all the way from genetic gene/protein expression over lab data up to clinical diagnostic, longitudinal, and behavioral data. Again, all analysis results are stored together with links to the original data, and extracted relationships are fed into the knowledge base.

Bayesian techniques in GeneSim are equipped with a number of key differentiating features. One branch of features includes a framework that enables assessment of confidence levels for extracted relationships by multiple criteria, including nonparametric bootstrap and dimensional bootstrap on feature partial directed acyclic graphs [DS04]. A second feature is the possibility to learn even very large interaction networks, far beyond 10,000 nodes, which is of particular importance in the world of high-dimensional molecular-biological and biomedical data. Also Markov models have been developed further according to the special needs of the field: learning decomposable models are used [DSTS04], which describe the data in terms of interacting functional modules instead of individual entities. Taking into account the fact that many biomolecules act cooperatively as groups (e.g., protein complexes, transcriptional regulation of gene expression, protein degradation, etc.) or functional modules, decomposable models are centered around this concept of modularity. In addition, the technique is able to deal with continuous data in a nonparametric way.

9.2.2 Text Management

A second information source that enters the GeneSimKB is encoded in scientific articles, which offer a huge body of knowledge about biomedical relationships. Relationships are often validated by experimental methods and therefore represent a reliable information source. However, usually each document provides statements about a restricted problem space only. GeneSim provides support that helps link the space of scientific literature to the space of topics being investigated by a user. When entering results from data-driven analysis to the GeneSim knowledge base, one or several publications of the group that had generated the data are linked to these results. Hence, on access to the knowledge base, either locally stored or publicly available text documents are provided, making the rich source of biomedical literature easily accessible. However, the large volume of articles available online generates additional complications for their interpretation. For example searching for the keyword "breast cancer" in PubMed retrieves 153,739 documents,[1] which makes it difficult to extract the relevant information and necessitates sophisticated text mining techniques [KAV05] to support the information extraction task.

GeneSim addresses this information overload by supporting document clustering based on textual features and additional meta-information (Figure 9.1c). As a result, to each entity or relationship queried by the user, a small cluster of—often only five to ten—scientific documents highly relevant to it is provided. The text management system also offers named entity recognition (NER), a text mining technique that learns to automatically recognize terms of a certain kind in full text. For example, the NER module can be trained to detect and highlight all names of genes, proteins, and diseases. Like this, the user can retrieve a number of documents related to, say, a protein-protein interaction, and can automatically find highlighted in the texts of the associated documents which other entities have been discussed in relation to the proteins considered primarily.

9.2.3 Human Experts

The success of a biomedical knowledge base as a tool for biomedical R&D relies on the quality of the provided knowledge derived either from raw data or from unstructured text as described above. However, as biological measurements and biomedical text are "noisy" and incomplete, the derived knowledge might be uncertain and incomplete as well. Beliefs and statements from domain experts (e.g. clinicians or lab investigators) can improve the

---

[1] Search done on October 10, 2006.

quality of the existing knowledge base and can furthermore provide new knowledge. The GeneSim platform offers the classical option to manually enter curated relationships by a human expert (Figure 9.1d) if allowed by the access control system. Entry of expert knowledge is supported by the GeneSimWeb portal solution, which also provides the general front end for navigation across data and knowledge bases. The structure of the information is guided by the proprietary ontology, which assures a consistent representation of knowledge. Together with the relationship itself, the user can also enter additional information, such as the level of confidence in this information, quantitative information, and links to documents and literature.

Together with credit-scoring mechanisms for contributions made, human experts can thus improve the quality of the knowledge base, which in turn leverages their own work, a win-win situation. Evidence for the positive effect of massive collaboration on the quality of knowledge bases is coming from different projects such as, for example, Open Cyc [Ope06] or Open Mind [Sto94], or from biomedical data repositories such as Geo or ArrayExpress [GEO06, Arr06], where people are encouraged to upload their own measured gene expression data.

9.2.4 GeneSim Knowledge Base: An Example

GeneSimKB (Figure 9.1e) stores information about relationships between entities at three different levels: the logic/semantic level, the probabilistic level, and the biochemical level (see Figure 9.2). Entities are matched between all three layers, where possible. In contrast, the type of knowledge about the relationships is different in each layer.

The semantic level (Figure 9.2, top) stores relationships that reflect some common sense from the corresponding biological or medical community. Statements can link all kinds of entities. Typically, knowledge at the semantic level is entered by a human expert based on his or her own knowledge or after consulting the scientific literature. It is qualitative and fragmentary by nature, but typically represents experimentally validated information. By default, the knowledge is also qualitative by nature, but can be enriched by annotations such as confidence levels. For example, it might be commonly accepted that a certain variation of "gene a" leads to a genetic predisposition for "disease a". At the same time, it is known that "disease a" can be diagnosed with some sensitivity and specificity by the outcome of "blood value a".

The semantic level is complemented by the probabilistic level, where knowledge about relations discovered from data is stored (Figure 9.2, middle). Typically, results from the GeneSim model learner and from statistical tests are entered here. In contrast to the semantic level, probabilistic knowledge is uncertain by definition, reflecting the variation and noise present in measured data, but the networks of relationships entered here usually cover a large number of entities and relationships. In addition, they can bridge the gap

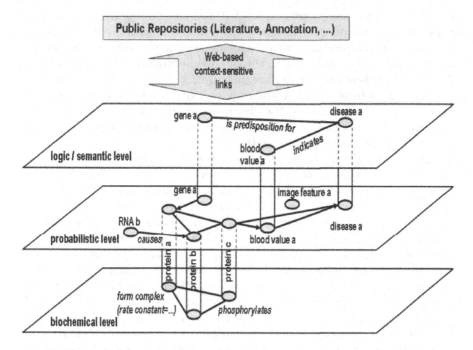

Fig. 9.2. Three-layer vertical integration of the knowledge representation scheme of GeneSimKB. Information about relationships is kept coherently at the biochemical, the probabilistic, and the semantic levels. Coherence is schematically represented by vertical cylinders between nodes. Entities are denoted in boldface, relationships in italics. For details, see the text.

between the microscopic molecular, the mesoscopic laboratory, and the macroscopic clinical worlds by means of quantitative probabilistic relationships. For example, one might wish to know by which mechanism "gene a" affects "disease a" in order to develop a more accurate diagnostic test for the disease or in order to discover molecular targets for treatment with stronger effects and reduced side effects. Form the statistical level, it becomes apparent that "gene a" affects the activity of "protein a", which is part of a triplet of "proteins a, b, and c". This triplet, executed by "protein c", causes both the change in the "blood value a" and "disease a" itself. As a consequence, it is reasonable to test whether the co-occurrence of all three proteins (a, b, c) might be a better diagnostic test or biomarker than the established blood test. Finally, it might be detected that only one genetic variant of "gene a" produces a strongly active "protein a", which might explain the mechanism by which the risk for disease a is much higher for one allele of "gene a" than for the other. In this example, it is further discovered that high levels of "RNA b" reliably cause an increase of "protein b" activity but have no other known effect. This suggests, that a drug that silences "RNA b", as could be done by suitable small interfering RNA [DT04], would deactivate the protein triplet (a,b,c), and thereby interrupt the pathogenic pathway from "gene a" to "disease a", but probably would not cause strong side effects. This process of propagation of an intervention through the network and calculation of the possible effects is referred to as the exploration of "in silico what-if scenarios". It is important to note that inference in the web of relationships, which has been formulated explicitly in the illustrative example here, is actually done automatically and quantitatively by means of probabilistic inference with the GeneSim explorer (see the next section).

The third layer is the biochemical level. It provides the basis for the quantitative simulation of biochemical reaction networks. The knowledge stored in this layer focuses on the molecular-biological and eventually meso-scopic scales of description, and investigated networks are usually small in size. However, this level is the only one to allow a direct analysis of biochemical cellular processes and the simulation of effects of biochemical intervention. Knowledge at this level is typically entered by a human expert or is extracted from the literature. In the example outlined here, the biochemical mechanism by which proteins "a, b, c" cooperate to cause "disease a" is to be investigated. Assume that the expert knows that proteins "a" and "b" form a complex with certain reaction constants and that only this complex can act as a kinase. This kinase attaches a phosphate group to a target enzyme—here "protein c"—and thereby transforms this protein into its active, pathogenic form. Having set up this reaction network, we wish to explore whether or not silencing of "RNA b" could be an effective therapy for "disease a". For example, the extent to which the production rate of "protein b" needs to be reduced in order to effectively deactivate the disease-relevant pathway can be explored.

9.2.5 Visualization, Exploration and Simulation Tools

Visualization

In general, the web of mutual relationships stored in GeneSimKB is large, dense, of different quality and level of quantification, and originates from different sources. The purpose of the services mentioned is to support the user in making efficient use of the knowledge stored in GeneSimKB. Having in mind an interaction network consisting of hundreds to thousands of entities and thousands to tens of thousands of relationships, it is obvious that visualization features are needed that allow different summarizing views on that network. GeneSim provides an integrative visualization engine (Figure 9.1f) that focuses on a network view of the relationship web: entities are identified with nodes and relationships with edges of a graph. The views provided are sensitive to the quality of knowledge available. For example, if relationships originate from pairwise statistical tests, a correlation network is shown (e.g., Figure 9.6), whereas a network from statistical models is visualized as a partially directed graph (e.g., Figure 9.7). Where available, additional information is provided as well; for example, confidence levels are assigned to statistically extracted relationships. On mouse-click, the nodes provide context-sensitive links to internal and/or external repositories, providing further information (e.g., literature, annotation) about the corresponding entity (e.g., SNP, gene, protein, lab value or disease; see Figure 9.1g and Figure 9.8). The most useful respective repositories are automatically recognized and provided to the user. Where possible, information about relationships from external sources is also included in the web and can be followed up interactively. The integrative visualization engine also supports the presentation of results obtained from the GeneSim explorer and operates as its graphical user interface.

Exploration

The GeneSim explorer focuses on the quantitative statistical exploitation of entity-relationship networks (Figure 9.1h). It automatically calculates predictions on the basis of the causal and/or Markov graphical probabilistic models stored in the knowledge base (predictive modeling). More than one model about any given topic is usually present, and these model networks were obtained from more than one source. Predictions using the GeneSim explorer are obtained by averaging over all predictive models. In this sense, the outcomes reflect the "common sense" of a whole set of different knowledge sources (e.g., different studies from different institutes). It is worth noting that this approach also deals with uncertain or conflicting information in a coherent way: by averaging the model, the confidence in information that conflicts in different models is decreased, while consistent information reaches a high level of confidence. Different models can also be weighted differently if further information about their credibility or reliability is available. For the examples shown here, however, we did not differentiate between information sources according to their quality.

In essence, the explorer enables one to interactively conduct "in silico what-if" scenarios. The user can apply an intervention to one or a group of entities. For example, a genetic variation can be fixed to a certain allele, meaning that the disease mechanisms for a patient group with a certain genotype are being investigated. Also, gene or protein expressions can be kept constant at a certain level, corresponding to a biological knock-out, RNA-interference, or transfection experiment. Similarly, a disease subtype might be specified to explore how this subtype differs from other subtypes. Based on these interventions, the explorer determines to what extent other entities in the network will be affected by these interventions. In particular, this enables the researcher (i) to assess the selectivity and sensitivity of a biomarker candidate, (ii) to explore the effects and side effects of a drug application, and (iii) to analyze the strengths and origins of a genotype-phenotype association on a large scale. In other words, a very large (combinatorial) number of interventions can be tested in an exhaustive search with the goal of finding an optimal drug candidate, biomarker, or genotype-phenotype association.

To quantify the strength of the effect of an intervention E, the *intervention score*

$$S(E,t) = \begin{cases} \frac{P(t|E)-P(t)}{1-P(t)} & P(t|E) > P(t) \\ \frac{P(t|E)-P(t)}{P(t)} & \text{otherwise} \end{cases} \qquad (9.1)$$

for an observable t given intervention E is defined [DS04]. The observables t can be the states of an entity or a set of entities or a quantity derived therefrom, such as a user-specified drug-effect or side-effect measure. $P(t)$ denotes the likelihood of the state t without intervention, whereas $P(t|E)$ is the likelihood of t under intervention E. The intervention score is in the range $[-1, 1]$, representing a probabilistic score that corresponds to the normalized increase or decrease of the probability for the variable state t caused by the intervention E. If the visualization engine is used in the context of predictive modeling, the marginal probabilities of the states of each entity are shown as a pie chart centered at the corresponding node (see Figure 9.3).

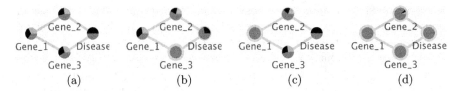

(a)   (b)   (c)   (d)

Fig. 9.3. Small example network (a) with three genes and their effect on a disease under several different interventions: overexpression of gene *Gene_3* (b), overexpression of gene *Gene_1* (c) and combined over-expression of genes *Gene_1* and *Gene_3* (d).

When an intervention has been imposed, the resulting posterior state probabilities are shown and the nodes are surrounded by a colored border, the thickness of which encodes the corresponding interventional score. The score is calculated for each state of a node. The maximum absolute value of all scores for one node is illustrated by the thickness of the border. By applying this method over and over again for a large number of interventions, we can generate a score-ranked list of potential origins for a phenotypic effect.

Example

We demonstrate the general procedure of modeling interventions on the basis of a very small example network consisting of three genes (*Gene_1*, *Gene_2*, *Gene_3*) and a phenotypic variable (*Disease*) representing a disease. This network, shown in Figure 9.3a, models the underlying regulatory relationships between the genes and their relations to the phenotypic effect *Disease*. The network structure supposes a direct influence of *Gene_2* and *Gene_3* on *Disease*, whereas *Gene_1* has only a regulatory influence on *Gene_2* and *Gene_3*. The visualization engine displays the marginal probabilities for the different activation states encoded in the toy dataset as a pie chart for each node. For the gene nodes, the "dark grey" sector denotes the fraction overexpressed, the "light grey" sector the fraction underexpressed, and the "black" sector the fraction of normal expressed samples. For the binary node *Disease*, the "dark grey" sector denotes the probability for gastric cancer.

One goal of modeling interventions is the identification of potential causative disorders in gene expression leading to a disease. Let us first model such an intervention by forcing gene *Gene_3* to the level *overexpressed*. Figure 9.3b shows the global effect on the other genes and the disease, quantitatively indicated by the thickness of each node's circular ("bright grey" in Figure 9.3) border, which reflects the interventional score. A comparison of the pie chart of the original probability distribution of *Disease* (Figure 9.3a) with its intervened counterpart (Figure 9.3b) suggests that a high expression of *Gene_2* has a promoting impact on the disease. Whereas a change of *Gene_1* alone has virtually no influence on the disease probability (Figure 9.3c), the combined overexpression of *Gene_1* and *Gene_3* has an impact even higher than *Gene_3* alone (Figure 9.3d). This example illustrates the capabilities of modeling interventions based on Bayesian networks, namely simulating the effect of an intervention on genes over a cascade of relationships with other genes in between.

Simulation

Ab initio calculations of the dynamics in molecular interaction networks, either free or under external influence, can be conducted by the GeneSim simulator (Figure 9.1i). The simulator is an agent-based environment that automatically constructs a set of elementary reaction-kinetic equations from a list of molecules, external influences, and biochemical interaction specifications. The framework treats transcriptional regulation, any order enzymatic reactions, multiple competitive and/or cooperative binding, secretion, and interfaces to macroscopic quantities in a unified way. What-if scenarios in small-to-medium interaction networks can be simulated quantitatively with a minimum of approximations. The next section provides a real-world example: the exploration of molecular mechanisms involved in gastric cancer. The example illustrates the modes of operation of GeneSim explorer, a platform-independent Java application that operates on the basis of the GeneSimKB.

9.3 Exemplifying Knowledge Discovery Workflow

Here we exemplify the way different GeneSim components work by describing a typical workflow (Figure 9.4) that aims at discovering new aspects of a complex disease, namely gastric cancer.

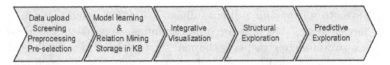

Fig. 9.4. Example workflow for knowledge discovery and exploitation.

The study proceeds from a gene expression dataset [HTT+02] that is uploaded to the BioChipDB repository. Initial screening results in a preselection of genes and phenotypic variables included for further study. From this subgroup, Bayesian networks are obtained by structure learning and yield a set of relationships to be stored in the knowledge base. The example focuses on the use of the GeneSim explorer, where different network views on that knowledge and a predictive model scenario are carried out.

9.3.1 Preprocessing and Visualization of Microarray Data

The study starts from a gastric cancer dataset with 30 patients and 7.129 genes [HTT+02] containing the expression profiles of 8 noncancerous gastric tissues and 22 primary human advanced gastric cancer tissues. Not all genes measured by the 7.129 probes are involved in the disease processes to be investigated here; hence genes that are highly differentially expressed between healthy and cancerous tissues are preselected. Out of the 7.129 measured genes, those 101 genes that best differentiate between the two phenotype states were selected using Student's t-test and were accepted for further analysis. The gene expression levels of the final dataset (101 genes × 30 samples) were first normalized to a gene-wise mean value of zero and unity standard deviation and then discretized to three levels (overexpressed, unchanged and underexpressed) by using the gene-wise negative and positive standard deviations of the normalized expression levels as thresholds for underexpression and overexpression.

Figure 9.5 shows the expression levels of the 15 genes (rows) with the highest differential expression across the 30 patients (columns).

The phenotypic state of a measured sample is marked by a colored label on the bottom of each sample (column). A "black" label denotes a measurement of a healthy tissue and a "grey" label a measurement of a cancer tissue. The names of the measured genes are given on the right-hand side of each row that contains the expression levels. The expression levels are color coded: "black" indicates an unchanged state of the expression level, "bright grey" an underexpressed gene, and "darker grey" an overexpressed gene.

Following statistical testing and gene preselection, a first network view using the visualization engine can be performed to screen the dependencies present in the data. The visualization engine provides a graphical view of correlations between genes based on expression measurements. The correlation coefficient is commonly used for clustering the expression profiles and/or array

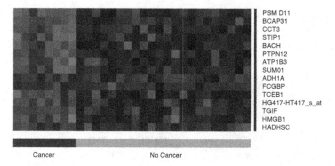

Fig. 9.5. Expression profiles for the 15 highest differentially expressed genes with respect to gastric cancer across 30 samples. "Black" indicates an unchanged state of the expression level, "bright grey" areas denote an underexpressed gene, and "darker grey" an overexpressed gene. Each sample is annotated with its phenotypic state, which is color coded at the bottom (black denotes healthy and grey gastric cancer).

profiles according to their similarity. Motivated by the assumption that genes with similar activity profiles have similar genetic or biological properties, clustering leads to a grouping of biologically similar genes. State of the art two-dimensional clustering based on the Pearson correlation coefficient, as used also in the original publication [HTT$^+$02], is provided by the visualization engine.

In addition to clustering, the visualization engine supports a network-centered view on the correlation structure. For that purpose, each gene is represented as a node in a network, connected by edges that represent the strength of the pairwise correlation coefficients of genes according to their expression data. The GeneSim explorer allows one to define a threshold for the correlation coefficient such that only edges coding for correlations above this threshold are displayed. The correlation network for the gastric cancer data with a threshold of 0.76 for the strength of the correlation coefficient is shown in Figure 9.6.

At the bottom right area of the figure, one can see a group of three nodes, representing the highly correlated genes *COL4A1* and *COL4A2*. Gene *COL4A2* appears twice in the clique because its expression level was measured by two different probes on the microarray. Using this graphical presentation of correlation between genes, and with the ability to dynamically choose a threshold for the coefficient, one can quickly obtain an overview about similarities in expression profiles and therefore about assumed biological functional proximity.

9.3.2 Learning a Network Model

Pairwise correlation analysis can account neither for statistics of higher order as seen in relationships between multiple (more than two) entities nor causal

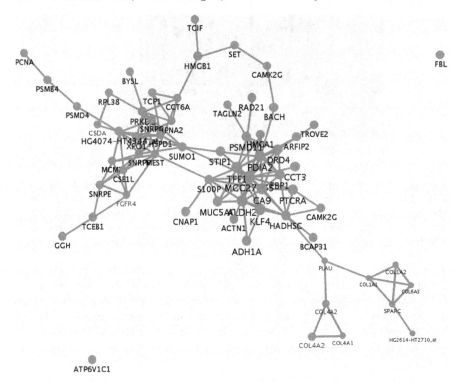

Fig. 9.6. Correlation network of the 101 selected gastric cancer genes. Edges represent a strong Pearson correlation between the expression profiles of a pair of genes that exceeds a threshold of 0.76 for the minimum absolute value of the coefficient.

influences. Therefore, a full statistical model is learned from the data by the GeneSim model learner. The dataset is comprised of the 101 preselected genes plus the phenotypic disease state (healthy or cancer) for each sample. In the resulting graphical model, each of the 101 genes is represented as a single node in the graph. This part of the graph represents the molecular part of the relationship web. The single node corresponding to the disease state, marked by the binary variable *Gastric_Cancer*, reflects the macroscopic, phenotypic part of the relationship web. The task of the model learner is to extract the network of relationships between these nodes as well as their characteristics from the data. Here the structures and parameters of a set of 40 networks have been learned for reasons of multiple robustness testing. As a result, the model learner yields a set of statistical relationships among the gene nodes and between genes and the disease node. In contrast to any pure pairwise correlations, these relationships can bind multiple nodes together because the learned statistical data model captures statistics of any order. The set of resulting relationships is stored as a so-called feature partial directed acyclic graph (fPDAG) [DSS04], comprised of a set of conditional probability tables, in the GeneSimKB.

9.3.3 Integrative Visualization

Figure 9.7 shows how the set of relations found by the model learner are displayed in the network view of the visualization engine.

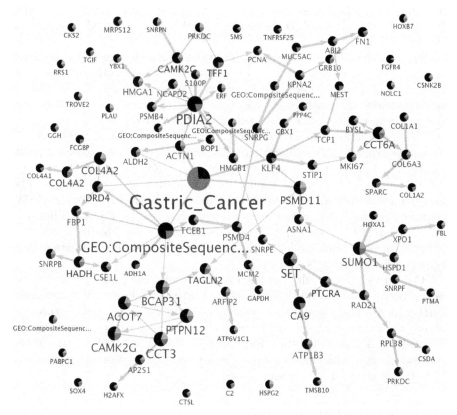

Fig. 9.7. Structure of relationships for the network containing 101 preselected genes and the disease state *Gastric_Cancer*, as shown by the visualization engine. The thickness of each line indicates the statistical confidence of the corresponding relationship. The direction of an arrow indicates a learned causal influence rather than a pure associative relation.

The set of gene and disease nodes (spots) is interconnected by a set of statistical relationships, indicated by grey lines. The thickness of each line encodes the confidence level, on the basis of the data, in the presence of the corresponding relationship. Arrows, where present, indicate a causal influence of one entity on the other rather than a pure statistical association.

The graphical user interface (GUI) allows the user to specify a minimum confidence threshold that can be adjusted, suppressing all relationships with confidence levels below this threshold.

The view on the structure of the network can help identify salient local network structures. For example, some genes maintain a particularly high number of links with other genes, referred to as their "betweenness centrality" or node degree. The node degree is encoded in the size of each node in the visualization. It has been discussed that the node degree can serve as an important indicator for the general importance of a molecule for cellular function [BO04, SDSG05]. For example, gene *PDIA2* is classified as important by this criterion.

In addition, the network-centric visualization provides an intuitive summary of the genetic pathways that directly or indirectly influence the disease state. For example, *PDIA2* has no strong direct link to the disease node; however, three other genes, namely *PSMD11*, *KLF4*, and *ACTN1*, are strongly related to gastric cancer, indicated by highly confident edges in Figure 9.7. This prediction matches well the GO annotation that annotates *KLF4* as a repressor of cell proliferation (GO:0008285). The oncogenic property of *ACTN1* is indicated by its GO annotation (GO:0051271, GO:0042981). *ACTN1* plays a role in the regulation of apoptosis and cell motility. The successful identification of these genes by the full network model is remarkable because standard differential expression analysis ranks *PSMD11* but not *KLF4* or *ACTN1* among the 15 most significant genes. This indicates that a full learned network model allows a much more powerful exploration than pure correlation analysis.

Guided by these results, we fetch further known information about these genes. By context-sensitive links to separate internal and external repositories, further information about the corresponding node is fetched. Figure 9.8 shows a zoomed-in version of the gastric cancer network together with the online-fetched gene annotation for *PSMD11*. It is annotated as part of the proteasome 26S, which plays a critical role in the degradation of proteins and therefore is involved in a variety of critical pathways.

9.3.4 Modeling Interventions

We now demonstrate how the GeneSim explorer supports online in silico modeling of interventions by its easy-to-use graphical user interface. For this purpose, we use the previously described gastric cancer network. By applying Student's *t*-test on the complete gastric cancer dataset, the proteasome subunit *PSMD11* is returned as the highest-ranked gene according to the *p*-value (see Figure 9.5, top row). In addition, structural network analysis reveals a strong relationship with the gastric cancer phenotype. We therefore proceed with an interventional study of the S26 proteasome and determine the effect seen when all proteasome subunits of the network, *PSMD11*, *PSMD4*, and *PSMB4*, are clamped to the overexpressed state. By right-clicking on the

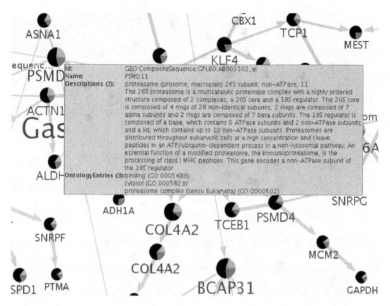

Fig. 9.8. Zoom of the same network as in Figure 9.7, with integrated information about gene *PSMD11* displayed. By positioning the mouse cursor on the node, further information, including GO annotation and descriptions, is fetched automatically from external databases and textually represented in the GUI of the explorer, as is shown for the gene *PSMD11* (text box).

PSMD11 node, the GeneSim explorer opens a dialog that can be used to fix the expression level of the gene to a specific value (see Figure 9.9).

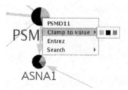

Fig. 9.9. Online in silico interventional modeling in the GeneSim explorer. The state of an entity can be set by right-clicking on the entity node. The figure shows the pop-up menu for the gene *PSMD11*, providing the possibility to clamp the gene to the state "normalexpressed" ("black"), "underexpressed" ("light grey"), or "overexpressed" ("dark grey").

We first choose "dark grey" (representing overexpressed) to estimate the effect of an overexpression of *PSMD11* on gastric cancer. By the same procedure, the two other subunits are clamped to overexpressed. The result of the intervention can be seen in Figure 9.10b.

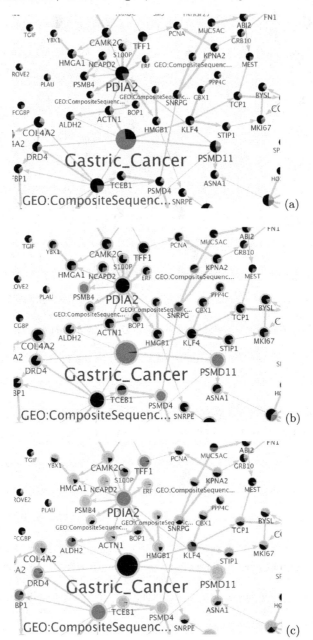

Fig. 9.10. (a) Part of the network structure shown in Figure 9.7. (b) Same network as in (a), where genes *PSMD11*, *PSMD4*, and *PSMB4* are kept fixed at the over-expressed state. (c) Same network as in (a), where genes *PSMD11*, *PSMD4*, and *PSMB4* are kept fixed at the underexpressed state. Visualization is in the same format as in Figure 9.3.

It shows a strong increase in the likelihood for node *Gastric_Cancer* to be in the "on" state (98%), as compared with a value of 73% for the unclamped case in Figure 9.10a. Consequently, the in silico enforced overactivity of the S26 proteasome (E) yields a high intervention score for gastric cancer (t), indicated by the circular ("bright grey") border around the *Gastric_Cancer* node. Moreover, if the same genes are deactivated (clamped to underexpressed; see Figure 9.10c), the result is exactly the opposite: the probability of gastric cancer shrinks dramatically to 1.7%. The influence of changes in S26 activity on cancer probability is stronger than for any of a large number of other interventions that have been tested manually. We therefore conclude that this in silico interventional study predicts the S26 proteasome to be a central pathogenic factor for gastric cancer. In fact, it has been shown that inhibition of proteasome function in gastric cancer cells induces apoptosis [FWW+01]. Proteasomal inhibitors have since then been biotechnologically developed as the FDA-approved anti-myeloma drug Velcade® (bortezomib, Ortho Biotech/Millennium Pharmaceuticals) and are currently being tested in clinical trials as a gastric cancer anti-tumor drug.

9.4 Summary

In this chapter, we have introduced for the first time the GeneSim IT platform to support molecular medicine and pharmaceutical research. The goal of this platform is not to integrate all possible knowledge about life processes, medical diagnosis, and treatment. Instead, it exploits context sensitivity, learning, and intelligent computing to provide slim but highly relevant collections of knowledge and information designed to be of highest relevance for the expert working on the solution for a given biomedical problem. The platform positions itself as a portal solution that combines data-driven modeling, learning, and knowledge discovery with links to databases, knowledge repositories, and literature collections, integrated in a central knowledge base.

The GeneSim knowledge base serves as the blackboard on which knowledge relevant to a topic is collected at three different levels of detail and complexity. It collects the information required to assess the genetic predisposition of individuals for curable diseases, enabling early preventive measures. It provides the basis for the discovery of diagnostically and therapeutically relevant relationships between clinical and molecular states of a patient. GeneSim aims to help cover the increasing need for intelligent computing in the biomedical world, which undoubtedly will pave the way to more efficient and effective health care delivery by molecular medicine approaches of the 21st century.

References

[AHR01]   AHRQ. *Reducing and Preventing Adverse Drug Events to Decrease Hospital Costs*, volume 1 of *Research in Action*. Agency for Healthcare Research and Quality, Rockville, MD, March 2001. http://www.ahrq.gov/qual/aderia/aderia.htm.

[Arr06]   ArrayExpress. Technology gets under the skin, 2006. http://www.ebi.ac.uk/arrayexpress/ (last accessed October 2006).

[BAD+05]   C.A. Ball, I.A.B. Awad, J. Demeter, J. Gollub, J.M. Hebert, T. Hernandez Boussard, H. Jin, J.C. Matese, M. Nitzberg, F. Wymore, Z.K. Zachariah, P.O. Brown, and G. Sherlock. The Stanford Microarray Database accommodates additional microarray platforms and data formats. *Nucleic Acids Research Database Issue*, 33:D580–D582, 2005.

[BHQ+01]   A. Brazma, P. Hingamp, J. Quackenbush, G. Sherlock, P. Spellman, C. Stoeckert, J. Aach, W. Ansorge, C.A. Ball, H.C. Causton, T. Gaasterland, P. Glenisson, F.C.P. Holstege, I.F. Kim, V. Markowitz, J.C. Matese, H. Parkinson, A. Robinson, U. Sarkans, S. Schulze-Kremer, J. Stewart, R. Taylor, J. Vilo, and M. Vingron. Minimum information about a microarray experiment (MIAME)–toward standards for microarray data. *Nature Genetics*, 29:365–371, 2001.

[BO04]   A.L. Barabasi and Z.N. Oltvai. Network biology: understanding the cell's functional organization. *Nature Reviews Genetics*, 5:101–113, 2004.

[Bro99]   T.A. Brown. *Genomes*. Bios Scientific Publishers, Oxford, 1999.

[BST+05]   T. Barrett, T.O. Suzek, D.B. Troup, S.E. Wilhite, W.C. Ngau, P. Ledoux, D. Rudnev, A.E. Lash, W. Fujibuchi, and R. Edgar. NCBI GEO: mining millions of expression profiles database and tools. *Nucleic Acids Research Database Issue*, 33:D562–D566, 2005.

[But01]   D. Butler. Publication of human genomes sparks fresh sequence debate. *Nature*, 409(6822):747–748, February 2001.

[DS03]   M. Dejori and M. Stetter. Bayesian inference of genetic networks from gene expression data: convergence and reliability. In Hamid R. Arabnia, Rose Joshua, and Youngsong Mun, editors, *Proceedings of the 2003 International Conference on Artificial Intelligence (IC-AI'03)*, volume 1, pages 323–327, Las Vegas, Nevada, USA, 23–26, June 2003. CSREA Press.

[DS04]   M. Dejori and M. Stetter. Identifying interventional and pathogenic mechanisms by generative inverse modeling of gene expression profiles. *Journal of Computational Biology*, 11:1135–1148, 2004.

[DSS03]   M. Dejori, B. Schürmann, and M. Stetter. Bioanalogue technologies and solutions. In W. Greiner and J. Reinhardt, editors, *Idea Finding Symposium of the Frankfurt Institute for Advanced Studies (FIAS)*, pages 57–66. EP Systema Bt., Debrecen, 2003.

[DSS04]   M. Dejori, B. Schürmann, and M. Stetter. Hunting drug targets by systems-level modeling of gene expression profiles. *IEEE Transactions on Nano-Bioscience*, 3:180–191, 2004.

[DSTS04]   M. Dejori, A. Schwaighofer, V. Tresp, and M. Stetter. Mining functional modules in genetic networks by decomposable models. *OMICS: A Journal of Integrative Biology*, 8:176–188, 2004.

[DT04]   Y. Dorsett and T. Tuschl. siRNAs: applications in functional genomics and potential as therapeutics. *Nature Reviews Drug Discovery*, 3:318–329, 2004.

[ELS06]   ELSSE. Entrez: the life sciences search engine, 2006. http://www.ncbi.nlm.nih.gov/gquery/gquery.fcgi (last accessed October 2006).

[EPM06] EPM. Entrez PubMed, 2006. http://www.ncbi.nlm.nih.gov/entrez/query.fcgi?DB=pubmed (last accessed October 2006).

[ESN06] ESNP. Entrez SNP, 2006. http://www.ncbi.nlm.nih.gov/entrez/query.fcgi?db=Snp (last accessed October 2006).

[FWW⁺01] X.M. Fan, B.C. Wong, W.P. Wang, X.M. Zhou, C.H. Cho, S.T. Yuen, S.Y. Leung, M.C.M. Lin, H.F. Kung, and S.K. Lam. Inhibition of proteasome function induced apoptosis in gastric cancer. *International Journal of Cancer*, 93:481–488, 2001.

[GEO06] GEO. Gene expression omnibus, 2006. http://www.ncbi.nlm.nih.gov/geo/ (last accessed October 2006).

[GO06] GO. Gene ontology, 2006. http://www.geneontology.org/ (last accessed October 2006).

[HBB⁺05] R. Hillestad, J. Bigelow, A. Bower, F. Girosi, R. Meili, R. Scoville, and R. Taylor. Can electronic medical record systems transform healthcare? An assessment of potential health benefits, savings, and costs. *Health Affairs*, 24(5):1103–1117, 2005.

[HGP03] HGP. Human genome project, 2003. http://www.genome.gov/ (last accessed October 2006).

[HTT⁺02] Y. Hippo, H. Taniguchi, S. Tsutsumi, N. Machida, J.M. Chong, M. Fukayama, T. Kodama, and H. Aburatani. Global gene expression analysis of gastric cancer by oligonucleotide microarrays. *Cancer Research*, 62(1):233–240, January 2002.

[HW00] D. Hanahan and R.A. Weinberg. The hallmarks of cancer. *Cell*, 100:57–70, 2000.

[IHP06] IHP. International HapMap project, 2006. http://www.hapmap.org/ (last accessed October 2006).

[Ins99] Institute of Medicine. *To Err Is Human: Building a Safer Health System.* The National Academies Press, Washington, DC, 1999.

[JO02] S. Jakobzone and H. Oxley. Ageing and healthcare costs. *International Politics and Society*, 1, 2002. http://www.fes.de/ipg/ipg1_2002/ZEITSCHRIFT.HTM (last accessed October 2006).

[KAV05] M. Krallinger, R. Alonso Allende, and A. Valencia. Text-mining approaches in molecular biology and biomedicine. *Drug Discovery Today*, 10:439–445, 2005.

[KEG06] KEGG. Kyoto encyclopedia of genes and genomes, 2006. http://www.genome.jp/kegg/ (last accessed October 2006).

[MSH06] MSH. Medical subject headings, 2006. http://www.nlm.nih.gov/mesh/ (last accessed October 2006).

[NCB06] NCBI. National center for biotechnology information, 2006. http://www.ncbi.nlm.nih.gov/Sitemap/index.html (last accessed October 2006).

[Ope06] OpenCyc, 2006. http://www.opencyc.org/ (last accessed October 2006).

[SDD03] M. Stetter, G. Deco, and M. Dejori. Large-scale computational modeling of genetic regulatory networks. *Artificial Intelligence Review*, 20:75–93, 2003.

[SDSG05] J. Scholz, M. Dejori, M. Stetter, and M. Greiner. Noisy scale-free networks. *Physica A*, 350:622–642, 2005.

[SMVC04] J. Shendure, R.D. Mitra, C. Varma, and G.M. Church. Advanced se-
          quencing technologies: methods and goals. *Nature Reviews Genetics*,
          4:335–344, 2004.
[SPD06]   SPD. Swiss prot database, 2006. `http://www.ebi.ac.uk/swissprot/`
          `access.html` (last accessed October 2006).
[Sto94]   D.G. Stork. Using open data collection for intelligent software. In
          R. Lopez de Mantaras and D. Poole, editors, *Proceedings of the AAAI
          Spring Symposium on Acquiring (and Using) Linguistic (and World)
          Knowledge for Information Access*, pages 367–373, Palo Alto, CA, 1994.
          Morgan Kaufmann, San Francisco.

10

Artificial Intelligence and DNA Computing

Zoheir Ezziane

College of Information Technology, University of Dubai, P.O. Box 14143, Dubai, United Arab Emirates, zezziane@ud.ac.ae

Summary. DNA computing is a relatively new computing paradigm that has attracted great interest in the computing community. Its inherent capacity for vast parallelism, the scope for high-density storage and its intrinsic ability for potentially solving many combinatorial problems are just some of the reasons for this. Computing power alone, however, may not be enough for solving many computing problems today. This is true, in particular, for problems requiring a degree of cleverness or intelligence. It is at this juncture where DNA computing and artificial intelligence meet. This chapter investigates the potential and advances of DNA computing related to artificial intelligence.

10.1 Introduction

DNA (deoxyribonucleic acid) computing is a new computation paradigm that proposes using molecular biology tools to solve mathematical problems. Computing with DNA offers a totally new means of looking at and performing computations. The key idea is that data can be encoded in DNA strands, while molecular biology laboratory techniques (called bio-operations) that involve manipulation of DNA strands in test tubes can be used to imitate arithmetical and logical operations.

Besides the novelty of the approach, and in spite of the technical difficulties that arise from the error rates of bio-operations, there are several reasons why computing with DNA might have advantages over silicon-based computing. These include memory capacity, massive parallelism, and power requirements. Indeed, one gram of DNA, which when dry would occupy a volume of approximately one cubic centimeter, can store as much information as approximately one trillion CDs. In addition, computing with DNA provides enormous parallelism. Adleman's first DNA computing experiment [Adl94] solved an instance of the Directed Hamiltonian Path Problem (HPP) that was carried out in one-fiftieth of a teaspoon of solution, and approximately 1014 oriented edges were simultaneously concatenated in about one second. It is not clear whether the fastest available supercomputer is capable of such a speed.

DNA molecules have the potential to perform calculations many times faster than the world's most powerful electronic computers. DNA might one day be integrated into a computer chip to create a so-called biochip that will push computers even faster. DNA molecules have already been harnessed to solve NP problems. A certain quantity of energy is required while performing DNA computations. Normally one joule is sufficient for approximately 2×10^{19} ligation operations, while existing supercomputers operate in the significantly smaller range of 10^9 operations per joule. The enormous information storage capacity of DNA and the low energy dissipation of DNA processing have led to an explosion of interest in massively parallel DNA computing. For serious advocates of the field, however, there never was a question of brute search with DNA solving the problem of exponential growth in the number of alternative solutions indefinitely. As a result, artificial intelligence (AI) techniques were used to tackle the combinatorial problem in DNA computing [IPZ01, SKK+99, Ezz06b].

The remainder of the chapter has the following structure. Section 10.2 briefly introduces DNA computing. Section 10.3 investigates the relationship between DNA computing and artificial intelligence. Section 10.4, finally, ends the chapter with conclusions.

10.2 DNA Computing

The field of DNA computing emerged as a fascinating combination of computer science and molecular biology. The field is not only an exciting technology for information processing but also a catalyst for knowledge transfer between information processing, nanotechnology, and biology. This area of research has great potential to change our perception of the theory and practice of computing [Ezz06b].

10.2.1 DNA Structure

DNA encodes the genetic information of cellular organisms. It consists of polymer chains known as DNA strands. Each strand may be viewed as a chain of nucleotides, or bases, attached to a sugar-phosphate backbone. An n-letter sequence of consecutive bases is known as an n-mer, or an oligonucleotide (or oligo) of length n.

DNA stores information that can be processed via enzymes and nucleic acid interactions. A strand of DNA is encoded with four bases (nucleotides), represented by the letters A, T, C, and G. Each strand, according to chemical convention, has a 5' and a 3' end, and therefore any single strand has a natural orientation. Figure 10.1 presents a DNA molecule composed of ten pairs of nucleotides. Bonding occurs by the pairwise attraction of bases; A bonds with T, and G bonds with C. The pairs (A, T) and (G, C) are therefore known

$$5'\text{-}\ A\ A\ C\ C\ C\ T\ C\ G\ C\ C\ \text{-}3'$$
$$3'\text{-}\ T\ T\ G\ G\ G\ A\ G\ C\ G\ G\ \text{-}5'$$

Fig. 10.1. Example DNA molecule.

as complementary base pairs. Such "double-stranded" DNA is also sometimes depicted in the following form $\frac{AACCCTCGCC}{TTGGGAGCGG}$.

Researchers in DNA computing develop algorithms that solve problems using the encoded information in the sequence of nucleotides that make up DNA's double helix and then break and make new bonds between them to satisfy the problem constraints and then ultimately reach the answer.

Since the space between nucleotides is about 0.35 nanometers, a DNA molecule has a massive data density, estimated as one bit per cubic nanometer, and the amount of information in a gram of DNA could reach exabytes [CWD04]. For example, let us assume that there is one base per square nanometer; the data density will exceed one million Gbits per square inch. Thus, this density exceeds that for a typical high-performance hard drive, which is about 7 Gbits per square inch. In addition, DNA computing is also massively parallel and can reach approximately 10^{20} operations per second compared with existing teraflop supercomputers.

10.2.2 Solving Combinatorial Problems Using DNA Computing

Various DNA computing methods were employed in complex computational problems such as the Hamilton path problem (HPP) [Adl94], maximal clique problem [OKLL97], satisfiability problem (SAT) [LWF+00], and chess problems [FCLL00]. The advantage of these approaches is the vast parallelism inherent in DNA-based computing, which has the potential to yield vast speedups over silicon-based computers for such search problems.

Adleman [Adl94] considered a very simple instance of the directed traveling salesman problem (TSP), also called HPP, and then applied a DNA computing technique to solve it. This has been a true beginning of data processing and communication on the level of biological molecules. This problem can be characterized by a door-to-door salesman who must visit several connected cities without going through any city twice. The TSP appears to be an easy puzzle; however, the most advanced supercomputers would take years to calculate the optimal route for 50 cities [Par03].

Using DNA to solve this problem starts with assigning a genetic sequence to each city. For example, the city of Dubai might be coded CGCAGA. If two cities connect, then the connecting genetic sequence is assigned the first three letters of one city and the last three letters of the other. For example, if Dubai is connected to Paris, the first three letters of Dubai (CGC) would connect to the last three letters of Paris (AGA). A single strand of DNA does not yield much power. But DNA can be replicated, so that you can have as much

DNA as needed to perform incredibly difficult tasks. And the strange property of a DNA computer is that it can test all the solutions simultaneously—a truly parallel task. Figure 10.2 provides a pseudo–code style representation of Adleman's approach to the HPP. Figure 10.3 illustrates an actual instance of HPP that was solved by Adleman (the dashed lines in the figure represent the Hamiltonian path).

Algorithm: Adleman-HPP;
Start
    Generate strands encoding random paths
    Keep only the potential solutions
    Monitor the quantities of DNA generated for the specific graph
    Remove strands that do not encode the HPP
    if Strand encodes HPP **then** Identify uniquely the HP solution
      else Discard the strands
End

Fig. 10.2. An outline to Adleman's approach to the HPP.

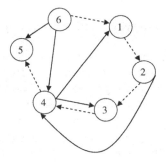

Fig. 10.3. Instance of the HPP solved by Adleman (source [Ezz06b]).

In a matter of seconds, the process of DNA hybridization starts off by replicating the initial input DNA sequences to reach trillions of new sequences. Eventually, this process ends by finding a new DNA sequence strand that represents a solution to the problem. However, when using Adleman's method in solving a 200-city TSP, the quantity of DNA might outweigh Earth itself. Another challenge in DNA computing is the error rate that occurs within each operation as the number of iterations increases.

Generally, all NP problems can be efficiently transformed to HPP [Lip95]. Additionally, it was shown how a DNA computing technique can be used to solve a two-variable SAT problem. Later, Sakamoto et al. [SKK+99] demonstrated how NP-complete problems can be solved by a single series of successive transitions, combined with parallel overlap assembly and some other operations. This method suffered from the additional time needed on successive transitions when more transitions are required.

The feasibility of autonomous molecular computing has been explored by Sakamoto et al. [SGK+00]. This method uses hairpin formation by single-stranded DNA molecules. Consequently, molecular biology techniques were used to solve the SAT problem, in which a given Boolean formula was examined autonomously, based on hairpin formation by the molecules that represent the formula. They illustrated how to reduce the number of laboratory steps required for computation through testing numerous clauses in the particular formula simultaneously.

The comparison between sequential computing and DNA computing in terms of the number of steps needed to solve a particular problem is fairly interesting. Since DNA sequences are able to encode each possibility in a single DNA molecule, all possibilities need a comparatively small space for a much larger problem size than in sequential computing. For example, the method used by Liu et al. [LWF+00] needed only 91 steps to find solutions, while a sequential computer would have required 1.6 million steps. Consequently, in order to improve DNA computing, the following points need to be explored: (1) discover smaller molecules; and (2) improve chemical methods to prepare and filter out the final solutions.

Cryptography is another area where DNA computing has been used. It has been estimated that in order to factor a 1000-bit number using Adleman's experiments [Adl94], 10^{200000} liters of solution would be needed [Bea94]. Nevertheless, in an experiment Adleman [Adl96] demonstrated that a DNA computing method is able to search for 256 DES (data encryption standard) keys and yet occupy only a small set of test tubes.

10.3 Intelligent DNA Computing

Subsequent to Adleman's experiment [Adl94], various combinatorial problems have been proposed using DNA computing, such as the 3-SAT problem [BCJ+02], the maximal clique problem [OKLL97], and the knight problem [FCLL00]. The existence of parallelism and molecules suitable for high-density computation let DNA computers solve NP problems in polynomial increasing time, while a conventional Turing machine requires exponentially increasing times [IPZ01, SKK+99, Ezz06b].

A selection process during a DNA computing method eliminates all incorrect DNA sequences from a pool of all candidate solutions. The size of this pool increases exponentially with the number of variables in the calculation. As a result, the use of a brute-force method becomes inefficient to deal with the increase of the problem size. Hence, the application of artificial intelligence (AI) methods to a small initial pool of DNA sequences will provide a final solution without enumerating all candidate solutions [Ezz06a].

10.3.1 Learning Methods with DNA Molecules

Neural Networks

Neural networks represent prospective candidates in making DNA computing more efficient [RHHE94, FH95]. Farhat and Hernendez [FH95] considered a logistic network consisting of a coupled population of externally driven logistic processing elements (LPEs) or "neurons" with quantized interactions between them. The interactions are modeled after the encoding of genetic information in molecular biology (i.e., as in DNA molecules in terms of four nucleotide bases). They presented an approach on what could be a useful parallel in the dynamics of neural networks that employ functionally complex processing elements with special forms of interaction matrix and certain features of encoding information in molecular biology.

Farhat and Hernendez [FH95] compared and analyzed the behavior of a neural network with enzyme-activated reactions in molecular biology. This analysis provided a conceptual framework for the development of specific ideas for incorporating molecular computing concepts into neural networks.

Version Space Learning

Learning can be formulated as a search for a hypothesis in the space of possible hypotheses that are consistent with the training examples. Mitchell [Mit97] proposed version space learning (VSL) as a method for representing the hypothesis space. This method maintains the general boundary and the specific boundary to represent the consistent hypotheses consisting of conjunctions of attribute values. However, the size of the boundaries can increase exponentially in some cases, which represents a major challenge to solve [Hau88]. Subsequently, Hirsh [HMP97] illustrated that if the consistency problem (that is, whether there exists a hypothesis in the hypothesis space that is consistent with the example) is tractable, the boundaries are not needed and new examples can be classified only by positive examples and negative examples.

Lim et al. [LYJ+03] used a version space (VS) in inductive concept learning to represent the hypothesis space, where the goal concept is expressed as a conjunction of attribute values. In order to tackle the issue of the size of the version space and the number of attributes, they presented an efficient method for representing the version space with DNA molecules and demonstrated its effectiveness by experimental results.

The DNA computing method can be used to implement the VSL without maintaining boundary sets by exploiting the huge number of DNA molecules to maintain and search the version space. To use the massive parallelism of DNA molecules efficiently, Lim et al. [LYJ+03] used an encoding scheme and presented an efficient and reliable method to express the hypothesis in the version space. The experiments showed that an encoding scheme can help make the number of necessary sequences increase linearly, not exponentially, with the number of attributes. This approach has successfully reduced the VSL to two primitive set operations of intersection and difference as well as predicting the classification of new examples. For example, if a positive example is given, the learning algorithm selects all hypotheses that classify the example as positive in VS. Similarly, if a negative example is given, it eliminates all hypotheses that classify the example as positive in the version space.

Mitchell [Mit97] used different methods to classify new examples using current VS: the VS classifies the new example as positive if it has at least one hypothesis that classifies the example as positive and classifies it as negative when there are none. Lim et al. [LYJ+03] used the majority-voting method, where the new example is classified as the majority of hypotheses in the VS.

Sakakibara [Sak00] and Hagiya et al. [HAK+99] show how it is possible to learn a concept of predefined form from training examples and adopt the general framework of generate-all-solutions and search similar to the experiments performed by Adleman [Adl98]. Sakakibara [Sak00] proposed a technique to express the k-term DNF with DNA molecules, to evaluate it, and to learn a consistent k-term DNF with the given examples. In addition, Hagiya et al. [HAK+99] designed a technique to evaluate a μ-formula and to learn a consistent μ-formula with whiplash PCR.

There are a few challenging issues to undertake in VSL using DNA computing: (1) conduct experiments where an attribute could have more than two values and deal with generalization properly [Hir94]; (2) since Lim et al. [LYJ+03] conducted their experiments using only affinity separation by magnetic bead, this reveals that microreactors [NGM01] represent a potential alternative to be explored during the learning process.

Bayesian-Based Learning Algorithm

Zhang and Jang [ZJ05a] developed a molecular evolutionary algorithm inspired by directed evolution and derived its molecular learning rule from Bayesian decision theory. They investigated through simulation the convergence behaviors of the molecular Bayesian evolutionary algorithm on a concrete problem from statistical pattern classification and focused on the probabilistic formulation of the pattern classification problem. They developed a molecular algorithm for learning probabilistic pattern classifiers and derived from Bayesian decision theory a rule for setting the learning parameters for evolving the classifier using a probabilistic DNA library.

Throughout the VSL approach proposed by Lim et al. [LYJ+03], the training examples are stored one copy for each instance. Zhang and Jang [ZJ05a] use many copies for each training example, and the number of copies of library elements is updated as new training examples are observed so that their frequency is proportional to their probability of observation. VSL does rote learning and thus is very fast in storage but very slow in recall since classification computation is done from scratch. Zhang and Jang [ZJ05a] update the probabilistic library on learning. On recall, their method works like a look-up table, but the probabilistic distribution of the data in the library facilitates classification computation.

Zhang and Jang [ZJ05a] presented a DNA computing algorithm that evolves probabilistic pattern classifiers from training data. Using a Bayesian-based theory, they derived the rule for determining the learning-rate parameter and showed this is related to the number of copies of matched molecules in the DNA library. They also performed simulations to evaluate the performance and stability of the molecular Bayesian evolutionary algorithm.

10.3.2 Evolutionary Computing

Evolution is a concept that achieves adaptation through the interplay of selection and diversity. The tendency of evolving populations to minimize the sampling of large, low-fitness individuals suggests that a DNA-based evolutionary approach might be effective for an exhaustive search. According to modern biological understanding, evolution is only responsible for the complexity included in the structure and behavior of biological organisms. However, evolution itself is a simple process that can occur in any population of imperfectly replicating entities where the right to replicate is determined by a process of selection.

Genetic Algorithms

The genetic algorithm (GA) [Hol75, Gol89] is a model of machine learning that derives its behavior from a metaphor of the processes of evolution in nature. This is done by the creation within a machine of a population of individuals represented by chromosomes, essentially a set of character strings that are analogous to the base-4 chromosomes that are available in DNA. The individuals in the population then go through a process of evolution. The evolution starts by creating a population of solutions and then applies genetic operators such as mutation and crossover to evolve the solutions in order to find the best one(s). Of all evolutionarily inspired approaches, GAs seem particularly suited to implementation using DNA. This is because genetic algorithms are generally based on manipulating populations of bit strings using both crossover and mutation operators [CAL$^+$99].

The combination of the massive parallelism and high storage density inherent in DNA computing with the direct search capability of GAs represent major advantages for DNA-GA approaches. GA is one of the possible ways to break the limits of the brute-force method in DNA computing [YC04]. One gram of single-stranded DNA is approximately 1.8×10^{21} nucleotides, or about 10^{22} bytes. Individuals and answers can be encoded in DNA molecules using binary representations. Larger populations can carry on larger ranges of genetic diversity and hence can generate high-fitness chromosomes in fewer generations, thus effectively reducing the size of the search space. Furthermore, experimenting with in vitro operations on DNA inherently involves errors. In a sense, errors may be regarded as a factor contributing to genetic diversity.

A DNA-based GA was proposed as an application of an evolution program searching for good encodings [DMR+97]. Yoshikawa et al. [YFU97] combined the DNA-encoding method with the pseudobacterial GA. Chen et al. [CAL+99] proposed the laboratory implementation of the DNA-GA for some simple problems such as the Max-1s, the royal road, and the cold war problems. Wood et al. [WCA+99] designed and implemented a DNA-based in vitro genetic algorithm for the Max-1s problem. Wood and Chen [WC99] proposed and implemented a DNA strand design suited for the royal road problem using a genetic algorithm where in vitro evolution started with a randomized population of DNA strands. A few years later, Rose et al. [RHDS02] proposed a DNA-based in vitro genetic algorithm for the HPP.

Evolutionary and genetic DNA computing were proposed to solve the maximum clique problem [YC04]. Yuan and Chen [YC04] designed a DNA best GA for the maximal clique problem, which was capable of producing a correct solution within a few cycles at high probability. Their simulation indicated the time requirement of their approach was approximately a linear function of the number of vertices in the network.

Wood et al. [WBK+01] employed in vitro evolutionary DNA computing to learn game playing and find adaptive game-theoretic strategies. They applied their approach to the game of poker, where they constructed two single-stranded DNAs to represent the two possible plays. Stojanovic and Stefanovic [SS03] designed a DNA computer named MAYA capable of playing tic-tac-toe.

Ren et al. [RDYS03] proposed a new approach to the virus DNA-based evolutionary algorithm (VDNA-EA) to implement self-learning in a class of Takagi-Sugeno (T-S) fuzzy controllers. The VDNA encoding method was used to encode the design parameters of the fuzzy controllers, which has shortened the code length of the DNA chromosome. The frameshift decoding method was used to decode the DNA chromosome into the design parameters of the fuzzy controllers. Those methods have made the genetic operators capable of operating at the gene level within the VDNA-EA approach. Computer simulation demonstrated the effectiveness of this method in designing automatically a class of T-S fuzzy controllers.

Molecular (Genetic) Programming

Genetic programming (GP) [Koz92] is the extension of the genetic model of learning into the space of programs. That is, the objects that constitute the population are not fixed-length character strings that encode possible solutions to the problem at hand but are programs that, when executed, "are" the candidate solutions to the problem. These programs are expressed in genetic programming as parse trees rather than as lines of code. Figure 10.4, for example, would represent the simple program "$w - x + y \times z$".

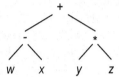

Fig. 10.4. Parse tree for $w - x + y \times z$.

Zhang and Jang [ZJ05b] presented an evolutionary method, called molecular programming, for learning genetic programs using DNA computing technology. The approach describes a representation method that makes use of the molecular DNA structures while maintaining the advantages of variable-length encoding capability of GP. It also uses a genetic program representing a decision list of variable length, and the whole population takes part in making probabilistic decisions. The representation of program structure via a decision lists is distinguished from other GP approaches.

The use of DNA computing technology makes the design of the evolutionary operators very different from the conventional GP and other evolutionary computing methods. The possibility of synthetic DNA molecules and their manipulation by biochemical techniques in a test tube allows the use of huge population sizes. Most of the operators, such as reproduction and selection, are massively parallel. Examples of biochemical techniques for in vitro molecular computing include: (1) the massively parallel matching and selection based on the A-T and G-C molecular recognition capability of DNA molecules; (2) the PCR-based exponential reproduction of fitter programs; and (3) the global search capability coming from the population size.

For the purpose of illustration, Figure 10.5 depicts two DNA molecules corresponding to a set of a decision list.

DL1: $(x_1 = 1, x_2 = 1, y = 1)$
DL2: $(x_2 = 1, x_3 = 0, y = 0)$

DL1: AATT<u>CC</u>CCAA<u>CC</u>AAGG<u>CC</u>
DL2: CCAA<u>CC</u>AAAA<u>GG</u>AAGG<u>GG</u>

Fig. 10.5. Two decision lists (DL1 and DL2), and corresponding DNA molecules. We use x_1 = AATT, x_2 = CCAA, x_3 = AAAA, y = AAGG, 0 = <u>GG</u>, and 1 = <u>CC</u>.

The DNA code represents a DNA sequence representing a combination of markers for diagnosing a disease. For example, a program ($x_1 = 1, x_2 = 1, y = 1$) in the form of a "decision list" (DL) denotes a decision rule saying "diagnose the DNA sample as positive for disease y if it contains the two markers x_1 and x_2".

The in vitro evolution of DNA-encoded genetic programs opens up a possibility of using GP in biotechnology and nanotechnology, where DNA is used as the structural material to be designed. Lately, Yokobayashi et al. [YWA02] have used evolutionary computing in designing novel molecules; and Kloster and Tang [KT04] have used evolutionary computing in studying natural behaviors of DNA.

Enzyme Genetic Programming

Genetic programming copies the process and genetic operators of biological evolution but does not take any motivation from the biological representations to which they are applied. It can also be argued that the program representation GP uses is not well-suited to evolution.

Artificial evolution can be applied to any structure that can be represented by a computer, including computer programs. GP is an approach in evolutionary computing that evolves programs and other executable structures.

Enzyme genetic programming is described by Lones and Tyrrell [LT04] as a form of genetic programming that not only mimics biological representations in an attempt to improve the evolvability of programs but also evolves executional structures using a GA. It is also an approach to evolutionary computing motivated by the metabolic processing of cells. The use of a program representation and development process derived from biology is distinguished from GP approaches. The aim of this approach is to capture the elements of biological representations that contribute to their evolvability and adapt them for artificial evolution. The resulting system represents an executable structure as a collection of enzyme-like computational elements that interact with one another according to their own interaction preferences.

The aim of enzyme genetic programming is to identify principles of biological representations thought to contribute to their evolvability and adapt these principles to improve the evolvability of representations in GP. In addition, the intention of this approach is not to produce an exact model of these biological representations but only to mimic those constructs and behaviors that might improve GP. One of the most interesting properties of enzyme genetic programming is probably that the context of each component within a program is independent of its position within the genome. Moreover, the context of a component is recorded by means of a description independent of any particular program and, as a result, the role of a component can be preserved following recombination [LT04].

10.4 Conclusions

DNA computing relies on biochemical reactions of DNA molecules and may result in incorrect or undesirable computations due to its technological difficulty. Sometimes DNA computing fails to generate identical results for the same problem and algorithm. Also, some DNAs can be wasted performing undesirable reactions. To overcome these drawbacks, much work has focused on improving the reliability and efficiency of DNA computing using artificial intelligence.

These practical incentives and the fascination of being able to perform computations with DNA molecules have inspired many researchers to pursue the challenging topic of DNA computing. It is anticipated that the pioneering research in this field of intersection between computer science and molecular biology will have great significance in many aspects of science and technology. Indeed, DNA computing sheds new light on the very nature of computation and opens prospects for computability models very different from the traditional ones. In an optimistic way, one may think of an analogy between the work of researchers in this area and the work on finding models of computation carried out in the 1940s that laid the foundation for the design of today's silicon-based computer.

In this chapter, we explored ways of encoding information in DNA sequences, DNA computing methods, classes of problems that can be solved by DNA computing, various AI techniques that helped reduce the time and space in solving some NP problems, and the feasibility and advantages of a DNA computer. While still in their infancy, it is anticipated that DNA computers will be capable of storing billions of times more data than silicon-based computers. Nowadays scientists are using genetic material to create nanocomputers that might take the place of silicon-based computers in the next decade.

References

[Adl94]   L. Adleman. Molecular computation of solutions to combinatorial problems. *Science*, 266:1021–1024, 1994.

[Adl96]   L.M. Adleman. Statement, Cryptographer's Expert Panel, RSA Data Security Conference, San Francisco, CA, January 1996.

[Adl98]   L.M. Adleman. Computing with DNA. *Scientific American*, 279(2):34–41, August 1998.

[BCJ+02]   R.S. Braich, N. Chelyapov, C. Johnson, P.W.K. Rothermund, and L. Adleman. Solution of a 20-variable 3-SAT problem on a DNA computer. *Science*, 296:499–502, 2002.

[Bea94]   D. Beaver. Factoring: the DNA solution. In J. Pieprzyk and R. Safavi-Naini, editors, *Proceedings of the 4th International Conference on the Theory and Applications of Cryptology*, pages 419–423, Wollongong, Australia, 1994. Springer–Verlag, New York.

[CAL+99]   J. Chen, E. Antipov, B. Lemieux, W. Cedeno, and D. Wood. DNA computing implementing genetic algorithms. In L.F. Landweber, E. Winfree, R. Lipton, and S. Freeland, editors, *Evolution as Computation*, pages 39–49. Springer–Verlag, New York, 1999.

[CWD04]   J. Chen, Y. Wang, and R. Deaton. Large scale genomic monitoring or profiling using a DNA-based memory and microarrays. In *Proceedings of the 24th Army Science Conference*, Orlando, 2004. Available at `http://www.asc2004.com/Manuscript/SessionA/AP-06.pdf` (last accessed August, 2006).

[DMR⁺97] R. Deaton, R.C. Murphy, J.A. Rose, M. Garzon, D.R. Franceschetti, and S.E. Stevens Jr. A DNA based implementation of an evolutionary search for good encodings for DNA computation. In *Proceedings of the IEEE International Conference on Evolutionary Computation*, pages 267–271, Indianapolis, IN, 1997. IEEE Computer Society Press, New York.

[Ezz06a] Z. Ezziane. Applications of artificial intelligence in bioinformatics: a review. *Expert Systems with Applications*, 30(1):2–10, 2006.

[Ezz06b] Z. Ezziane. DNA computing: applications and challenges. *Nanotechnology*, 17:R27–R39, 2006.

[FCLL00] D. Faulhammer, A.R. Cukras, R.J. Lipton, and L.F. Landweber. Molecular computation: RNA solutions to chess problems. *Proceedings of the National Academy of Sciences USA*, 97:1385–1389, 2000.

[FH95]   N.H. Farhat and E.D.M. Hernandez. Logistic networks with DNA-like encoding and interactions. In J. Mira and F.S. Hernandez, editors, *Proceedings of the International Workshop on Artificial Neural Networks*, volume 930 of *Lecture Notes In Computer Science*, pages 215–222, Malaga, Spain, 1995. Springer–Verlag, Berlin.

[Gol89]   D.E. Goldberg. *Genetic Algorithms in Search, Optimization and Machine Learning*. Addison-Wesley, Reading, MA, 1989.

[HAK⁺99] M. Hagiya, M. Arita, D. Kiga, K. Sakamoto, and S. Yokoyama. Towards parallel evaluation and learning of Boolean μ-formulas with molecules. *DNA Based Computers III*, 48:57–72, 1999. DIMACS Series in Discrete Mathematics and Theoretical Computer Science.

[Hau88]   D. Haussler. Quantifying inductive bias: AI learning algorithms and Valiant's learning framework. *Artificial Intelligence*, 36:177–221, 1988.

[Hir94]   H. Hirsh. Generalizing version spaces. *Machine Learning*, 17(1):5–45, 1994.

[HMP97]   H. Hirsh, N. Mishra, and L. Pitt. Version spaces without boundary sets. In *Proceedings of the 14th National Conference on Artificial Intelligence (AAAI97)*, pages 491–496. AAAI Press/MIT Press, Cambridge, MA, 1997.

[Hol75]   J.H. Holland. *Adaptation in Natural and Artificial Systems*. MIT Press, Cambridge, MA, 1975.

[IPZ01]   R. Impagliazzo, R. Paturi, and F. Zane. Which problems have strongly exponential complexity? *Journal of Computer and System Sciences*, 63(4):512–530, 2001.

[Koz92]   J. Koza. *Genetic Programming: On the Programming of Computers by Means of Natural Selection*. MIT Press, Cambridge, MA, 1992.

[KT04]   M. Kloster and C. Tang. Simulation and analysis of in vitro DNA evolution. *Physical Review Letters*, 92(3):038101, 2004. Epub.

[Lip95]   R.J. Lipton. DNA solution of hard computational problem. *Science*, 268:542–545, 1995.

[LT04]   M.A Lones and A.M. Tyrrell. Enzyme genetic programming. In M. Amos, editor, *Cellular Computing*, Series in Systems Biology, pages 19–42. Oxford University Press, Oxford, 2004.

[LWF⁺00]   Q. Liu, L. Wang, A.G. Frutos, A.E. Condon, R.M. Corn, and L.M. Smith. DNA computing on surfaces. *Nature*, 403:175–179, 2000.

[LYJ⁺03]   H.W. Lim, J.E. Yun, H.M. Jang, Y.G. Chai, S.I. Yoo, and B.T. Zhang. Version space learning with DNA molecules. In H. Masami and O. Azuma, editors, *8th International Workshop on DNA Based Computers: DNA Computing*, volume 2568 of *Lecture Notes in Computer Science*, pages 143–155. Springer–Verlag, London, 2003.

[Mit97]   T.M. Mitchell. *Machine Learning*. McGraw-Hill, New York, 1997.

[NGM01]   D. van Noort, F.U. Gast, and J.S. McCaskill. DNA computing in microreactors. In G. Goos, J. Hartmanis, and J. van Leeuwen, editors, *Proceedings of the 7th International Meeting on DNA Based Computers*, pages 128–137. Springer, Berlin, 2001.

[OKLL97]   Q. Ouyang, P.D. Kaplan, S. Liu, and A. Libchaber. DNA solution of the maximal clique problem. *Science*, 278:446–449, 1997.

[Par03]   J. Parker. Computing with DNA. *EMBO Reports*, 4(1):7–10, 2003.

[RDYS03]   L. Ren, Y. Ding, H. Ying, and S. Shao. Emergence of self-learning fuzzy systems by a new virus DNA-based evolutionary algorithm. *International Journal of Intelligent Systems*, 18:339–354, 2003.

[RHDS02]   J.A. Rose, M. Hagiya, R.J. Deaton, and A. Suyama. DNA-based in vitro genetic program. *Journal of Biological Physics*, 28:493–498, 2002.

[RHHE94]   M.F. Russo, A.C. Huff, C.E. Heckler, and A.C. Evans. An improved DNA encoding scheme for neural network modeling. In P. Werbos, H. Szu, and B. Widrow, editors, *Proceedings of the International Neural Network Society Annual Meeting*, pages 354–359, San Diego, CA, 1994. Lawrence Erlbaum Associates. I/354–I359.

[Sak00]   Y. Sakakibara. DNA computing. volume 2054 of *Lecture Notes in Computer Science*, chapter Solving computational learning problems of Boolean formulae on DNA computers, pages 220–230. Springer–Verlag, Berlin, 2000.

[SGK⁺00]   K. Sakamoto, H. Gouzu, K. Komiya, D. Kiga, S. Yokoyama, T. Yokomori, and M. Hagiya. Molecular computation by DNA hairpin formation. *Science*, 288:1223–1226, 2000.

[SKK⁺99]   K. Sakamoto, D. Kiga, K. Komiya, H. Gouzu, S. Yokoyama, S. Ikeda, H. Sugiyama, and M. Hagiya. State transitions by molecules. *Biosystems*, 52:81–91, 1999.

[SS03]   M.N. Stojanovic and D. Stefanovic. A deoxyribozyme-based molecular automaton. *Nature Biotechnology*, 21:1069–1074, 2003.

[WBK⁺01]   D.H. Wood, H. Bi, S.O. Kimbrough, D. Wu, and J. Chen. DNA starts to learn poker. In G. Goos, J. Hartmanis, and J. van Leeuwen, editors, *Proceedings of the 7th International Meeting on DNA-based Computers*, pages 23–32, Tampa, 2001. Springer, Berlin.

[WC99]   D.H. Wood and J. Chen. Physical separation of DNA according to royal road fitness. In *Proceedings of IEEE Conference on Evolutionary Computation*, pages 1016–1025, Washington DC, 1999. IEEE Computer Society Press, New York.

[WCA⁺99]   D.H. Wood, J. Chen, E. Antipov, W. Cedeno, and B. Lemieux. A DNA implementation of the Max 1s problem. In W. Banzhaf, J. Daida, A.E. Eiben, M.H. Garzon, V. Honavar, M. Jakiela, and R.E. Smith, editors, *Proceedings of the Genetic and Evolutionary Computation Conference*, pages 1835–1842, Orlando, 1999. Morgan Kaufmann, San Francisco.

[YC04]   L. Yuan and F. Chen. Genetic algorithm in DNA computing: a solution to the maximal clique problem. *Chinese Science Bulletin*, 49(9):967–971, 2004.

[YFU97]   T. Yoshikawa, T. Furuhashi, and Y. Uchikawa. The effects of combination of DNA coding method with pseudo-bacterial GA. In *Proceedings of the IEEE International Conference on Evolutionary Computation*, pages 285–290, Indianapolis, Indiana, USA, 1997. IEEE Computer Society Press, New York.

[YWA02]   R. Yokobayashi, R. Weiss, and F.H. Arnold. Directed evolution of a genetic circuit. *Proceedings of the National Academy of Sciences USA*, 99(26):16587–16591, 2002.

[ZJ05a]   B.T. Zhang and H.Y. Jang. DNA computing. In C. Ferretti, G. Mauri, and C. Zandron, editors, *A Bayesian algorithm for in vitro molecular evolution of pattern classifiers*, volume 3384 of *Lecture Notes in Computer Science*, pages 458–467. Springer–Verlag, Berlin, 2005.

[ZJ05b]   B.T. Zhang and H.Y. Jang. Molecular programming: evolving genetic programs in a test tube. In H.G. Beyer, editor, *Proceedings of the 2005 Conference on Genetic and Evolutionary Computations (GECCO'05)*, pages 1761–1768, Washington DC., 2005. ACM Press.

Part V

Artificial Intelligence in Challenging
Environments

Ambient Intelligence: The Confluence of Ubiquitous/Pervasive Computing and Artificial Intelligence

Juan Carlos Augusto

School of Computing and Mathematics, Faculty of Engineering, University of Ulster, Shore Road, Newtownabbey, Co. Antrim BT37 0QB, Northern Ireland, jc.augusto@ulster.ac.uk

Summary. We elaborate on recent developments in the area of "ambient intelligence". Our work includes descriptions of possible applications, a general architecture that can help to define such systems, and the computational process that can link perception through sensors with actuation after decision making.

11.1 Introduction

"Computers will be everywhere," I heard when I was young. The prediction was at that time repeated as a mantra with a mix of admiration, fear, and resignation. Nowadays computers are already influencing our daily lives and there is substantial effort directed at increasing the way they help our society. In particular, technology is being developed that will allow people to be surrounded by an artificial environment that assists them proactively. Whether it is our home anticipating our needs and forecasting dangers, a transport station facilitating commuting, or a hospital room helping to care for a patient, there are strong reasons to believe that our lives are going to be transformed in the coming decades by the introduction of a wide range of devices that will equip many diverse environments with computing power. These computing devices are coordinated by intelligent systems that integrate the resources available to provide an "intelligent environment". This confluence of topics has led to the area of "ambient intelligence".

This chapter explores various scenarios of ambient intelligence and a basic architecture that supports such systems. We also provide some technical details on how these systems work. Section 11.2 reviews the basic concepts associated with ambient intelligence. Different instances of such systems are explained to illustrate how ambient intelligence can be applied in different environments. Section 11.3 examines a basic architecture for ambient intelligence systems, and Section 11.4 shows how this architecture accommodates different scenarios. One of those scenarios is developed in more detail in Section 11.5, where we illustrate how particular contexts of interest can be represented and incorporated into a rule-based language in order to trigger appropriate and timely reactions from the system. Finally, Section 11.6 provides some reflections on this chapter and the area of ambient intelligence itself.

11.2 Ambient Intelligence

"Ambient intelligence" (AmI) [Gro01, AC07] is growing quickly as a multi-disciplinary approach that can allow many areas of research to have a significant beneficial influence on our society. The basic idea behind AmI is that by enriching an environment with technology (mainly sensors and devices interconnected through a network), a system can be built to make decisions to benefit the users of that environment based on real-time information gathered and historical data accumulated.

Ambient intelligence has a decisive relationship with many areas in computer science. The relevant areas are depicted in Figure 11.1.

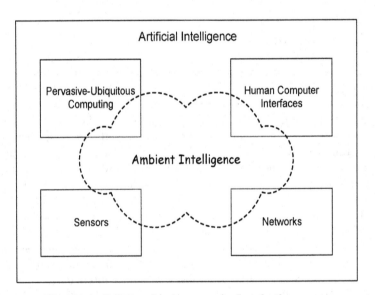

Fig. 11.1. Relationship between AmI and other areas.

Here we must add that while AmI is connected to all those areas, it should not be confused with any of them in particular. Networks, sensors, interfaces, ubiquitous or pervasive computing, and artificial intelligence (AI) are all relevant, but none of them conceptually covers AmI. It is AmI that puts together all these resources to provide flexible and intelligent services to users acting in their environments.

As Raffler succinctly expressed [Raf06], AmI can be defined as:

A digital environment that supports people in their daily lives in a non-intrusive way.

It is aligned with the concept of the *"disappearing computer"* [Wei91, SN05]:

The most profound technologies are those that disappear. They weave themselves into the fabric of everyday life until they are indistinguishable from it.

The notion of a disappearing computer is directly linked to the notion of "ubiquitous computing" [Wei93], or "pervasive computing" [SM03], as IBM called it later on. Some authors equate "ubiquitous computing" and "pervasive computing" with "ambient intelligence". Here we argue that ubiquitous[1]/pervasive[2] systems are different, as they emphasize the physical presence and availability of resources and miss a key element: the explicit requirement of *"intelligence"*. This, we think, is the grounds of artificial intelligence [RN03] and should not be ignored. Here we refer to artificial intelligence in a broad sense, encompassing areas such as agent-based software and robotics. What matters is that AmI systems provide flexibility, adaptation, anticipation, and a sensible interface in the interest of human beings. The same observations can be made about alternatives to *"ubiquitous"* or *"pervasive"* such as the most recent, and less used, term *"everyware"* [Gre06].

This chapter will be based on a more suitable definition that emphasizes intelligence as a fundamental element of an AmI system:

A digital environment that proactively, but sensibly, supports people in their daily lives.

In order to be sensible, a system has to be intelligent. That is how a trained assistant (e.g., a nurse) typically behaves. It will help when needed but will refrain from intervention unless it is necessary. Being sensible demands recognizing the user, learning or knowing her or his preferences, and the capability to exhibit empathy with the user's mood and current overall situation.

Although ambient intelligence will be used to describe this area of research in Europe, similar developments in the United States and Canada will be referred to as *"smart environments"* or *"intelligent environments"*. We keep

---

[1] *Ubiquitous*: adj. present, appearing, or found everywhere (The Oxford Pocket Dictionary of Current English, 2006).

[2] *Pervasive*: adj. (esp. of an unwelcome influence or physical effect) spreading widely throughout an area or a group of people (The Oxford Pocket Dictionary of Current English, 2006).

here the European denomination, as it emphasizes the intelligence factor of these systems as opposed to the physical infrastructure.

Important for ubiquitous/pervasive computing are the "5Ws" (who, where, what, when and why) principle of design [Bro03] as follows.

Who: The identification of a user of the system and the role that user plays within the system in relation to other users. This can be extended to identifying other important elements such as pets, robots, and objects of interest within the environment.

Where: The tracking of the location where a user or an object is geographically located at each moment during system operation. This can demand a mix of technologies; for example, technology that may work well indoors may be useless outdoors and vice versa.

When: The association of activities with time is fundamental to building a realistic picture of a system's dynamics. For example, users, pets, and robots living in a house will change location very often, and knowing when those changes happened and how long they lasted is fundamental to understanding how an environment is evolving.

What: The recognition of activities and tasks users are performing is fundamental in order to provide appropriate help if required. The multiplicity of possible scenarios that can follow an action makes this very difficult. Spatial and temporal awareness help to achieve task awareness.

Why: The capability to infer and understand intentions and goals behind activities is one of the hardest challenges in the area but no doubt a fundamental one that allows the system to anticipate needs and serve users in a sensible way.

An important aspect of AmI has to do with interaction. On one side, there is a motivation to reduce the human-computer interaction (HCI) [DFAB03], as the system is supposed to use its intelligence to infer situations and user needs from the recorded activities, as if a passive human assistant were observing activities unfold with the expectation to help when (and only if) required. On the other hand, a diversity of users may need or voluntarily seek direct interaction with the system to indicate preferences, needs, etc. HCI has been an important area of computer science since the inception of computing as an area of study. Today, with so many gadgets incorporating computing power of some sort, HCI continues to thrive as an important area.

Let's examine in the following section what the possible intelligent environments can be. Later sections will look more closely at how AmI can be implemented in those environments and how AmI can help our society in these environments.

11.2.1 Smart Homes

An example of an environment enriched with AmI is a "smart home" [AN06]. By "smart home" here we understand a house equipped to bring advanced services to its users. Naturally, how smart a house should be to qualify as a smart home is, so far, a subjective matter. For example, a room can have a sensor to decide when its occupant is in or out and on that basis keep lights on or off. However, if sensors only rely on movement and no sensor in, say, the door, can detect when the person left, then a person keeping the body in a resting position while reading can confuse the system, which will leave the room dark. The system will be confusing absence of movement with absence of the person, and that inference will certainly not be considered as particularly "bright", despite the lights.

The technology available today is rich. Several artifacts and items in a house can be enriched with sensors to gather information about their use and in some cases even to act independently without human intervention. Some examples of such devices are electrodomestics (e.g., cooker and fridge), household items (e.g., taps, bed, and sofa), and temperature-handling devices (e.g., air conditioning and radiators). Expected benefits of this technology can be: (a) increased safety (e.g., by monitoring lifestyle patterns or the latest activities and providing assistance when a possibly harmful situation is developing), (b) comfort (e.g., by adjusting temperature automatically), and (c) economy (e.g., controlling the use of lights). There are a plethora of sensing/acting technologies, ranging from those that stand alone (e.g., smoke or movement detectors), to those fitted within other objects (e.g., a microwave or a bed), to those that can be worn (e.g., shirts that monitor heartbeat). For more about sensors and their applications, the reader may like to consider [Wan04] and [NA06].

Recent applications include the use of smart homes to provide a safe environment where people with special needs can have a better quality of life. For example, in the case of people at early stages of senile dementia (the most frequent case being elderly people suffering from Alzheimer's disease), the system can be tailored to minimize risks and ensure appropriate care at critical times by monitoring activities, diagnosing interesting situations, and advising the caregiver. There are already many ongoing academic research projects with well-established smart homes research labs in this area, for example Domus [PMG+02], Aware Home [ABEM02], MavHome [Coo06], and Gator Tech Smart Home [HME+05].

11.2.2 Other Environments and Applications for AmI

Other applications are also feasible and relevant, and the use of sensors and smart devices can be found in:

- *Health-related applications.* Hospitals can increase the efficiency of their services by monitoring patients' health and progress by performing automatic analysis of activities in their rooms. They can also increase safety by, for example, only allowing authorized personnel and patients to have access to specific areas and devices.

- *Public transportation sector.* Public transport can benefit from extra technology, including satellite services, GPS-based spatial location, vehicle identification, image processing, and other technologies to make transport more fluent and hence more efficient and safe.
- *Education services.* Education-related institutions may use technology to track students' progress on their tasks, frequency of attendance at specific places and health-related issues such as advising them on their diet with regard to their eating habits and dietary choices.
- *Emergency services.* Safety-related services (e.g., fire brigades) can improve the reaction to a hazard by locating the place more efficiently and also by preparing the way to reach the place in connection with street services. The prison service can also quickly locate a place where a hazard is occurring or is likely to occur and prepare better access to it for security personnel.
- *Production-oriented places.* Production-centered places such as factories can self-organize according to the production/demand ratio of the goods produced. This will demand careful correlation between the collection of data through sensors within the different sections of the production line and the pool of demands via a diagnostic system that can advise the people in charge of the system at a decision-making level.

Well-known leading companies have already invested heavily in this area. For example, Philips [Phi06] has developed smart homes for the market that include innovative technology on interactive displays. Siemens [Sie06] has invested in smart homes and in factory automation. Nokia [Nok06] also has developments in the area of communications, where the notion of ambience is not necessarily restricted to a house or a building. VTT has developed systems that advise inhabitants of smart homes on how to modify their daily behavior to improve their health [VTT06].

In the next section, we give one step in the direction of identifying some of the important issues and how to consider them explicitly within a system.

11.3 AmI Architecture

So far, the design of AmI systems is quite informal and lacks any agreed conceptualization or prescriptive standards that could help in building such systems. This section therefore aims to identify the main components of AmI systems. We explore a basic architecture for the specification of AmI systems, a triplet,

$$AmISystem = \langle E, IC \rangle$$

such that:

$$
\begin{array}{ccc}
E & \xrightarrow{} & I \\
& IC & \\
\underbrace{} & \xleftarrow{} & \underbrace{} \\
\textit{Environment} & \underbrace{} & \textit{Interactors} \\
& \textit{Interaction} & \\
& \textit{Constraints} &
\end{array}
$$

where E is the environment, for example a house, a hospital, a factory, a street, a city, an airplane, an airport, a train, or a bus station. E is defined by an ontology that can be as detailed as needed and include a variety of physical entities that are known to the system and their relevant attributes. Examples of such entities could be a table, a sink, a tap, a pet, or a robot. Many associated concepts may also be important for the system to understand the role and interrelationships of those entities. For example, areas of the house, interconnection of rooms, and location of doors and windows can be fundamental for the system to predict where activities are developing and what their nature is. If the system is linking activities in a smart home with a group of caregivers (e.g., nurses and relatives), then a hierarchy of care can be used to decide who is the primary contact and how to react if that person is not reachable in an emergency.

The interaction constraints (ICs), specify the possible ways in which elements of E and I can interact with each other. Some elements to be specified are $\langle S, A, C, IR \rangle$, where:

S is a set of sensors. They can be represented as Boolean or real functions and represent devices that can obtain information from the environment; for example, a thermostat or a movement sensor. The range of available elements is wide, and some devices can, for example, take the blood pressure of a patient. A video camera and other image processing devices will be considered a type of sensor despite the complexity of their input, which can range from shapes and contours given by thermo-cameras to real images.

A is a set of actuators. Sensors are usually conceived as passive observers, but some of them are associated with complex mechanisms that also embed the capacity to act on the environment; for example, to interrupt the flow of water in a tap.

C is a set of contexts of interest. A context can be defined as a Boolean specification denoting, for example, particular situations involving objects, sensors, users, places, and so on. Here the principle of "5Ws" (who, where, what, when and why) can be applied as pillars of the system's awareness. It is important for the system to identify who is doing what at a given place and time and for which purpose in order to judge the best possible way to assist users.

IR is a set of interaction rules. Here we are not committing to a particular language at the moment. They can be ECA (event-condition-action) [PD99] or agent-oriented rules [Woo02]. They are the logical core of the system, as they specify the way in which elements listed in previous sets can be related and the effects of those relations.

I is a set of interactors (usually beneficiaries; it can be people, pets, or robots). They can interact with the system. Each is uniquely identified, if possible; otherwise they are considered "anonymous" or as belonging to a group with specific properties of interaction assigned (e.g., caregivers). While the description at E is internal to the AmI system, I is the description of the interactors, which lies outside the system. This internal description is usually not known or available to the AmI system.

Figure 11.2 illustrates an abstract depiction of an AmI system highlighting the elements mentioned in the AmI architecture. All the essential elements are depicted there at physical and logical levels. The environment comprises an individual, four objects, two sensors, and three actuators. The logical level specifies contexts of interest and a set of rules to link the activities at the physical level with the interaction rules that will govern changes at the logical level of the system.

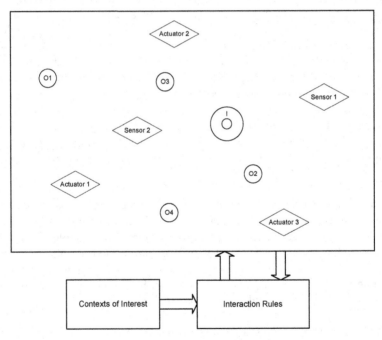

Fig. 11.2. An abstract AmI system.

The forthcoming section describes how this architecture can be used to highlight and specify the essential components of an AmI system and their interrelationships.

11.4 AmI Scenarios

AmI systems can be deployed in many possible environments. Below we describe some of these environments in order to better illustrate the scope of the basic architecture presented earlier.

Scenario 1: An instance of the concept of ambient intelligence is a smart home. See, for example, Figure 11.3.

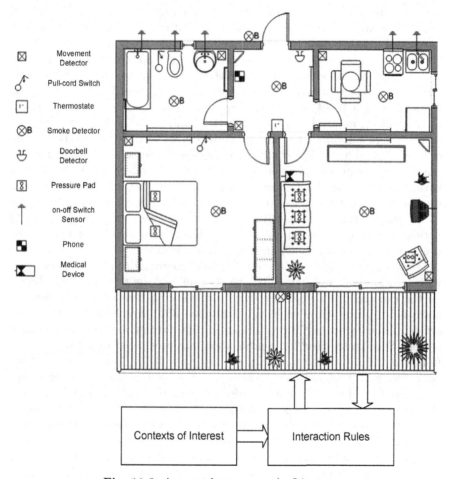

Fig. 11.3. A smart home as an AmI instance.

Here an AmI specification may include the following details. The meaningful environment E is the house, including the backyard and a portion of the front door, as these areas also have sensors. Elements of O are plants, furniture, and so on. There are three interactors depicted and therefore I has three elements: a person in the bedroom and a cat and a floor-cleaning robot in the living room. There are also multiple sensors in S: movement sensors, pull-cord switch, smoke detector, doorbell detector, and pressure pad, plus switch sensors for taps, a cooker, and a TV. In addition, there is a set of actuators A, as the taps, cooker, and TV also have the capacity to be turned on and off without human assistance. Medical devices can also exhibit autonomous behavior by making recommendations before and after their use. Contexts of interest listed in C can be "cooker is left on without human presence in the kitchen for more than 10 minutes" or "occupant is still sleeping after 9AM". Interaction rules specified in IR may consider that "if occupant is in bed and is later than 9AM and contact has been attempted unsuccessfully then caregiver should be notified".

Scenario 2: Let us consider a specific room of a hospital as the environment, with a patient being monitored for health and security reasons. Objects in the environment are furniture, medical equipment, and specific elements of the room such as a toilet, and a window. Interactors in this environment will be the patient, relatives and caregivers (e.g., nurses and doctors). Sensors can be movement sensors and wristband detectors for identifying who is entering or leaving the room and who is approaching specific areas such as a window or the toilet. Actuators can be microphones within the toilet to interact with the patient in an emergency. Contexts of interest can be "the patient has entered the toilet and has not returned after 20 minutes" or "frail patient left the room". Interaction rules specified in IR can consider, for example, that "if patient is leaving the room and status indicates that this is not allowed for this particular patient then nurses should be notified".

Scenario 3: Assume a central underground coordination station is equipped with location sensors to track the location of each unit in real time. Based on the time needed to connect two locations with sensors, the system can also predict the speed of each unit. Examples of objects in this environment are tracks and stations. Interactors are trains, drivers, and command center officers. Sensors are used for identification purposes based on ID signals sent from the train. Other signals can be sent as well (e.g., emergency status). Actuators will be signals coordinating the flow of trains and messages that can be delivered to each unit in order to regulate their speed and the time they have to spend at a stop. Contexts of interest can be "delays" or "stopped train". One interaction rule can be "if line blocked ahead and there are intermediate stops describe the situation to passengers".

Scenario 4: Let's assume a primary school where students are monitored to best advise them on balancing their learning experience. The objects within a classroom or playground are tables and other available elements. The interactors are students and teachers. The sensors will identify who is using what scientific kit, and that in turn will allow monitoring of how long students are involved with a particular experiment. Actuators can be recommendations delivered to wristwatch-like personalized displays. Contexts of interest can be "student has been with a single experimentation kit for too long" or "student has not engaged in active experimentation". The first context will trigger a rule "if student has been interacting with one single kit for more than 20 minutes advise the student to try the next experiment available", while the second one will require a message to a tutor, such as "if student S has not engaged for more than 5 minutes with an experiment then tutor has to encourage and guide S".

Scenario 5: When a fire brigade has to act, then the environment can be a city or a neighborhood. Streets can be equipped with sensors to measure passage of traffic within the areas through which the fire brigade truck might go in order to reach the place where the emergency is located. Objects here will be streets and street junctions. Interactors will be cars. Actuators can be traffic lights, as they can help speed the fire brigade through. A context will be a fire occurring at peak time with a number of alternative streets to be used. An interaction rule can be "if all streets are busy, use traffic lights to hold traffic back from the vital passage to be used".

Scenario 6: If a production line is the environment, then different sensors can track the flow of items at critical bottlenecks in the system, and the system can compare the current flow with a desired benchmark. Decision makers can then make decisions on how to proceed and how to react to the arrival of new materials and to upcoming demands. Different parts of the plant can be activated or deactivated accordingly. Similarly, sensors can provide useful information on places where there has been a problem and the section has stopped production, requiring a deviation in flow. Objects here are transportation belts and elements being manufactured, while actuators are the different mechanisms allowing or disallowing the flow of elements at particular places. A context can be "a piece of system requiring maintenance", and a related interaction rule can be "if section A becomes unavailable then redirect the flow of objects through alternative paths".

In addition, we need to go beyond the enumeration of parts and the description of their roles to provide a computational layer so that intelligent behavior can result synergetically from their interactions. The next section considers this interaction at a higher logical level, assuming the existence of an appropriate middleware level that can pass information to the reasoning system as meaningful temporally tagged events.

11.5 AmI Architecture at Work

Let's assume a house like the one in Figure 11.3, inhabited by an elderly person who requires assistance for daily living in order to minimize hazards and to detect and react to undesirable situations. We have described the elements of the AmI architecture in Section 11.3, and here we look closer at the representation and use of "context" and "interaction rules", which are key components in the computational realization of any AmI architecture. Some examples of contexts, or situations, of interest are:

- leaving the cooker unattended while preparing a meal,

- not taking a phone call,

- not walking to the front door when the doorbell rings,

- sequence of vital signs indicating possible health deterioration,

- not eating with the expected frequency or at the expected time,

- not bathing with the expected frequency,

- going to the toilet too frequently,

- wandering (especially during the night),

- attempting to leave the house at inconvenient times (e.g., 12AM—6AM),

- detection of an intruder, and

- medication intake compliance.

These contexts then can be used to direct the interaction rules, which will provide the right reactions in the right contexts. For contexts and interaction rules to be of any use, they have to be described in a way that can be processed by computers. We do not aim to be prescriptive here, so the language used in this chapter has to be interpreted simply as one possibility.

Consider the following general language $\mathcal{E}$ based on a formalization of temporal notions presented in natural language expressions. This language allows us to distinguish two key notions: event-forming and state-forming phenomena [Gal05]. $\mathcal{E}$ will be used here to define the sublanguage to be used for complex event detection and for condition specification. The reader can find more technical details of the language in [Gal05] and the computational tools associated with it in [GAG00] and [GAG01].

Temporal representations in $\mathcal{E}$ are in the form of instants $t][t+1$ or intervals $[t, t']$. Here t is an abstract unit of time arbitrarily selected according to the application; therefore, in between t and $t+1$ we can assume, for example, that one second, one minute, or ten seconds have elapsed.

It is not possible to give full coverage of all the operators here, so we just list a few operators that are mentioned in the rules given below.

Ingr(S): Occurs at $n][n+1$ iff $\neg S$ holds on $[n, n]$ and S holds on $[n+1, n+1]$.

Trans(S_1, S_2): If S_1 and S_2 are two mutually incompatible states, then the event $Trans(S_1, S_2)$ has:

1. an instantaneous occurrence at $n][n+1$ iff S_1 holds on $[n, n]$ and S_2 holds on $[n+1, n+1]$.
2. a durative occurrence in $[m, n]$ iff S_1 holds on $[m-1, m-1]$, S_2 holds on $[n+1, n+1]$, and both $\neg S_1$ and $\neg S_2$ hold on $[m, n]$.

Po(S): Occurs on $[m, n]$ iff S holds throughout $[m, n]$, and $\neg S$ holds on both $m-1$ and $n+1$.

For(S, d): Occurs on $[m, n]$ iff $n - m = d - 1$, S holds throughout $[m, n]$, and $\neg S$ holds on both $m-1$ and $n+1$.

GSC(E_1, E_2): If E_1 is instantaneous and E_2 is durative, then **GSC(E_1, E_2)** occurs on $[m, n]$ iff there is an integer k, where $m \leq k \leq n$, such that E_1 occurs at $m-1][m$ but at no instant $l-1][l$ where $m < l < k$ and E_2 occurs on $[k, n]$ but not on any interval $[p, q]$ where $m \leq p < q$. Note: see [Gal05] for the definition of **GSC** in the three other remaining possibilities regarding E_1 and E_2 being instantaneous or durative.

Consec-I(E, N): If E is an instantaneous event, then:

1. **Consec-I($E, 2$)** occurs on $[m, n]$ iff E occurs on both $m-1][m$ and $n][n+1$.
2. **Consec-I(E, k)**, with $k > 2$, occurs on $[m, n]$ iff there is an integer p where $m < p \leq n$ such that E occurs at $m-1][m$ but not at any instant between m and p and **Consec-I($E, k-1$)** occurs on $[p, n]$.

$\mathcal{E}$ has been integrated into an "active database" [PD99] framework to define a language $\mathcal{L}$ where interaction rules can be specified that denote how contexts can be used to trigger decisions and reactions on behalf of the AmI system. These rules have the typical format adopted in the active databases literature,

ON *event* IF *condition* THEN *action*,

meaning that whenever *event* is detected, if *condition* holds, then *action* is applied [AN04]. Assuming there is a nonempty and finite set of ECA rules, $R = \{R_1, R_2, \ldots, R_n\}$ with n a natural number, where each rule R_i for $1 <= i <= n$ is of the form specified in [AN04], the general algorithm of the process monitoring and triggering rules can be briefly described as follows. Each time an event arrives, the ON clauses are checked and, from those rules in the subset of R: $R' = \{R_{i_1}, \ldots, R_{i_m}\}$ having a complex event definition detected, the conditions stated in the IF clause are checked. For those rules in the subset of R': $R'' = \{R_{j_1}, \ldots, R_{j_n}\}$ with their conditions satisfied the actions stated in the THEN clause are applied. Let us consider that the set of actions in the rules of R'' is $A'' = \{A_{j_1}, \ldots, A_{j_n}\}$. Then in our system all actions in A'' will be performed atomically in sequence. The system combines an active database where the events are collected to record sensors that have been stimulated and a reasoner that will apply spatio-temporal reasoning and other techniques to make decisions. A typical information flow for AmI systems is depicted in Figure 11.4.

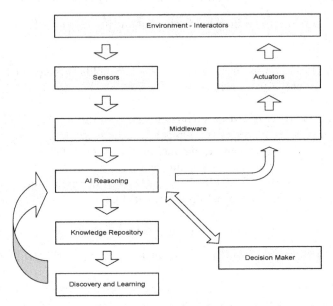

Fig. 11.4. Information flow in AmI systems.

As the interactors perform their tasks, some of these tasks will trigger sensors, and these in turn will activate the reasoning system. Storing the frequency of activities and decisions made during relevant parts of the system's lifetime allows the system to learn information that is useful to decision makers (e.g., for doctors and nurses to decide if a change in the medication of a patient suffering Alzheimer's disease may be needed). It also allows learning that can improve the system itself (e.g., to make interaction rules more personalized and useful for a particular person). For example, peoples' habits in winter are different than in summer in terms of their usual time to get up or the time they spend watching TV or sleeping. The next scenario is about monitoring whether the person living in the smart house reacts as expected to normal situations. A lack of response can be used as a possible indicator that the person is unwell and is worth investigating if that is the case.

If there is an ingression to a state where doorbell has been rung and is not followed by an ingression to a state were the person goes to the door in a reasonable time, say 5 mins, while it is known that the person is at home and is not hearing impaired then apply the procedure to deal with a potential emergency and separately try alternative ways of contact (e.g., visually or by phone).

Let us consider sensors `doorbell_rang` and `at_outside`, and let us assume we keep Boolean variables in our system to indicate different characteristics of the person inhabiting the house; for example, `hearing_problems` indicates the person is known to be hearing impaired. Variable `at_home` can be inferred from the status of any of the other sensors detecting the passage of people through doors. Passing through the front door to go out of the house means `at_home` becomes false and `at_outside` becomes true. Suppose then the recording of events:

	at_kitchen	doorbell_rang
0] [1	on	
1] [2	on	
2] [3	on	on
3] [4	on	on
4] [5	on	on
5] [6	on	
6] [7	on	
7] [8	on	
8] [9	on	
9] [10	on	
. . .		

which can be summarized as:

```
0] [1  at_kitchen_on
1] [2  dummy_event
2] [3  doorbell_on
3] [4  doorbell_on
4] [5  doorbell_on
5] [6  dummy_event
6] [7  dummy_event
7] [8  dummy_event
8] [9  dummy_event
9] [10 dummy_event
       . . .
```

where we use the following notational conventions: $t]$ $[t+1$ *sensor_on* means *sensor* has been activated, $t]$ $[t+1$ *sensor_off* means *sensor* has been deactivated, and $t]$ $[t+1$ `dummy_event` means no new sensors are activated. In the rule below, `occurs(ingr(doorbell_rang_on)`, `2][3)` denotes the instant between intervals 2 and 3 at which the doorbell was off and then on, while a predicate `occurs(trans(at_reception, at_outside), [5,7])` would represent a sensor activation indicating the person has opened the kitchen door and moved from the kitchen to the reception area between intervals 5 and 7. A transition will generally be instantaneous, but if the transition is detected by an RFID sensor located at the door between the kitchen and the reception area, then the person staying for a while under the door can cause the sensor to be permanently activated for a little while.

```
ON (occurs(ingr(doorbell_rang_on), I1a][I1b) ∧
     ¬ (occurs(trans(at_reception, at_outside), [I1b,Now]) ∨
        occurs(trans(X,at_reception), [I1b,Now])) )
IF (moreThanNUnitsElapsed(I1b, Now, 5 mins) ∧
    holds(at_home, [I1a,I1b]) ∧
    ¬ holds(hearingProblems, [I1a,I1b]))
THEN (TryAlternativeWaysOfContact)
```

The scenario below represents a situation where the above rule will be triggered at 8][9, as the person has remained in the kitchen for more than 5 units of time despite somebody ringing the bell:

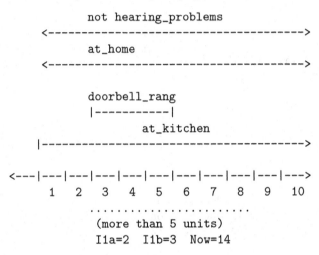

```
            not hearing_problems
    <-------------------------------------->
            at_home
    <-------------------------------------->

            doorbell_rang
            |-----------|
                at_kitchen
    |-------------------------------------->

<---|---|---|---|---|---|---|---|---|---|--->
    1   2   3   4   5   6   7   8   9   10
        . . . . . . . . . . . . . . . . .
            (more than 5 units)
        I1a=2  I1b=3  Now=14
```

Contexts defined by an activity being developed within a given period of time can also be considered:

If there is an ingression to a state where the person is in bed during the daytime and stays in bed for more than 3 hours then raise a warning.

Let us assume we have the events:

	in_bed	day_Period
...		
7][8		true
8][9		true
9][10		true
10][11		true
11][12		true
12][13		true
13][14	on	true
14][15	on	
15][16	on	
16][17	on	
...		

which can be summarized as:

```
7] [8  day_Period
8] [9  dummy_event
9] [10 dummy_event
10] [11 dummy_event
11] [12 dummy_event
12] [13 dummy_event
13] [14 in_bed_on
14] [15 in_bed_on
15] [16 in_bed_on
16] [17 in_bed_on
    ...
```

and can be represented in $\mathcal{L}$ as:

```
ON (occurs(ingr(inbed_on), I1a][I1b) ∧
    occurs(for(inbed_on, 3), I1b][I2))
IF ¬ during([I1b,I2], day_Period)
THEN (ApplyPossibleUnwellPatientProcedure ∧
    TryContact)
```

and depicted as below:

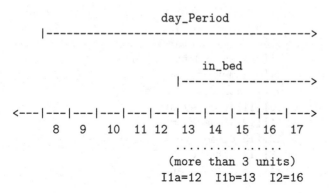

Let us consider now that we include in the system a rule capturing that:

If there is an ingression to a state where the cooker is in use, followed by the person going out of the kitchen without returning to it for more than 10 minutes, then apply a procedure to deal with a potential hazard and separately try to make personal contact.

Let us assume we have the following events sent from our middleware system to the AmI reasoner: at_kitchen_on, cooker_on, at_reception_on, at_toilet_on, tapSinkBathroom_on, at_bedroom_on and inbed_on. Suppose the following sequence of events arrives at the AmI system (tapSinkBathroom is shortened to tapSinkBathR):

	at_kitchen	cooker	at_reception	at_toilet	tapSinkBathR	at_bedroom	inbed
0][1	on						
1][2	on						
2][3	on	on					
3][4	on	on					
4][5		on	on				
5][6		on		on			
6][7		on		on	on		
7][8		on		on			
8][9		on		on			
9][10		on	on				
10][11		on					
11][12		on				on	
12][13		on				on	
13][14		on				on	on
14][15		on				on	on
. . .							

For simplicity, we summarize this as follows:

```
 0] [1 at_kitchen_on
 1] [2 dummy_event
 2] [3 cooker_on
 3] [4 dummy_event
 4] [5 at_reception_on
 5] [6 at_toilet_on
 6] [7 tapSinkBathroom_on
 7] [8 tapSinkBathroom_off
 8] [9 dummy_event
 9] [10 at_reception_on
10] [11 dummy_event
11] [12 at_bedroom_on
12] [13 dummy_event
13] [14 inbed_on
14] [15 dummy_event
   . . .
```

Then we can write in $\mathcal{L}$:

```
ON (occurs(ingr(cooker_in_use), I1a][I1b) ∧
    occurs(trans(at_kitchen, at_reception), I2a][I2b))
IF (earlier(I1b, I2b) ∧
    ¬ holds(at_kitchen, [I2b,Now]) ∧
    moreThanNUnitsElapsed(I2b, Now, 10 mins))
THEN (ApplyPossibleHazardProcedure ∧ TryContact)
```

Assuming each primitive event takes one unit of time to arrive, then by the time the person is in bed at time 13, the condition that more than 10 units have elapsed since the person turned the cooker on without returning to the kitchen is satisfied. All the conditions will be fulfilled for our rule to be triggered. This scenario can be graphically depicted as:

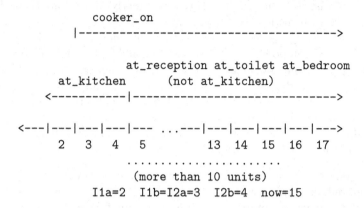

```
                cooker_on
        |------------------------------------------->


                     at_reception at_toilet at_bedroom
           at_kitchen        (not at_kitchen)
        <-----------|------------------------------->

  <---|---|---|---|--- ...---|---|---|---|---|--->
       2   3   4   5          13  14  15  16  17
                    ........................
                    (more than 10 units)
        I1a=2  I1b=I2a=3  I2b=4  now=15
```

Operators in $\mathcal{E}$ can also be composed at arbitrary nesting levels capturing many different situations. As an example of a slightly more involved non-primitive event detection, we can combine the operators **Po**, **GSC**, and **Consec-I** as:

```
occurs( po(gsc(ingr(change_of_medication),
             consec-i(high_blood_pressure,2)),
        [(2007,8,22,13,00,00), (2007,8,23,13,00,00)] ) )
```

to express that an occurrence of two consecutive high blood pressure records have been detected after a change in medication has been detected during the interval [(2007,8,22,13,00,00), (2007,8,23,13,00,00)].

The scenarios described through $\mathcal{L}$ and the examples of complex events that can be detected with $\mathcal{E}$ provided above are only a few samples of what can be achieved. It was not the aim of this section to impose a specific language, in this case $\mathcal{E}$, but to illustrate some of the things that can be done and stimulate constructive reflection on these matters. It is clear, that there is much to do yet. For example, while $\mathcal{E}$ is well-equipped for time-related issues, it lacks explicit constructs for spatially related concepts. Some spatial representation and reasoning can be made; for example, it is possible to represent that a person is in an area (e.g., the kitchen) and makes a transition to another area (e.g., reception). But if we want to detect wandering, we need specific ways to represent trajectories and ways to detect them. Given space restrictions, we cannot fully develop an AmI architecture. Instead we listed and briefly exemplified some expected features of it with emphasis on context awareness and hope it inspires further developments in this area.

11.6 Conclusions

In this chapter, we have reviewed the notion of ambient intelligence and associated concepts. We highlighted that an essential component of the area is the distribution of technology intelligently orchestrated to allow an environment to benefit its users.

We have also proposed an architecture that demands explicit reasoning about the main components of an AmI system and highlighted the importance of having a specific language to define contexts and rules of interaction governing the AmI system. These concepts were illustrated with several possible scenarios, in particular with different situations related to a smart home system.

AmI is still in its infancy and there is much to do. Future challenges include answering the following questions:

- How do we develop a software engineering framework capable of producing more reliable AmI systems?
- How do we achieve proper detection of meaningful events (for example, to ensure medication is actually swallowed by a patient)?
- How do we avoid undesirable effects (for example, a fly opening a curtain because it activates a movement detector)?
- How can a system self-monitor (for example, to infer if a sensor is not working properly)?
- How do we combine preferences in a group (for example, when suggesting TV programs)?
- How do we anticipate needs that are realistic projections of a context (for example, predicting the behavior of other drivers)?
- How do we detect and adapt to the changing needs and preferences of a user or group of users (people change preferences and needs due to a multiplicity of factors such as weather, economic situation and mood)?
- How do we achieve a sensible level of intervention (too much is over-whelming, and with too little the user may be unprotected)?

These questions will increase the predictability of AmI systems being deployed. Since these systems are autonomous and proactive, the issue of predictability and reliability should not be underestimated if we want the environments where we live and work to be of real help.

Acknowledgments

The author would like to express his gratitude to Dr. Alfons Schuster and the reviewers for their valuable suggestions on how to improve this chapter.

References

[ABEM02] G.A. Abowd, I. Bobick, E. Essa, and W. Mynatt. The aware home: developing technologies for successful aging. In K. Haigh, H. Yanco, B. Brumitt, M. Coen, and V. Lesser, editors, *Proceedings of AAAI Workshop on Automation as a Care Giver*, pages 1–7. AAAI Press, Menlo Park, CA, Alberta, Canada, July 2002.

[AC07] J.C. Augusto and D. Cook. *Ambient Intelligence: Applications in Society and Opportunities for AI*. IJCAI, Hyderabad, India, January 2007. Lecture notes for the tutorial given during the 20th International Joint Conference on Artificial Intelligence (IJCAI 2007).

[AN04] J.C. Augusto and C.D. Nugent. The use of temporal reasoning and management of complex events in smart homes. In R.L. de Mántaras and L. Saitta, editors, *Proceedings of the European Conference on Artificial Intelligence (ECAI 2004)*, pages 778–782, Valencia, Spain, August 2004. IOS Press, Amsterdam.

[AN06] J.C. Augusto and C.D. Nugent. *Designing Smart Homes: The Role of Artificial Intelligence*, volume 4008 of *Lecture Notes in Artificial Intelligence*. Springer-Verlag, Berlin, 1st edition, 2006.

[Bro03] K. Brooks. The context quintet: narrative elements applied to context awareness. In *Proceedings of the 10th International Conference on Human–Computer Interaction (HCI 2003)*, pages 1213–1217, Crete, Greece, 2003. Lawrence Erlbaum Associates, Mahwah, NJ.

[Coo06] D. Cook. Health monitoring and assistance to support aging in place. *Journal of Universal Computer Science*, 12(1):15–29, 2006.

[DFAB03] A. Dix, J. Finlay, G.D. Abowd, and R. Beale. *Human–Computer Interaction*. Prentice–Hall, Englewood Cliffs, NJ, 3rd edition, 2003.

[GAG00] R. Gómez, J.C. Augusto, and A. Galton. Implementation and testing for a set of event detection operators. Technical Report 398, School of Engineering and Computer Science, University of Exeter, United Kingdom, 2000. http://www.infj.ulst.ac.uk/~jcaug/rr398.pdf.

[GAG01] R. Gómez, J.C. Augusto, and A. Galton. Testing an event specification language. In *Proceedings of the 13th International Conference of Software Engineering and Knowledge Engineering (SEKE 2001)*, pages 341–346, Buenos Aires, Argentina, 2001.

[Gal05] A. Galton. Eventualities. In M. Fisher, D.M. Gabbay, and L. Vila, editors, *Handbook of Temporal Reasoning in Artificial Intelligence*, pages 25–28. Elsevier, Amsterdam, 2005.

[Gre06] A. Greenfield. *Everyware: The Dawning Age of Ubiquitous Computing*. Peachpit Press, Sebastopol, CA, 2006.

[Gro01] IST Advisory Group. The European Union report, scenarios for ambient intelligence in 2010, 2001. ftp://ftp.cordis.lu/pub/ist/docs/istagscenarios2010.pdf.

[HME+05] A. Helal, W. Mann, H. Elzabadani, J. King, Y. Kaddourah, and E. Jansen. Gator tech smart house: a programmable pervasive space. *IEEE Computer Magazine*, 38(3):64–74, March 2005.

[NA06] C.D. Nugent and J.C. Augusto, editors. *Proceedings of the 4th International Conference on Smart Homes and Health Telematic (ICOST2006)*, volume 19 of *Assistive Technology Research*, Belfast, June 2006. IOS Press, Amsterdam.

[Nok06]   Nokia, 2006.   http://www.research.nokia.com/research/projects/
            sensorplanet/index.html.

[PD99]   N.W. Paton and O. Diaz. Active database systems. *ACM Computing
            Surveys*, 31(1):63–103, 1999.

[Phi06]   Philips, 2006. http://www.research.philips.com/technologies/syst_
            softw/ami/background.html.

[PMG+02]   H. Pigot, A. Mayers, S. Giroux, B. Lefebvre, V. Rialle, and N. Noury.
            Smart house for frail and cognitive impaired elders. In *First International
            Workshop on Ubiquitous Computing for Cognitive Aids (UbiCog'02)*,
            September 2002. Goteborg, Sweden.

[Raf06]   H. Raffler. Other perspectives on ambient intelligence. Password Mag-
            azine, Issue 23, 2006.   http://www.research.philips.com/password/
            archive/23/pw23_ambintel_other.html.

[RN03]   S.J. Russell and P. Norvig. *Artificial Intelligence: A Modern Approach.*
            Prentice–Hall, Englewood Cliffs, NJ, 2nd edition, 2003.

[Sie06]   Siemens, 2006.   http://www.networks.siemens.de/smarthome/en/
            index.htm.

[SM03]   D. Saha and A. Mukherjee. Pervasive computing: a paradigm for the
            21st century. *IEEE Computer*, 36(3):25–31, March 2003.

[SN05]   N. Streitz and P. Nixon. Introduction. *Communications of the ACM*,
            48(3):32–35, March 2005. Special issue: The disappearing computer.

[VTT06]   VTT, 2006. http://www.vtt.fi/uutta/2006/20060602.jsp.

[Wan04]   R. Want. RFID—a key to automating everything. *Scientific American*,
            290:46–55, January 2004.

[Wei91]   M. Weiser. The computer for the twenty-first century. *Scientific Ameri-
            can*, 165:94–104, 1991.

[Wei93]   M. Weiser. Hot topics: ubiquitous computing. *IEEE Computer*,
            26(10):71–72, 1993.

[Woo02]   M. Wooldridge. *An Introduction to Multiagent Systems.* John Wiley and
            Sons, New York, 2002.

Artificial Intelligence for Space Applications

Daniela Girimonte and Dario Izzo

European Space Agency, Advanced Concepts Team, ESTEC, EUI-ACT,
Keplerlaan 1, 2201 AZ Noordwijk, The Netherlands,
daniela.girimonte@esa.int, dario.izzo@esa.int

Summary. The ambitious short-term and long-term goals set down by the various national space agencies call for radical advances in several of the main space engineering areas, the design of intelligent space agents certainly being one of them. In recent years, this has led to an increasing interest in artificial intelligence by the entire aerospace community. However, in the current state of the art, several open issues and showstoppers can be identified. In this chapter, we review applications of artificial intelligence in the field of space engineering and space technology and identify open research questions and challenges. In particular, the following topics are identified and discussed: distributed artificial intelligence, enhanced situation self-awareness, and decision support for spacecraft system design.

12.1 Introduction

In the second half of 2003, the European Space Agency (ESA) delivered a roadmap, in the framework of the Aurora program, to bring humans to explore Mars within the next few decades [MO03]. The plan included the successful implementation of several flagstone missions as stepping stones for achieving this final ambitious goal. A few months later, with the vision delivered by U.S. president George W. Bush, the National Aeronautics and Space Administration (NASA) also started to draft plans for the manned exploration of Mars [Bus04]. Their vision included the establishment of a human base on the Moon, among several other advanced preparatory steps. The return of humans to the Moon and a future manned mission to Mars therefore seem to be likely achievements we may witness in the next few decades. At the same time, even more ambitious plans and missions are being conceived by farsighted researchers who dream about the exploration and colonization of even farther planets.

In the framework of these more or less concrete future scenarios, the consolidation of artificial intelligence methods in space engineering is certainly an enabling factor. As an example, the reader may think of a future mission to Mars. This will probably be constituted by a large number of heterogeneous space agents (intended to be satellites, humans, robots, modules, sensors, and so on). In such a scenario, the round-trip communication delay time, depending on the relative positions of Mars and Earth, would range from 6.5 minutes to 44 minutes approximately. Besides, communication with Earth would not be possible at all during a 14 day period every Mars synodic period (approximately 2.1 years). Clearly, for such a mission to happen, the single space agents must be able to make autonomous decisions, to interact harmoniously with each other, and to be able to determine their own health status so as to properly plan their actions. Unfortunately, if we take a look at the current state of the art of artificial intelligence applications in space engineering, we can identify several open issues and showstoppers. Actually, it seems that we are far away from the desirable situation in which these methods can be considered as off-the-shelf tools available to space engineers.

This chapter is addressed to the artificial intelligence community in order to create an awareness of the many open research questions and challenges in the space engineering community. In order to achieve this task, the chapter focuses on a few niche applications only, namely distributed artificial intelligence for swarm autonomy and distributed computing, and enhanced situation self-awareness and decision support for spacecraft system design. Our survey aims to give the reader a general overview of these topics by pointing out some of the relevant activities within the international space community and as such is not intended to cover the entire array of all artificial intelligence applications in space. For example, we deliberately omitted in this discussion research on automated planning and scheduling, which is traditionally the most studied field within artificial intelligence for space, and we refer interested readers to other resources such as the proceedings of the International Workshop on Planning and Scheduling for Space (e.g., 1997, 2000, 2004, and 2006).

12.2 Distributed Artificial Intelligence

At the end of the 1980s, the artificial intelligence community started wondering whether intelligence had to be strictly related to reasoning. Failures in constructing agents able to interact with the environment in real-time following high-level decisions derived via symbolic reasoning led to a new approach in the design of robot control systems: "behavior based" robotics [Bro91]. Starting from the simple observation that most of what we do in our daily lives is not related to detailed planning but rather to instinctual reactions to an unstable and changing environment, behavioral robotics introduced, for the first time, the notion of "emerging" intelligence. Researchers were forced to observe that, in some systems, intelligence could emerge from the interaction with the environment and from indirect relations between system parts and that, in general, intelligence could not always be easily located in one particular part of the system studied. The idea of intelligence residing in a distributed form throughout an agent started the study of intelligent systems made by more than one agent. Hence, "distributed artificial intelligence" (DAI) developed as a discipline studying systems made up of a number of diverse agents that despite their individuality are able to achieve common global tasks. In the following sections, we mainly touch upon two topics of DAI systems for space applications: swarm intelligence and distributed computing.

12.2.1 Swarm Intelligence

There is no common agreement on the definition of swarm intelligence. Definitely a subcategory of distributed artificial intelligence, we define swarm intelligence as the emerging property of systems made by multiple identical and noncognitive agents characterized by limited sensing capabilities. This definition, nearly a description of biological swarm intelligence, stresses the necessity of having agents that interact locally with the environment and between themselves. It may be argued that algorithms historically considered at the center of swarm intelligence research, such as "particle swarm optimization" (PSO) [KE95], sometimes lack this property, which therefore should not be required in the definition.[1] Others would instead take the opposite direction in requiring that the local interaction happen only indirectly through an intentional modification of the environment (stigmergy [TB99]). Other issues arise when trying to decide whether deterministic systems should be excluded from the definition of swarm intelligence. These pages may not be a suitable place to settle or discuss these issues, and we therefore ask the reader to be forgiving should our view not be fully satisfactory to him or her.

Whatever definition one wishes to adopt, a number of features of swarm intelligence are certainly attractive to the space engineering community. The space environment typically puts stringent constraints on the capabilities of single satellites, robots, or anything that needs to survive in space (space agents). Space agents are particularly limited in terms of mobility (propellant- and power-limited), communication (power-limited), and size (mass-limited). At the same time, a high level of adaptability, robustness, and autonomy is required to increase the chances of success of operating in a largely unknown environment. Similar characteristics are found in the individual components of a biological swarm. Moreover, a number of space applications are naturally based on the presence of multiple space agents. The first commercial application proposed and realized for satellite systems was that of Arthur C. Clarke and was a satellite constellation providing global communication services by means of three satellites put in a geostationary orbit [Cla45]. Since then, a large number of constellations have been deployed to provide global communication, navigation, and Earth observation services.

---

[1] The so-called social component in the PSO algorithm requires at each step for each agent to know the best solution found so far by the entire swarm. Interagent communication is, in this case, direct and unlimited in range.

More recently, the idea of a number of satellites flying in formation has been used in a number of missions for applications ranging from x-ray astronomy (XEUS) to differential measurements of the geomagnetic field (CLUSTER II), space interferometry, the search for exoplanets (DARWIN), and others. All these missions [2] are able to meet their requirements without making use of an emerging property that can be regarded as swarm intelligence. On the other hand, if available, swarm intelligence methods would represent an attractive design option allowing, for example, achievement of autonomous operation of formations. Simple agents interacting locally could be considered as a resource rather than overhead. At the same time, one would be able to engineer systems that are robust, autonomous, adaptable, distributed, and inherently redundant. Besides, swarms allow for mass production of single components, thus promising mission cost reduction, and represent highly stowable systems, thus allowing reduced launch costs. Recently, these motivations led a number of researchers to simulate some degree of swarm intelligence in a number of space systems and to investigate their behavior.

Kassabalidis et al. [KEM+01] studied the routing problem in wireless communication networks between satellites or planetary sensors. He applied ant-inspired algorithms to achieve a great efficiency in networks that are spatially distributed and changing over time. This type of research is targeted at applications such as those being developed by the NASA sensorweb project [CCD+05]. Distributed cooperative planning between satellites belonging to the same constellation has also been studied, introducing swarm intelligence at the level of coordinated planning [DVC05] (for a typical case study, see Fuego, studied by Escorial et al. [ETR+03]). Recent work on intersatellite communication in constellations observed the birth of emerging properties from a more or less complex system of rules and behaviors [BT07] programmed in the autonomous planners onboard the satellites. More generally, any problem of autonomy for satellite constellations is a problem of distributed artificial intelligence, where the possibility of communication between agents (ISL-intersatellite links) or between an agent and a central planner (ground station) is limited by the complex dynamics of the system and by the agent design.

Another field where swarm intelligence provides a possibility to improve current technology is that of relative satellite motion control. When a system of many satellites has to move in a coordinated way, the control action selected by each satellite may take into account the decisions made by the others at different levels. The information exchanged with the other swarm components is useful but not necessary to define the geometric and kinematical representation of the time-varying environment, which will then influence the satellite action selection. Many studies dealing with terrestrial robot navigation [Kha86], with spacecraft proximity and rendezvous operations [McI95], and self-assembly structures in space [McQ97] have taken the ap-

---

[2] At the time of writing, CLUSTER II is the only one operational.

proach of defining an artificial potential field to model the environment. The control action is then chosen to follow the steepest descent of the defined potential. Another approach to the action selection problem, based on dynamic systems theory, was introduced by Schoner [SD92]. In this approach, the state-space contains behavioral variables such as heading directions or velocities. All the contributions given by each behavior are combined by means of weighting parameters into a final dynamical system that defines the course of behaviors that each agent will follow. The weighting parameters can be evaluated by solving a competitive dynamic system operating on a faster timescale. Recently, other approaches have been proposed, in particular for space applications, attempting to obtain some degree of decentralized coordination in a group of satellites. Lawton and Beard [RB04, LYB03] introduced what they call a "virtual structure" method to design a decentralized formation control scheme. Their method aims at reaching a unique final configuration in which each satellite has its position preassigned. When a swarm of homogeneous agents is considered and the task is given to acquire a certain final geometry, the final positions occupied by each agent in the target configurations should be chosen in an autonomous way and should be part of the global behavior emerging from the individual tasks assigned. This result is actually possible using a technique [IP07] developed at ESA and inspired by swarm aggregation results [Gaz05] for terrestrial robots. Introducing a behavioral component that accounts for the differential gravity typical of orbital environments, the algorithm allows one to obtain, in a given countable number of final formations, a swarm whose emerging behavior is the solution of the target allocation problem and the acquisition and maintenance of the final formation.

Figure 12.1 illustrates two examples of orbital swarms controlled by this algorithm with the addition of a limited amount of hierarchy in the swarm to allow the lattice formation [IP07]. Note that, in the first case, the swarm autonomously selects its final arrangement from $2.81 \cdot 10^{41}$ different final possible configurations. In the second case, this number is $4.16 \cdot 10^{29}$. A behavior-based control approach for satellite swarms has also been shown to be useful in controlling highly nonlinear systems such as those derived by introducing electrostatic interactions between swarm agents [PIT06].

12.2.2 Distributed Computing

A second example of distributed artificial intelligence with specific applications to space systems, and in particular to trajectory design [IM05], is that of distributed computing. The possibility of sharing the memory and the computing resources of a large network of simple computers is clearly appealing for any kind of application. On the other hand, not every problem is suitable for being solved in a distributed computing environment. The problem structure has to be such as to allow its subdivision into packages that have little or no dependency between each other. This requirement is the main limitation to

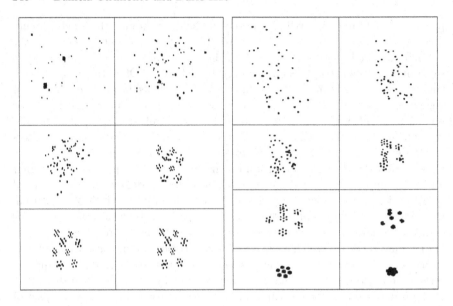

Fig. 12.1. Two examples of orbital swarms assembling a given structure (source: [IP07]).

the use of distributed computing. The forthcoming sections introduce, briefly, two examples of space applications suitable for distributed computations.

Analysis of Large Quantities of Data

The main purpose of most of the commercial satellites currently orbiting Earth is to provide data. Satellites continuously download data to ground stations in a nonprocessed format (usually, few data manipulations are made by the not too powerful computers onboard satellites). ESA's ENVISAT satellite alone generates 400 terabytes of data each year [FGL+03]. The data are then processed sequentially by computers and the results stored again in mass memories together with raw ones. Over the years, these data accumulate to the point that deletion is sometimes necessary (also due to changes in storage technology). Sophisticated analysis of these datasets can take as long as years to complete, often making the analysis itself obsolete before it has even been concluded. Distributed computing therefore becomes a useful tool to allow efficient use of satellite data, the main asset of the space business. Earth observation data coming from European satellites have already been made available in a computer grid [FGL+03], sharing processing power, memory storage, and processed data. A dedicated generic distributed computing environment that uses the idle CPU time of ESA internal personal computers has also been tested already [IM05] on problems such as ionospheric data processing and Monte Carlo simulations of constellation architectures

[IMN05]. In these types of applications, as no dependency is present between the different parts of the computations, little distributed artificial intelligence is actually present. The huge problem is just divided into small isolated subproblems that, in turn, are solved by different machines located in various parts of a common network. From the technological point of view, the challenges in these types of distributed computations (and the part where artificial intelligence could play a role) are mainly in the coordination of network traffic, in resource sharing, and in the reconstruction of the whole solution from the different parts returned by the different machines.

Distributed Solving of Global Optimization Problems

Distributing global optimization tasks over a large network of computers is certainly more elaborate, as it introduces a dependency between the different computations. Global optimization problems can be found everywhere in industrial processes. Many of the issues engineers face during spacecraft design are global optimization problems. Most notably, global optimization seems to be essential in preliminary trajectory optimization [MBNB04]. Essentially, this can be considered in the rather generic form

$$\text{min} : \mathbf{f}(\mathbf{x})$$
$$\text{subject to} : \mathbf{g}(\mathbf{x}) \leq 0$$

with $\mathbf{x} \in \mathcal{U} \subset \mathrm{R}^n$. The problem dimension n depends on the type of trajectory considered and can be as low as 2 but also on the order of thousands.

In order to visualize, for the reader, the problem of trajectory optimization, Figure 12.2 illustrates an example of an optimized interplanetary trajectory. Since the first applications of evolutionary strategies to trajectory design [RC96], heuristic optimization techniques such as differential evolution, simulated annealing, particle swarm optimization, and genetic algorithms have proven to be quite effective in providing preliminary solutions to trajectory problems [BMN+05, DRIV05]. The complete automatization of the optimization process, however, is not yet possible, as the existing algorithms are incapable of replacing the acute reasoning necessary to locate the best possible transfer between celestial bodies. A recent attempt to capture some expert knowledge and to use it to prune the search space in a trajectory problem, called "multiple gravity assist" (MGA), has managed to reduce the MGA problem complexity to polynomial time [IBM+07]. In other cases, NP-complexity cannot be avoided, and the global optimization of an interplanetary trajectory may be untractable for a single machine. Fortunately, global optimization algorithms such as evolutionary algorithms and branch-and bound-based techniques are suitable for distributed environments [GP02, AF98], drastically improving the performance of the search and thus alleviating the "curse of dimensionality". A first attempt to use this possibility in a spacecraft trajectory optimization problem has been performed by ESA

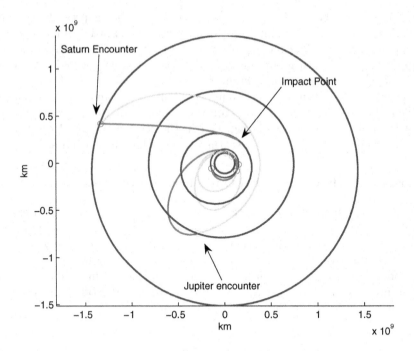

Fig. 12.2. An optimized Earth-Venus-Earth-Venus-Earth-Jupiter-Saturn-asteroid trajectory.

researchers, who solved a complicated MGA transfer distributing a differential evolution algorithm in a small number of personal computers. The problem solved[3] using the distributed version of differential evolution was inspired by the 1st Global Trajectory Optimization Competition (GTOC1), an annual event established in 2005 to make international research groups compete to find the best solution to the same trajectory design problem. Depending on the type of spacecraft one is considering (the main difference being the possibility of having impulsive or continuous velocity changes), the mission goal (destination orbit and celestial body), and the launch window considered, the trajectory optimization problem's dimension and complexity vary a lot. As in many other fields, for trajectory optimization, too, there is no available algorithm that outperforms all others. Consequently, this often leaves one to try different techniques until finally the algorithm that in a particular problem performs best is found. In the attempt to make the entire problem-solving process entirely distributed, a novel approach is that of Vinko et al. [VIP07], who consider a central server and a number of clients, which evolve demes (subpopulations) extracted from a larger population stored in the server,

---

[3] There is actually no mathematical guarantee that the solution found is the global optimum, but the experiment improved previous solutions by approximately 10%.

which then takes care of the reinsertion of the demes. According to the results returned by the various clients in each given phase of the optimization process, the server updates the probabilities to allocate a given algorithm for the next subsearch request to a client. The resulting global optimization environment is able to understand and select the best-performing algorithm in each phase of the solution of a problem. A preliminary version of this intelligent server is being developed and tested [VIP07] for the final purpose of being able to automatically carry out the whole trajectory optimization process without any expert supervision.

12.3 Enhanced Situation Self-Awareness

Ideally, a spacecraft should be able to perform autonomous actions, determine its own health status, and eventually make decisions based on this enhanced self-awareness. Unfortunately, real space missions are instead strongly dependent on the ground segment and on the flight engineers who monitor the enormous amount of telemetry data sent back to Earth during spacecraft operation. This procedure, which requires large numbers of human experts, is of course cumbersome and time-consuming. Sometimes, it might take days before the data are processed, decisions are made, and uploaded commands reach the spacecraft, whereas during critical mission phases such as the launch, information must be processed and decisions make within seconds. Furthermore, humans are not always able to recognize anomalous situations, especially when these involve complex relationships among large numbers of variables. Autonomous systems for enhanced situation self-awareness are therefore a very important research topic in spacecraft engineering.

Classically, two major approaches can be described: model-based methods and data-driven (model-free) methods. Model-based methods use models of the hardware and the physical processes to track the states of the system and detect deviations from nominal behavior. These models are sometimes very expensive to produce because they largely depend on expert knowledge. Moreover, when applied to very complex systems such as spacecraft, they might fail to reproduce all the possible off-nominal modes for which accurate models are lacking most of the time.

On the other hand, data-driven approaches, based on data mining and machine-learning techniques, are not based on a physical system but rather on models that are inferred from the telemetry data (e.g., temperature sensor data). Many activities in this field are being carried out in the framework of the Integrated Vehicle Health Management (IVHM) program of NASA Ames Research Center for the Second Generation Reusable Launch Vehicle (RLV), crew, and cargo transfer vehicles [IVH06]. This program is dedicated to the development of highly integrated systems that will include advanced smart sensors, diagnostic and prognostic software for sensors and components, model-based reasoning systems for subsystem- and system-level managers, advanced onboard and ground-based mission and maintenance planners, and a host of other software and hardware technologies. These hardware and software technologies will provide both real-time and life-cycle vehicle health information, which will enable decision making.

12.3.1 Data-Driven Approaches

The application of data-driven approaches to flight time-series analysis is being researched extensively by the space engineering community for the autonomous identification of suspicious trends that might lead to malfunctions or losses. Only the preventive detection of these trends might allow the ground systems or the intelligent planner and scheduler of the spacecraft to take corrective actions. Most of the data-driven approaches used in daily spacecraft operations are based on unsupervised learning techniques since in safety-critical applications, such as space engineering, it is usually impossible to collect exhaustive datasets for the representation of all possible fault modes. Therefore, most of these methods and algorithms can detect anomalies and off-nominal trends but leave to the flight control operator the delicate task of interpretation. The forthcoming paragraphs introduce a few of these approaches. Far from being an exhaustive list, we intend to give the reader a flavor of some work done in this field.

In [Ive04], the authors propose an "inductive monitoring system" (ISM) to detect off-nominal behaviors. Flight data of past missions are used as training data for a clustering algorithm (i.e., K-means and density-based clustering) that identifies nominal behavior areas (the clusters) in the n-dimensional data space, where n is the number of sensor readings. The clusters, which, according to the authors, represent the ISM knowledge base, can be used for the real-time detection of anomalous behavior during a new flight. Once a new measurement vector is received, the knowledge base returns the cluster to which the vector would belong (according to some cluster limit, preidentified after training). When the membership in a specific cluster cannot be detected, the distance to the closest cluster (with respect to Euclidean metrics in the n-dimensional space) will give the control operator an idea of the system's deviation from its nominal behavior as represented by the training data. The algorithm is tested successfully on the data collected during mission STS-107 of the Columbia space shuttle, which exploded during reentry because of a breach in its thermal protection system [Geh03]. An approach very similar to the one just introduced is presented in [Sch05]. In this work, an unsupervised detection algorithm named Orca, developed by the authors on the basis of the nearest-neighbor approach, is applied to the test data of the space shuttle main engine and of a rocket engine stand.

The K-means clustering algorithm is also used in [VLFD05] on the space of the features extracted from the time series collected from past missions. The authors here make an attempt to find specific relations between fault occurrence and the trend of the parameters by inferring association rules from data by means of the a priori algorithm. Therefore, the fault occurrence data must be part of the training set so that the algorithm can be trained to recognize future similar events. Unexpected fault modes therefore cannot be detected by the algorithm.

12.3.2 Model-Based Approaches

Most of the model-based approaches for enhanced situation awareness that have been researched and developed in space systems in recent years used as a reference the Livingstone model-based diagnosis engine [WN96] and its successors Livingstone 2 (L2) and Livingstone 3 (L3). Livingstone flew on Deep Space 1, and L2 has been uploaded to the Earth Observing One (EO-1) satellite [HSC+04, CST+04] for the "autonomous sciencecraft experiment" (ASE), which provides an onboard planning capability. The task of these diagnosis engines is to predict nominal state transitions initiated by control commands monitoring the spacecraft sensors and, in the case of failure, isolate the fault based on the discrepant observations. Fault detection and isolation is done by determining a set of component modes, including most likely failures, which satisfy the current observations.

L3 is the most recent and advanced of these architectures and consists of three main components. The "system model" stores the model of the system and is responsible for tracking the modes of operation of the different components and determining the constraints that are valid at any point in time. The "constraint system" serves the role of tracking the overall system behavior using constraint programming techniques. It receives constraints from the system model indicative of the current configuration of the system and propagates these constraints to try to assign consistent values to variables in the system. When observations are different from propagated values for corresponding components, the "candidate manager" is responsible for generating candidate faults that resolve all the conflicts and that can possibly explain all of the inconsistencies. In order to deal with uncertainties, the dynamic behavior of the system is tracked through Bayesian approaches such as "particle filtering" in order to assign posterior probability distributions to the candidate faults [NDB04, NBB04].

Bayesian approaches are also used in [GIB06], where the authors present the preliminary results of dual filtering techniques for the detection of possible variations of the thermal properties of the spacecraft that result from variations of its physical properties and for determining a complete thermal mapping of the system. System and sensor uncertainties are taken into account in the lumped parameter modeling of the thermal system, and a dual unscented Kalman filter is run on the stochastic model in an alternating optimization fashion to estimate the thermal state and coefficients of the resulting thermal network from the readings of a few strategically placed thermal sensors. Events such as faults can be detected by the dual filter as well as new values of system parameters (e.g., radiative couplings) that result from a variation of the spacecraft geometry (e.g., from the deployment of antennas, solar panels, etc.). This method would be particularly attractive in networks whose state and parameters can be estimated by the filter using a minimal amount of readings. The relation between the network topology and this minimal number is therefore an issue strictly related to the observability of the system, which is here approached using graph theory.

12.4 Decision Support for Spacecraft System Design

As the complexity of space systems increases, innovative approaches to system design are needed to allow assessment of the largest possible number of design concepts at an early stage. In space system design, several disciplines corresponding to all different subsystems[4] must be considered, and the overall spacecraft is the result of a "multidisciplinary design optimization" (MDO) [BS02, Roy96]. MDO can be described as a methodology for the design of systems where the interaction between several disciplines must be considered and where the designer is free to significantly affect the system performance in more than one discipline. In this sense, the space design process is an integrated optimization [5] that receives as inputs the mission requirements in the form of constraints and produces as output an optimal design.

In the classical approach to MDO, each specialist would prepare a subsystem design relatively independently from the others using stand-alone tools. Design iterations among the different discipline experts would take place in meetings at intervals of a few weeks. This well-established approach has the drawbacks of reducing the opportunity to find interdisciplinary solutions and to create system awareness in the specialists. A considerable step toward a multidisciplinary approach in the early phases of space system design has been achieved through an MDO based on concurrent engineering, where a sequential iterative approach to system design is replaced by a parallel and cooperative approach. Design facilities where these methodologies are implemented are, among others, the ESA Concurrent Design Facility [BMO99], the NASA Goddard Integrated Mission Design Center [KMSR03], and the Concept Design Center at The AeroSpace Corporation [ADL98].

In these concurrent MDO approaches, however, the subsystem experts are the core of the decision process of the design. Over the last couple of years, much research has been dedicated to the achievement of decision support systems or that of autonomous system design methods, which try to capture the reasoning of the experts toward an optimal and robust design.

---

[4] A spacecraft is constituted by the following subsystems: attitude determination and control, telemetry tracking and command, command and data handling, power, thermal structures and mechanisms, and guidance and navigation [WL99].

[5] The term optimization is not used here in the strict mathematical sense but rather to indicate any procedure that aims to find a solution that is either optimal or suboptimal.

Therefore, the spacecraft design started to be viewed as the solution of an optimization problem under constraints: given a set of decision variables D (e.g., the dimension of solar arrays) and a set of constraints C on D (e.g., their volume and mass), the constrained optimization algorithm looks for the values of D that minimize or maximize an objective function $F(X)$ subject to C.[6] However, finding the optimal design point was revealed to be a very difficult task, and traditional global optimization approaches most of the time fail to find the global optimum in the design space [FCM+97]. To tackle this problem in spacecraft design, a quite common approach is based on the employment of heuristic solvers. The Jet Propulsion Laboratory implemented an optimization assistant (OASIS) that depending on the design problem selects and tunes either a genetic algorithm or a simulated annealing algorithm [FCM+97]. The goal of OASIS was to facilitate rapid "what-if" analysis of spacecraft design by developing a spacecraft design optimization system that maximizes the automation of the optimization process and minimizes the amount of customization required by the user. More recently, evolutionary algorithms have been used to evolve the design of the antenna that flew on NASA's Space Technology 5 (ST5) mission [HGLL06] and for trajectory design as discussed in the previous section.

The problem of tackling the conflicting situations that might emerge during the system design activity when interests from different disciplines must be harmonized in the same project or when different goals must be reached within the same mission has been studied in [AFA+04]. The neighborhood approach aims at finding by means of dedicated heuristics a set of "paretian" solutions at the system level. To efficiently reduce the total number of such solutions to a small subset that is to be considered "optimal" from the point of view of conflict reduction, "game theory" and "multicriteria decision analysis" are used.

Other approaches to autonomous space system design look not only at the achievement of an optimal design but also at its robustness with respect to uncertainties of the design variables and models involved in the design.[7] In this framework, the most common approach in space system design is essentially based on safety margins and expert knowledge. The safety margins, which are the most conservative way of handling uncertainties, identify the worst possible conditions that might be encountered during the operational phase in order for the resulting design to be adequate. Probabilistic approaches have been introduced in space system design as a consequence of the Challenger accident in 1986 [Fey86] and are essentially based on "probabilistic risk analysis" [PF93]. However, in general, the probability of infeasibility for a given design cannot be determined reasonably without knowing the joint

---

[6] In the case of spacecraft design, the objective function is most of the time the cost, which is ultimately proportionally linked to be the spacecraft's total mass.

[7] For an extensive qualitative and quantitative overview of these uncertainties, the reader may consult [Thu05].

distribution of the uncertain variables or having sufficient amounts of data samples from past observations. Sometimes, the probability model assumptions can be replaced by deterministic data, for which a rigorous worst-case analysis could be performed by using numerically reliable tools, such as verified interval calculations. In the most recent literature on system design under uncertainties, design variables are modeled by a range of values (intervals), by membership-degree functions of fuzzy sets [LF02], or by evidence theory [CCV07]. The European Space Agency's Advanced Concepts Team is assessing a promising new approach for an autonomous and robust design based on the concept of clouds [Neu04, DP05]. Clouds capture useful properties of the probabilistic and fuzzy uncertainties, enabling the user to utilize the collected empirical information (even if limited in amount) in a reliable and validated way. Being a hybrid between probabilistic and deterministic models, clouds can provide risk analysis using tools from optimization, in particular global optimization, and constraint satisfaction techniques. The numerical techniques for solving such problems have recently become much more reliable and powerful and allow one to compute bounds for the expected values of any multivariate functions of design processes and also for probabilities of qualitative statements involving design variables [NFD$^+$07].

12.5 Summary

The aim of this chapter is to give the reader an overview of some of the research carried out within the international space community on artificial intelligence. Having identified artificial intelligence as one of the enabling technologies for the achievement of the various short- and long-term goals of the international space agencies, we believe that a synergic effort of scientists from both fields is required to effectively tackle the numerous open issues and challenges in this area. In more recent years, we have observed a growing number of researchers getting interested in the benefits of using artificial intelligence methods for space applications. These applications go beyond the more classical automated planning and scheduling field and include different mission phases from conceiving the preliminary design to the mission operation phase.

References

[ADL98]   J.A. Aguilar, A.B. Dawdy, and G.W. Law. The Aerospace Corporation's concept design center. In *8th Annual International Symposium of the International Council on Systems Engineering*, volume 2. INCOSE Technical Working Group Papers, 1998. Published in CD-ROM.

[AF98]   I.P. Androulakis and C.A. Floudas. Distributed branch and bound algorithms in global optimization. In P.M. Pardalos, editor, *IMA Volumes in Mathematics and Its Applications*, volume 106, pages 1–36. Springer-Verlag, New York, 1998.

[AFA+04] V. Amata, G. Fasano, L. Arcaro, F. Della Croce, M.F. Norese, S. Palamara, R. Tadei, and F. Fragnelli. Multidisciplinary optimisation in mission analysis and design process. GSP programme ref. GSP 03/N16, contract number 17828/03/NL/MV, European Space Agency, Noordwijk, 2004.

[BMN+05] V.M. Becerra, D.R. Myatt, S.J. Nasuto, J.M. Bishop, and D. Izzo. An efficient pruning technique for the global optimisation of multiple gravity assist trajectories. In I. Garcia, L.G. Casado, E.M.T. Hendrix, and B. Toth, editors, *Proceedings of the International Workshop on Global Optimization*, pages 39–45, Almeria, Spain, April 2005.

[BMO99] M. Bandecchi, S. Melton, and F. Ongaro. Concurrent engineering applied to space mission assessment and design. *ESA Bulletin*, 99, September 1999. Available at http://esapub.esrin.esa.it/bulletin/bullet99.htm.

[Bro91] R.A. Brooks. Intelligence without reason. In J. Mylopoulos and R. Reiter, editors, *Proceedings of the 12th International Joint Conference on Artificial Intelligence*, pages 569–595, Sydney, Australia, August 1991. Morgan Kaufmann, San Mateo, CA.

[BS02] V. Belton and T.J. Stewart. *Multiple Criteria Decision Analysis: An Integrated Approach*. Kluwer Academic Publishers, Dordrecht, 2002.

[BT07] G. Bonnet and C. Tessier. On-board cooperation for satellite swarms. In D. Girimonte, D. Izzo, T. Vinko, S. Chien, and V. Kreinovich, editors, *Workshop on Artificial Intelligence for Space Applications at IJCAI'07*, pages 26–27, Hyderabad, India, January 2007. IJCAI.

[Bus04] G.W. Bush. A renewed spirit of discovery: the President's vision for U.S. space exploration. 2004.

[CCD+05] S. Chien, B. Cichy, A. Davies, D. Tran, G. Rabideau, R. Castano, R. Sherwood, D. Mandl, S. Frye, S. Shulman, J. Jones, and S. Grosvenor. An autonomous Earth-observing sensorweb. *IEEE Intelligent Systems*, 20(3):16–24, May–June 2005.

[CCV07] N. Croisard, M. Ceriotti, and M. Vasile. Uncertainty modelling in reliable preliminary space mission design. In D. Girimonte, D. Izzo, T. Vinko, S. Chien, and V. Kreinovich, editors, *Workshop on Artificial Intelligence for Space Applications at IJCAI'07*, pages 22–23, Hyderabad, India, January 2007. IJCAI.

[Cla45] A.C. Clarke. Extra-terrestrial relays. *Wireless World*, LI(10):305–308, October 1945.

[CST+04] S. Chien, R. Sherwood, D. Tran, B. Cichy, G. Rabideau, R. Castano, A. Davies, R. Lee, D. Mandl, S. Frye, B. Trout, J. Hengemihle, J. D'Agostino, S. Shulman, S. Ungar, T. Brakke, D. Boyer, J. Van Gaasbeck, R. Greeley, T. Doggett, V. Baker, J. Dohm, and F. Ip. The EO-1 autonomous science agent. In *Proceedings of the 3rd International Joint Conference on Autonomous Agents and Multiagent Systems*, pages 420–427, New York, New York, 19–23 July 2004. IEEE Computer Society, Washington, DC.

[DP05] D. Dubois and H. Prade. Interval-valued fuzzy sets, possibility theory and imprecise probability. In E. Montseny and P. Sobrevilla, editors,

              Proceedings of the International Conference in Fuzzy Logic and Technol-ogy, pages 314–319, Barcelona, Spain, 8–10 September 2005. Universitat Politènica de Catalunya.

[DRIV05] P. Di Lizia, G. Radice, D. Izzo, and M. Vasile. On the solution of interplanetary trajectory design problems by global optimisation methods. In I. Garcia, L.G. Casado, E.M.T. Hendrix, and B. Toth, xeditors, *Proceedings of the International Workshop on Global Optimization*, pages 159–164, Almeria, Spain, April 2005. Available at http://www.esa.int/gsp/ACT/publications/pub-mad.htm.

[DVC05]   S. Damiani, G. Verfaillie, and M.C. Charmeau. An Earth watching satellite constellation: how to manage a team of watching agents with limited communications. In *Proceedings of the 4th International Joint Conference on Autonomous Agents and Multiagent Systems, AAMAS*, pages 455–462, Utrecht, Netherlands, 25–29 July 2005. ACM Press, New York, NY.

[ETR⁺03] D. Escorial, I.F. Tourne, F.J. Reina, J. Gonzalo, and B. Garrido. Fuego: a dedicated constellation of small satellites to detect and monitor forest fires. *Acta Astronautica*, 52(9–12):765–775, 2003.

[FCM⁺97] A. Fukunaga, S. Chien, D. Mutz, R.L. Sherwood, and A.D. Stechert. Automating the process of optimization in spacecraft design. In *Proceedings of the IEEE Aerospace Conference*, volume 4, pages 411–427, Snowmass at Aspen, CO, 1–8 February 1997. IEEE, New York.

[Fey86]   R. Feynman. Report of the presidential commission on the space shuttle Challenger accident. Volume 2 (appendix f), U.S. Government Printing Office, Washington, DC, 1986.

[FGL⁺03] L. Fusco, P. Goncalves, J. Linford, M. Fulcoli, A. Terracina, and G. D'Acunzo. *ESA Bulletin*, 114:86–90, 2003.

[Gaz05]   V. Gazi. Swarm aggregations using artificial potentials and sliding mode control. *IEEE Transactions on Robotics*, 21(6):1208–1214, December 2005.

[Geh03]   H.W. Gehman. The Columbia accident investigation board report. Technical report, U.S. Government Printing Office, Washington, DC, 2003.

[GIB06]   D. Girimonte, D. Izzo, and L. Bergamin. Reasoning under an uncertain thermal state. In *Proceedings of the 57th International Astronautical Congress*, Valencia, Spain, 2–6 October 2006. International Astronautical Federation.

[GP02]   C.; Gagne and M. Parizeau. A new versatile C++ framework for evolutionary computation. In W.B. Langdon, E. Cantú-Paz, K. Mathias, R. Roy, D. Davis, R. Poli, K. Balakrishnan, V. Honavar, G. Rudolph, J. Wegener, L. Bull, M.A. Potter, A.C. Schultz, J.F. Miller, E. Burke, and N. Jonoska, editors, *Proceeding of Genetic and Evolutionary Computation Conference*, page 888, New York, NY, April 2002. Morgan Kaufmann, San Francisco, CA.

[HGLL06] G.S. Hornby, A. Globus, D.S. Linden, and J.D. Lohn. Automated antenna design with evolutionary algorithms. In *Proceedings of the AIAA Space Conference*, San Jose, California, 19–21 September 2006. Available at http://ase.arc.nasa.gov/publications.

[HSC⁺04] S.C. Hayden, A.J. Sweet, S.E. Christa, D. Tran, and S. Shulman. Advanced diagnostic system on Earth Observing One. In *Proceedings of the*

         AIAA Space Conference, 2004. Available at `http://ase.arc.nasa.gov/` `publications`.

[IBM+07] D. Izzo, V.M. Becerra, D.R. Myatt, S.J. Nasuto, and J.M. Bishop. Search space pruning and global optimisation of multiple gravity assist spacecraft trajectories. *Journal of Global Optimisation*, 38(2):283–296, June 2007.

[IM05] D. Izzo and M.Cs. Markot. A distributed global optimisation environment for the European Space Agency internal network. In I. Garcia, L.G. Casado, E.M.T. Hendrix, and B. Toth, editors, *Proceedings of the International Workshop on Global Optimization*, pages 133–140, Almeria, Spain, April 2005. Available at `http://www.esa.int/gsp/ACT/` `publications/pub-inf.htm`.

[IMN05] D. Izzo, M.Cs. Markot, and I. Nann. A distributed global optimiser applied to the design of a constellation performing radio-occultation measurments. In Univelt Inc., editor, *Proceedings of the 2005 AAS/AIAA Space Flight Mechanics Conference*, volume 121, pages 739–748, Tampa, Florida, 2005. AAS Publications Office. Paper AAS 05–150.

[IP07] D. Izzo and L. Pettazzi. Autonomous and distributed motion planning for satellite swarm. *Journal of Guidance Control and Dynamic*, 30(2):449–459, 2007.

[Ive04] I.L. Iverson. Inductive system health monitoring. In H.R. Arabnia and Y. Mun, editors, *Proceedings of the International Conference on Artificial Intelligence IC-AI'04*, volume 2, pages 605–611, Las Vegas, Nevada, 21–24 June 2004. CSREA Press.

[IVH06] Integrated vehicle health management (IVHM), March 2006. Available at `http://www.nasa.gov/centers/ames/research/`.

[KE95] J. Kennedy and R. Eberhart. Particle swarm optimization. In *Proceedings of the IEEE International Conference on Neural Networks*, volume 4, pages 1942–1948, Perth, Australia, 1995. IEEE, New York.

[KEM+01] I. Kassabalidis, M.A. El-Sharkawi, R.J. Marks II, P. Arabshahi, and A. Gray. Swarm intelligence for routing in communication networks. In *Proceedings of the IEEE Global Telecommunications Conference GLOBECOM*, volume 6, pages 3613–3617, San Antonio, TX, 25–29 November 2001. Available at `http://ieeexplore.ieee.org/xpls/abs_` `all.jsp?arnumber=966355`.

[Kha86] O. Khatib. Real-time obstacle avoidance for manipulators and mobile robots. *The International Journal of Robotics Research*, 5(1):90–98, 1986.

[KMSR03] G. Karpati, J. Martin, M. Steiner, and K. Reinhardt. The Integrated Mission Design Center (IMDC) at NASA Goddard Space Flight Center. In *Proceedings of the IEEE Aerospace Conference*, volume 8, pages 3657–3667. IEEE, New York, 8–15 March 2003.

[LF02] M. Lavagna and A.E. Finzi. A multi-attribute decision-making approach toward space system design automation through a fuzzy logic-based analytic hierarchical process. In T. Hendtlass and M. Ali, editors, *Proceedings of the 15th International Conference on Industrial and Engineering. Applications of Artificial Intelligence and Expert Systems*, volume 2358 of *Lecture Notes In Computer Science*, pages 596–606. Springer-Verlag, London, 17–20 June 2002.

[LYB03]   J. Lawton, B. Young, and R. Beard. A decentralized approach to elementary formation maneuvers. *IEEE Transactions on Robotics and Automation*, 17(6):933–941, 2003.

[MBNB04] D.R. Myatt, V.M. Becerra, S.J. Nasuto, and J.M. Bishop. Advanced global optimisation tools for mission analysis and design. Technical Report 03-4101, European Space Agency, Noordwijk, 2004. Available at `http://www.esa.int/gsp/ACT/ariadna/completed\_studies.htm`.

[McI95]   C. McInnes. Autonomous rendezvous using artificial potential functions. *Journal of Guidance Control and Dynamics*, 18(2):237–241, 1995.

[McQ97]   F. McQuade. Autonomous control for on-orbit assembly using artificial potential functions, 1997. PhD thesis, Faculty of Engineering, University of Glasgow, Scotland.

[MO03]   P. Messina and F. Ongaro. Aurora: the European space exploration programme. *ESA Bulletin*, 115:34–39, 2003.

[NBB04]   S. Narasimhan, L. Brownston, and D. Burrows. Explanation constraint programming for model-based diagnosis of engineered systems. In *Proceedings of the IEEE Aerospace Conference*, volume 5, pages 3495–3501, Big Sky, Montana, 6–13 March 2004. IEEE, New York.

[NDB04]   S. Narasimhan, R. Dearden, and E. Benazera. Combining particle filters and consistency-based approaches for monitoring and diagnosis of stochastic hybrid systems. In *Proceedings of the 15th International Workshop on Principles of Diagnosis DX'04*, Carcassonne, France, 23–25 June 2004. Available at `http://www.laas.fr/DX04/`.

[Neu04]   A. Neumaier. Clouds, fuzzy sets and probability intervals. *Reliable Computing*, 10:249–272, 2004.

[NFD+07] A. Neumaier, M. Fuchs, E. Dolejsi, T. Csendes, J. Dombi, B. Banhelyi, and Z. Gera. Application of clouds for modeling uncertainties in robust space system design. ACT Ariadna Research ACT-RPT-05-5201, European Space Agency, Noordwijk, 2007. Available at `http://www.esa.int/gsp/ACT/ariadna/completed\_studies.htm`.

[PF93]   M. Pate-Cornell and P. Fischbeck. Probabilistic risk analysis and risk based priority scale for the tiles of the space shuttle. *Reliability Engineering and System Safety*, 40(3):221–238, 1993.

[PIT06]   L. Pettazzi, D. Izzo, and S. Theil. Swarm navigation and reconfiguration using electrostatic forces. In *Proceedings of the 7th International Conference on Dynamics and Control of Systems and Structures in Space*, pages 257–268, Greenwich, UK, 16-20 July 2006. Cranfield University Press, London.

[RB04]   W. Ren and R.W. Beard. A decentralized scheme for spacecraft formation flying via the virtual structure approach. *AIAA Journal of Guidance, Control and Dynamics*, 27(1):73–82, January 2004.

[RC96]   G.A. Rauwolf and V.L. Coverstone-Carroll. Near optimal low-thrust orbit transfers generated by a genetic algorithm. *Journal of Spacecraft and Rockets*, 33(6):859–862, 1996.

[Roy96]   B. Roy. *Multicriteria Methodology for Decision Aiding*. Kluwer Academic Publishers, Dordrecht, 1996.

[Sch05]   M. Schwabacher. Machine learning for rocket propulsion health monitoring. *SAE Transactions*, 114(1):1192–1197, 2005.

[SD92]   G. Schoner and M. Dose. A dynamics systems approach to task level systems integration used to plan and control autonomous vehicle motion. *Robotics and Autonomous Systems*, 10(4):253–267, 1992.

[TB99]   G. Theraulaz and E. Bonebeau. A brief history of stigmergy. *Artificial Life*, 5(2):97–116, 1999.

[Thu05]   D.P. Thunnissen. Propagating and mitigating uncertainty in the design of complex multidisciplinary systems, 2005. PhD thesis, California Institute of Technology, Pasadena.

[VIP07]   T. Vinko, D. Izzo, and F. Pinna. Learning the best combination of solvers in a distributed global optimisation environment. Technical Report ACT-RPT-TV-5200-LBCSDGOE, ESA Advanced Concepts Team, Noordwijk, 2007.

[VLFD05] E. Vecchio, B. Lazzerini, S. Foley, and A. Donati. Spacecraft fault analysis using data mining techniques. In B. Battrick, editor, *Proceedings of the 8th International Symposium on Artificial Intelligence, Robotics and Automation in Space*, München, Germany, 5–8 September 2005. Published in CDROM.

[WL99]   J.R. Wertz and W.J. Larson. *Space Mission Analysis and Design*. Microcosm Press, Torrance, CA, 3rd edition, 1999. Space Technology Library.

[WN96]   B.C. Williams and P. Nayak. A model-based approach to reactive self-configuring systems. In *Proceedings of the 13th National Conference on Artificial Intelligence*, volume 2, pages 971–978, Portland, OR, 4–8 August 1996. AAAI Press/The MIT Press.

A

Abbreviations

AI = artificial intelligence
ANN = artificial neural network
ANS = autonomic nervous system
ATM = accelerating Turing machine
BCI = brain-computer interface
BOLD = blood oxygenation level dependent
CTM = conventional Turing machine
fMRI = functional magnetic resonance imaging
fPDAG = feature partial directed acyclic graph IM = infinite machine
ISM = infinite state machine
NIRS = near-infrared spectroscopy
SCP = slow cortical potentials
SMR = sensorimotor rhythm
TANN = tokenized artificial neural network

Index